WHAT IT MEANS TO BE A VOLUNTEER

NK LAURICELLA · DOUG ATKINS · JIM HASLAM · JOHNNY MAJORS

SON · RICHMOND FLOWERS · CHARLIE ROSENFELDER · STEVE K

DGE HOLLOWAY · MICKEY MARVIN · STANLEY MORGAN · LARRY S

WHITE · JIMMY COLQUITT · BILL MAYO · JOHNNIE JONES · TIM

EATH SHULER · JOEY KENT · PEYTON MANNING · JEFF HALL · TE

SON · DUSTIN COLQUITT · JAMES WILHOIT · ARRON SEARS · BEN

· JOHN MICHELS · HANK LAURICELLA · DOUG ATKINS · JIM HA

ON WIDBY · BOB JOHNSON · RICHMOND FLOWERS · CHARLIE R

MIE ROTELLA · CONDREDGE HOLLOWAY · MICKEY MARVIN · ST

IN · WILLIE GAULT · REGGIE WHITE · JIMMY COLQUITT · BILL

ERIC STILL · ANTONE DAVIS · HEATH SHULER · JOEY KENT · P

TRAVIS STEPHENS · JOHN HENDERSON · DUSTIN COLQUITT ·

ERT NEYLAND · HACK, MAC, & DODD · JOHN MICHELS · HANK

EVE DELONG · FRANK EMANUEL · RON WIDBY · BOB JOHNSON

LESTER MCCLAIN · BOBBY MAJORS · JAMIE ROTELLA · CONDE

IG COLQUITT · ROLAND JAMES · TIM IRWIN · WILLIE GAULT · R

RUCE WILKERSON · HARRY GALBREATH · ERIC STILL

N · DEON GRANT · DARWIN WALKER · TRAVIS STEP

D · HAYWOOD HARRIS · GENERAL ROBERT NEYLAND · HACK, MA

WHAT IT MEANS TO BE A
VOLUNTEER

PHILLIP FULMER
AND TENNESSEE'S GREATEST PLAYERS

RAY GLIER

TRIUMPH
BOOKS

For
Jessie Bond

Library of Congress Cataloging-in-Publication Data

Glier, Ray.
  What it means to be a Volunteer / Ray Glier.
    p. cm.
ISBN-13: 978-1-60078-069-1
ISBN-10: 1-60078-069-5
  1. Tennessee Volunteers (Football team) 2. University of Tennessee—Football—History. I. Title.
  GV958.U586G55 2008
  796.332'630976885—dc22

                                  2008015417

This book is available in quantity at special discounts for your group or organization. For further information, contact:

Triumph Books
542 South Dearborn Street
Suite 750
Chicago, Illinois 60605
(312) 939-3330
Fax (312) 663-3557

Printed in U.S.A.
ISBN: 978-1-60078-069-1
Design by Nick Panos.
Editorial production and layout by Prologue Publishing Services, LLC.
All photos courtesy of the University of Tennessee Sports Information office unless otherwise noted.

CONTENTS

FOREWORD

What It Means to Be a Volunteer

I'M NOT JUST PASSING THROUGH HERE. I'm not looking for the next job. This is my dream job, and this is my home. I told Vicki, my wife, when we were first married not to buy drapes for the house because I didn't know how long we would be here. I was a coach and, in this profession, things can happen. This was in 1981.

We've been here 26 years. Finally, we bought drapes.

Being a Vol is all about commitment, and that's something I have understood going all the way back to my prospect days when I was a high school student in lower middle Tennessee. I'm committed to Tennessee.

Coming out of high school, I looked at a number of schools, trying to decide where to go. Alabama had Coach Bryant. I loved him and their tradition, and they had just won a championship my senior year. I considered going there, but when I came to Knoxville and met with Coach Dickey, they had just come off a season in which they finished No. 2 in the country. I felt a great loyalty to the state of Tennessee and to the University of Tennessee. This is where I wanted to be.

I had been on campus just twice before, once at a game and again on a recruiting visit, and I could just feel that it was the right place. I had visited Georgia, Tennessee, Vanderbilt, and 'Bama. When I got here, I got into the passion of what Coach Dickey was doing, which was resurrecting the program. That loyalty and commitment have been here ever since.

When Coach Dickey took over in 1964, he really brought it from the ashes. They had gone through some tough times, so I was glad to be a part of bringing it back. We won an SEC championship in 1969 and had good

Phillip Fulmer was an undersized offensive lineman for Tennessee, but made a place for himself with commitment.

teams in 1970 and 1971. We had the winningest era in college football at that particular time in history, which was from 1967 to 1971. More wins than Texas, more wins than Ohio State. I was proud to be a part of that.

It took commitment to be able to come here and find a way to play. I came as a linebacker and tight end, but we had great linebackers, like Jack Reynolds, Steve Kiner, Jamie Rotella, James Woody, and Jackie Walker. All these guys were in the program. I needed to find a position other than linebacker, so I moved to offensive line and found a way as a 218-pound offensive guard to get into some games. I started just before the era when offensive linemen started to get bigger. I was captain in 1971, which is the greatest honor I've had in athletics.

After I was through playing, I got into coaching. Coach [George] Cafego took a special interest in me and taught me how to do all the scouting for the University of Tennessee. I was a graduate assistant, so I would come back Saturday night after games and stay up all night back in the day where you had to cut the film, splice it, and put it up on the wall, play by play. I would do a written scouting report and present it to the staff Sunday at 1:00 PM, for both sides of the ball.

Here I am, 21, 22, wet behind the ears, trying to present a scouting report to these coaches. I must have done a pretty good job, because Jim Wright took a job at Wichita State and offered me a job as offensive coordinator. I made $6,000. He took one salary, split it, and hired two of us—me and John Stuckey, whom I later hired here at Tennessee.

I was at Wichita State five years and had some chances to leave but just couldn't. Coach Wright had hired me, and I wanted to be loyal to him. In 1979, I went to Vanderbilt and was there about nine months when Coach Majors asked me to come back to Tennessee.

By the time I was 28, I was back here in Knoxville, and it was unbelievable to come back to where I had played and a place I loved.

When I got back, the first thing that struck me was how far things had fallen in terms of players since the early '70s. It wasn't where it had been at all. That was in 1980, and they were just getting things together again.

In 1985, we finally won the SEC championship and beat Miami in the Sugar Bowl, and that was a huge victory for the program.

My favorite tradition was running through the T before the game—I still get a big kick out of it. Coach Dickey started it. He started the checkerboard end zones, too.

I've probably run through the T more than anybody, except for our equipment manager and team doctor. You hear the crowd, you hear the band, and I think it's one of the greatest moments in college football; it's like dotting the *i* at Ohio State or having the 12th man at Texas A&M.

People all over the country will ask me about the checkerboard end zones and running through the T. Coach Majors, I think, started the Vol Walk where the players walk to the stadium through the crowd. The traditions here are a wonderful part of the program.

We've had some serious illnesses with teammates over the years, and we all get together and talk about where people are and what we can do to help. That's part of being in this program and playing for Tennessee. Ex-teammates looking out for one another is part of what it means to be a Volunteer.

We have a golf tournament every spring, and I'm in a great position because players are usually going to come through here. There are some we haven't seen for years, and we get a chance to catch up.

I've had chances at pro football and could have gone on to other schools, but with children and at the age they were, we chose not to move them. But it was also the passion of the program and the school itself that kept me here. The passion is huge.

Coach Fulmer hoists the national championship trophy celebrating Tennessee's perfect season in 1998.

Fulmer rejoices with fans following the Vols' victory in the Fiesta Bowl, which capped a perfect season in 1998.

It started with the administration and Andy Holt, who was the president. It carried on with Coach Dickey and on to athletic director Mike Hamilton and the current president, Dr. John Petersen.

When I played, it was a great time to be in college because you had all the Vietnam stuff going on and students taking over the administration building. It was a growing time for me. I opened my mind and changed my way of thinking about people.

Outside of my faith and family, coaching in this program has been the most important thing in my life. My wife and kids have been extremely patient, because being a part of this program means being committed and working until 2:00 or 3:00 in the morning or sleeping in your office some nights to get something the way you want it. I don't do that as much anymore.

Being a Vol means pushing yourself one more time for that next stop in recruiting and doing something else that makes a difference. That's what I mean when I say being a Vol means commitment.

We have great facilities and great tradition, but there has to be a commitment because while we have great high school coaches and some great players, we don't have a lot of great players compared to Florida, Pennsylvania, Texas, and Ohio. General Neyland really started the tradition of going to a lot of places to recruit outside of the Southeast and the state. He came from West Point and was accustomed to having players from around the country.

We can go to a lot of places because of where we are. We can go up and down the eastern seaboard. It's not that far to New Jersey, it's not that far to New York, and we can get into central Florida. We built on that recruiting base, and we have Tennessee's name out there all over the country. People ask me all the time about "Rocky Top" and how big the stadium is and how many people come to the games.

We have a quarterback from Oregon and a tailback from San Diego. Our heart and soul is Tennessee kids, but if you look at our team, 80 percent of them are from other places.

We are a melting pot, not just in the football program, but on the campus as a whole. It ends up being a tremendous growing experience, because when they get here their roommates or suitemates end up being from another part of the country. The kids from the North can't run home to be with high school buddies.

I remember when I was in school I could take somebody back to Winchester and the next spring break I might go to New Jersey. The diversity of the university and city is a great thing. People don't realize our campus has kids from every state in the union and 57 foreign countries.

We make sure the kids who come from outside the state know the tradition and get absorbed by what is going on here. They come for different reasons. Some see an opportunity for pro football, but I make sure they understand the traditions and why our game maxims are so important, and I want them to understand the history of General Neyland.

When they first set foot on campus, part of their orientation process is to learn who General Neyland was and what he meant to the program. We also try and teach them "Rocky Top."

Haywood Harris (longtime sports information director) meets with the freshmen every year and talks about the tradition. We try and give them the whys and explain where things came from. There are a lot of people who came before them who have worn the orange and white, and they need to

As an offensive line coach, Fulmer was a stickler for details and fundamentals in preparation for a game.

understand the spirit and that they are an extension of those people. Most of them pick up the words to "Rocky Top" and learn it.

People wonder how it got so big here on game days. Well, our geography is such that we can count western North Carolina, southwest Virginia, and north Georgia as part of our in-state area. There is a strong base of Tennessee people in those areas. It has helped that we have put a darn good product on the field for a number of years and that coming to a game here is a happening.

The fans are committed to the program and have a great passion for it. We don't spend state dollars or tax dollars, but we have one of the best facilities in the country because of the support of the fans. It allows us to stay on the cutting edge of technology, and we don't lose coaches to other programs with parallel moves.

When I first took over as head coach, there were some branding things we had, but I thought we needed a single symbol that was important to us. We went with the Power T, and that has become what people associate with Tennessee football. The T has been around since Coach Dickey put the T on the helmet in 1964.

To me, what it means to be a Volunteer has to do with pride, work ethic, and commitment—being proud of what we have accomplished over the years. It's pride in who I have played for and worked for and what we do on a daily basis.

—Phillip Fulmer

Phillip Fulmer played offensive line at Tennessee from 1969 to 1971. He became the head coach of the Vols in the middle of the 1992 season and was named National Coach of the Year for leading Tennessee to a perfect season and a national championship in 1998. Tennessee has finished a season ranked in the top 10 six times. Fulmer's record at Tennessee is 146–45 (.764), which is the third-highest winning percentage behind General Robert Neyland (.829), who coached 21 seasons, and John Barnhill (.846), who coached four seasons. Fulmer is the national spokesperson for the Jason Foundation, which works to prevent teen suicides. Fulmer has been on the board of directors for the Boys and Girls Clubs, American Football Coaches Association, and Child and Family Services.

ACKNOWLEDGMENTS

WHEN YOU START A BOOK, you don't just start at the beginning. You start at a place just before the beginning, where the spark lurks, the reason for doing something.

Jim Haslam, a former Tennessee player, a captain, has been around the program since 1947 and has seen the highs and the lows, the comings and the goings, the ins and the outs. We met for lunch.

He was the spark.

Haslam didn't just talk Tennessee football, he leaned forward and talked in earnest. In a 55-minute conversation, there was a passion about Tennessee football that burst through and told me, "I'm glad I signed the contract for this book."

The same day I talked to Haslam, I spent an hour with Phil Fulmer. Fans were starting to grumble because Tennessee had not won an SEC championship since 1998, and they were trying to get prepared for 2007 camp so they could get back into the championship picture. Fulmer took a lot of valuable time to be interviewed for this project.

Haslam and Fulmer have a deep appreciation for the roots of the program. It was easy for Haslam to recite the maxims that General Neyland, the true founder of the program, brought from West Point.

Fulmer spoke with a reverence for the program and what had been accomplished before him and the tradition he was trying to uphold, not just on the field, but off it.

When Haslam and I left Naples, the restaurant, he said, "Call me any time," and I did call. It was to get phone numbers for some of the great players from the '50s, and that is how this project inched forward.

Haslam, who is the founder and boss of Pilot Oil, gave me Hank Lauricella's phone number. Then I got John Michels's phone number, and away I went.

Haslam, Michels, and Lauricella were among the lynchpins of General Neyland's last national championship team in 1951. The project gained speed when I got into the era of the great All-American Johnny Majors, who almost won a Heisman Trophy. Then I got into the '60s with the renewal of Tennessee football under Doug Dickey, who is a Florida Gator, except you wouldn't know it from the admiration showed him by his former players.

I had to leap around—from the '60s to the '70s, from the '80s to the '90s, and back to the '70s—as I chased players for interviews. It went from Tim McGee and the Sugar Vols, back to the days of two-sport All-American Rod Widby, and ahead again to Peyton Manning–to–Joey Kent, the most prolific pass-catch combination in UT history.

The book is a collection of narratives of some of the most prominent players in the history of the Tennessee program. They are interviews done from July 2007 to November 2007, and the men I talked to were delighted to share their stories.

Doug Atkins, a fearsome defensive end from the '50s, was too ill to be interviewed, so I pieced together his story from a collection of newspaper clips.

If you don't see a player in the book who you thought should be in here, well, we tried to get him, or else he has passed away. There were a number of players who should be in this book but who, for one reason or another, were unable to participate in the interview process—players like Travis Henry, the all-time leading rusher; Al Wilson, the great linebacker who was the leader of the defense for the 1998 national championship team; the terrific linebackers Paul Naumoff, Keith DeLong, and Dale Jones; Curt Watson, an outstanding running back; and Dale Carter.

Jack Reynolds, as well, should be in this book. But I was warned that it was impossible to talk to Hacksaw. The great UT linebacker stays behind the curtain in the tropics and does not do interviews.

Two weeks before the deadline, I finally interviewed John Henderson, the 2000 Outland Trophy winner. Ryan Robinson, who is part of the Jacksonville

Jaguars media staff, and Tennessee defensive line coach Dan Brooks made it happen, along with Henderson, who provided terrific insight.

What made the Henderson "get" significant is that three days before I talked to him, I interviewed the only other Outland Trophy winner in UT history, Steve DeLong.

It would have been great to get the words of the All-American Reggie White, but he died suddenly in 2004. Jimmy Sexton, his friend and agent, and a former Vol manager, was gracious enough to give his thoughts on Reggie. Sexton also hooked me up with Dustin Colquitt, a punter for the Chiefs.

Craig Kelley of the Indianapolis Colts, who is considered one of the best public relations guys in the NFL, helped make the interview happen with Peyton Manning. Andrew Whalen, the communications director for Congressman Heath Shuler, connected me with the busy politician to make that interview go off smoothly, and I am grateful.

Haywood Harris, the former sports information director and Vols historian, gave me early traction and advice. Alan Carmichael and Cynthia Moxley, former newspaper people who have built a trustworthy public relations business in Knoxville, were instrumental in helping me get the phone numbers of former players, along with local lawyer Don Bosch.

Ben Byrd, a former colleague at *The Knoxville Journal* before it closed in 1991, also provided encouragement and insight, and he is included in this book.

The one person I would have loved dearly to get in this book was Russ Bebb, the former sports editor of *The Journal*, who has passed away.

Bud Ford, the Tennessee sports information director, deserves credit for this project because the Tennessee media guide still has every game score, starting lineups through the years, assistant coaches' names, where players were drafted, and all the awards they have won. A number of schools have started to use their so-called media guides as recruiting tools with a maddening number of pictures, and they have made the guides useless to the media. The UT media guide was priceless in going back in time with players as I interviewed them. John Painter of the UT SID office secured the long interview with Fulmer and always helped with questions.

My wife, Jessie Bond, gave me the nudge I needed to get into this project. She said it would be a great experience, and it was. Her moral support helped me through a long project.

I am most grateful to the players who shared their stories. The insights, the highs, the lows, and the appreciation of their teammates are all in this book.

I cover college football for newspapers and websites, and I have a skeptical disposition toward this monolith of college football. It has become a money grab and an arms race.

This book, more than anything, gives me a softer view of college football. It settles my apprehension—not completely, but a little—and reveals there is something still worthwhile underneath the glistening weight rooms, the seat licenses, and the largesse of recruiting. I will never know firsthand what it means to be a Volunteer, but I am certain now it is something quite special to nearly every kid who has come out of high school and worn the orange and white.

INTRODUCTION

WHEN DOUG DICKEY TOOK OVER as Tennessee's football coach for the 1964 season, there was an uneasy relationship between the new coach and his All-American lineman, Steve DeLong.

DeLong was a fierce player, a courageous player. He was determined and disciplined, and he was also one of the few talents on the squad Dickey inherited. The new coach wanted to make sure everyone knew who was in control when he met DeLong for the first time.

"I knew he was the head coach, he didn't have to tell me," DeLong said with a wry smile. "But I think he wanted to make sure the players were going to follow his line of thinking.

"I didn't like the way he went about things when he got there."

In that first year under Dickey, DeLong had one of the greatest seasons in Tennessee football history. A 6′3″, 235-pound middle guard, he won the Outland Trophy, just one of two players in the history of the UT program to win the prestigious award given to the nation's top interior lineman since 1946.

DeLong is in a wheelchair now, partially paralyzed after a fall when he was 59 years old.

And Doug Dickey?

DeLong looked up with a smile.

"If he has time, he comes to see me whenever he is in town," the legendary Vol said.

Is that what it means to be a Volunteer? I think it is.

The coach and player, once at odds, have a certain respect for one another.

There are stories of mutual respect throughout this book. If there was a common denominator in these narratives, it was that the Tennessee players included here always seemed to stop and consider others around them, whether it was their coaches, their teammates, or the fans.

That aspect gave an emotional tug to this project that will give the most jaded and cynical of sportswriters—me—a reason to pause and see another side of the college football player.

There are some things about Tennessee football not included in the narratives of the players in this book that can illustrate what it means to be a Volunteer. One is the Last Tackle Drill. You don't have to be a star or a starter to feel its emotion.

At the last practice of the regular season, Tennessee's seniors line up and, one by one, charge down a tunnel of teammates and crush a dummy dressed in the jersey of the opponent. Most years it was Vanderbilt. Lately it has been Kentucky.

Mike Cunningham, a walk-on, got to do the Last Tackle, and he will never forget it. He looked at the tackling dummy in a Vandy jersey, sprinted full speed, and mauled the thing. Haywood Harris, the Tennessee football historian, said emotion poured out of Cunningham.

That's what it means to be a Volunteer.

"Some guys would just push the tackling dummy over," Cunningham said. "I wanted to hit it. It was my last hurrah. You have to understand I fulfilled a dream by wearing that jersey, and I think that's why I hit the dummy so hard and why it was so emotional for me. It's a great program, and I was part of it."

What does it mean to be a Vol? Even for a brief moment?

A million dollars. That's what it means.

It's what somebody will give to have the tiniest of slices of being a Vol. A million bucks, just like that, smack on the table.

John Thornton, a Tennessee football fan, made a $1 million contribution to the Tennessee athletic department, but he requested that he be able to run through the T, that legendary band formation, which players run through before a game at Neyland Stadium.

The request was granted, and Thornton had his day in the spotlight. Imagine four years of that.

Thornton got to hear firsthand the thunderous ovation of more than 100,000 fans as Tennessee's team ran onto the field. If you have been on the field—and I have stood on the sideline during a game—it can bring chills.

So imagine what it means to be a Volunteer for two years, three years, four years, or a lifetime.

It means more than a million bucks. It means priceless stories and memories, and those stories and memories are inside this book in the narratives of some of the most prominent players in the history of the program.

The stories are *really* what it means to be a Volunteer.

One of the things you figure out is that once it was apparent General Robert Neyland's legacy could not sustain the dynasty in the mid-1960s and things started to unravel, the players took over. Except for a few modest years in the early '70s, and one down year recently, the program has thrived for 40 years.

It did not thrive under one legend, like Bear Bryant at Alabama. The program thrived from Doug Dickey to Bill Battle to Johnny Majors to Phil Fulmer. None of them is General Neyland. None of them was as large as Bear Bryant at Alabama, but they did not have to be because the players sustained the program and kept it right-side up for most of this 40-year run.

It is ironic that a Florida Gator, Dickey, the head coach from 1964 to 1970, pulled the program out of its rut. Tennessee had gone through a stretch (1958–1963) where it had just three winning seasons in six, and Dickey helped restore the prominence.

Neyland died in the middle of the downturn (1962), and the program was losing its allure. The Vols had stubbornly stuck to the single-wing and, Steve DeLong told me, there was some chaos on the coaching staff and within the athletic department.

Dickey was hired, and a switch was flipped. Dickey got the Tennessee program back in the black. One of the last schools to abandon the single-wing and move to a T formation offense (1963), the Vols rejoined the powerhouses of college football—Oklahoma, Notre Dame, and Alabama, among others.

It was during those Dickey years that Lester McClain became the first black player of significance in the Southeastern Conference. What Bryant couldn't make happen in Alabama, Dickey made happen in Tennessee.

McClain's courage had just as much to do with it. He looked back 40 years and said that somewhere on campus, perhaps in a heated argument, somebody stood their ground and said, "We will have a black player."

There is a twist to that story, and you will find it embedded in McClain's narrative, as well as the narrative of Richmond Flowers, the fast kid from Montgomery, Alabama, who turned down Bear Bryant's scholarship offer.

What was Bryant's response in later years to Flowers's snub? Read about it in Flowers's narrative.

There is something else about this program. The fans matter. They have a hand on the rudder, right along with the guys with the titles in the Tennessee administration.

It is simply referred to as "The Stop." UT defenders stop LSU All-American Billy Cannon at the goal line to upset the No. 1 Tigers 14–13 in 1959. Wayne Grubb, Charley Severance, and Bill Majors made the stop.

General Neyland on the sideline with All-American Hank Lauricella (No. 27).

The late Russ Bebb, the former sports editor and columnist of *The Knoxville Journal*, knew that as well as anyone. I called them readers, customers of *The Journal*. He knew they were fans first.

Bebb liked to empower these fans/readers. He made sure there was room for letters, and then one day he had an idea. It was an editorial in disguise.

He wanted to survey Tennessee football fans in 1990 on the new white jerseys with the orange numbers. The fans were grumbling, and so was Russ, who was a 60-something spotter/statistician for the Vol Network. He couldn't make out the jersey numbers from the press box. The fans he talked

General Neyland and the Vols have a fine time following another win.

to—and he talked to many—had the same problem. The orange was too light of a tone and nearly invisible in the upper reaches of that stadium.

I was the executive sports editor. My first thought when he presented the idea of the survey to me was, "No way, Russ."

I am from Fairfax, Virginia, not Tennessee. I was new to Knoxville. I had no idea you could do a survey about something as ordinary as football jerseys and incite so much passion.

Russ, of course, knew better. He knew Tennessee fans and he knew they wanted to be heard and have a place to vent, so we ran the survey.

There was an avalanche of mail. The surveys stuffed our mailbox for two weeks. This was before email, and Bebb would have a pile of letters from east Tennessee—and beyond—dropped on his desk each day. Served him right.

That's what it means to be a Volunteer. The passion of the fans seems endless.

I started at the paper in 1989, and I knew it was 24-hour Vols, but this survey, which seemed humdrum, hit me over the head.

I should have known. Randy Moore, who covered the Vols for *The Journal*, had to work from home in January. If he tried to handle the reporting on recruiting while in the office, he wouldn't get any work done because the phone rang off the hook.

That didn't stop the recruiting calls from coming in, which seemed like a nuisance at the time, but I should have been delighted at those calls. People were going to read the paper...and it wasn't even football season for crying out loud. It was January and early February.

That's what it means to be a Volunteer. People don't give it a rest.

There were all kinds of anecdotes about the passion and fury of Tennessee football fans. The most vivid for me was being on the sideline for the opening kickoff of the Florida game in Neyland Stadium in 1990. UT was No. 5. The Gators were No. 9. It was a night game, and UT fans had all day to get juiced up, if you know what I mean.

Tennessee's Dale Carter caught the kick against the sideline, darted upfield, and the noise that rose in that stadium was deafening. Carter scored to spark a 45–3 rout.

You don't just hear the noise inside Neyland Stadium, you feel it. The ground can shake. It shook that night.

Lou Holtz set up speakers inside the Notre Dame field house before the Irish came to play Tennessee in Neyland Stadium in 1990. He was trying to duplicate the noise level at UT for his practice.

I was in South Bend writing an advance story on Notre Dame for *The Journal*, and he didn't let me into practice, but I could hear the noise standing outside the Irish practice facility. After practice, I told him, "If your ears aren't hurting, it's not loud enough."

He yelled, "What?!" The noise had left him a little deaf.

I always maintained an objective stance toward Tennessee football as a journalist. Never rooted for them, never rooted against them.

But I always admired how much passion was stirred by the Big Orange. Friends up north would ask, "What's it like to watch a game with 100,000-plus in Neyland Stadium?" And I would tell them, "You have to go, just once." Buy a ticket.

Peyton Manning told me he never tries to explain it to his teammates on the Indianapolis Colts, the teammates that played in the Big Ten or Pac-10. He tells them, "Just go. Once."

The press box is halfway to the moon, and if I wasn't on a national deadline for *The New York Times* and didn't need a computer at my fingertips, I would find a way to watch the game from the aisleways or the field. Sometimes I will go out on the photo deck, in the open air, and get a hint of the passion.

Every time I see a Tennessee fan in Atlanta—you can spot them easily in the shirt, the hat, or something—I try and strike up a conversation. The first thing most of them will say is, "I am a huge Vol fan."

Is there any other kind?

The

FOUNDING
FATHERS

GENERAL ROBERT NEYLAND

(AS TOLD BY ROBERT NEYLAND JR.)

HEAD COACH
1926–1934 ★ 1936–1940 ★ 1946–1952

WHEN I WAS NINE YEARS OLD, I remember so well the first thrill of Tennessee football. It was when we played Alabama in Knoxville, and the second-string tailback Johnny Butler made a great run for a touchdown. I never forgot that. That run was lost for years, then someone found the film, and I watched it, and I said, "Hey, I remember that." Johnny was one of those guys who could break a run on you anytime.

That was in 1939, and the reason I remember it so well was that was the year we didn't even get scored on in the regular season. That was way before the soccer-style field-goal kickers who could kick long field goals and get a team on the scoreboard.

Somewhere along the line, my father just became convinced his teams would be built on defense, and that was how Tennessee was going to win football games. Bob Gilbert wrote a book called *Gridiron General*, and he pointed out that 60 percent of dad's wins were shutouts. He used to say there are more ways to score on defense than there are on offense. On defense, you

General Neyland's record at Tennessee was 173–31–12.

could recover fumbles, intercept passes, recover a fumble in end zone, block a kick. We frequently did score on defense.

His strength was not the pregame oratory to the players to get them ready to play. He didn't do that. He devoted the whole pregame talk to the players about going over fundamentals and our game plan. One time, he said, "Right before the game is a poor time to try and organize a team and get them motivated." He didn't feel like pep talks were the way to go.

West Point is where he met my mother. She came to a West Point dance with somebody else and she struck up a conversation with my father, and it went from there.

My father's success goes back to something he told me one time, which was that the key to winning and being successful at anything required him to do three things: organize, deputize, and supervise. That's what he did in football. He had everything organized and fine-tuned and had some great assistant coaches, so he supervised in those years. He left much of the on-field coaching to those coaches, but he had already told them in meetings what he expected and what he wanted. It goes back to organization and fundamentals.

I have been embarrassed more than a few times by people who were well-meaning who came up to talk to me and talked about him like he was a god. He certainly wasn't, as he would tell you.

The highlights of his career, of course, were the great times that came with winning. The bad part was that, when Tennessee lost, I felt like I lost a family member.

I went to a prep school in Chattanooga called Baylor and played football there. When it came time for college, I never did think about going anywhere else because I knew I would always be wondering what Tennessee was doing. So if I didn't make the team, that was okay, too, because I was going to live right there in Knoxville. I was on the second-team, which is right where I belonged. I didn't deserve to start. I was in the right place. My dad didn't treat me any better than the other players, and in fact, I had no real interaction with him because the assistant coaches did most of the on-field coaching.

My junior and senior years, 1952 and 1953, I lettered as a second-team wingback. I came in 1949 and redshirted in 1950.

Dad resigned following the 1952 season for health reasons, and the chief assistant, Harvey Robinson, took over, and we started to slide a little bit. The material wasn't as good. In 1950 and 1951 we were loaded, but those players had left.

Over the years, I have considered which of those last few teams of my father's were the best, and I would have to say the 1950 team was the best, even better than the 1951 team that won the national championship. They dropped the second game of the season to Mississippi State and then got better and better, climaxing with the big win over Texas in the Cotton Bowl. That might have been the win he was the happiest about of all the wins he had. He was a Texan, born in Greenville, so that was important for him to come home and get a win like that.

Texas, for that era, was a big, strong team. They were the favorite in that Cotton Bowl, but the single-wing with that double-team blocking just wore them down gradually. It was a fourth-quarter win.

Even as good as we were back in that era, a lot of our games were not sell-outs. It wasn't nearly as big as it is today. We might have sold out for Alabama, but not all the time. He didn't notice, I don't think, because he was all about the football. I don't think he would have been very comfortable today with all the media and the huge crowds. He was very camera-shy, anyway, and avoided the media as much as he could. He never felt comfortable around them and didn't like to talk.

Of course, there have been some down times, and we went through them in 1947 and 1948 when Tennessee had some very ordinary teams. There was a lot of talk around Knoxville that Dad had gotten too old and that he passed his prime and that they needed somebody else to get a different offense in there besides the single-wing.

My mother tried to get him to quit because of that pressure in the '40s. She felt the emotion of the losses, too, and didn't want him to have to deal with it.

When he was getting pressured, he went out and recruited that great class that came in with Hank Lauricella (1948). Things changed with that group because, when they got some experience, they were very, very good. Things really improved with the program, and there wasn't much talk anymore about Dad being past his prime.

His health started to decline, and he finally decided to resign following the 1952 season. He had liver problems and all, and on doctor's advice, he stepped down when he was 60. Dad became the athletic director for the rest of his time there, which was until 1962, when he died.

When we go into the stadium and watch a game there, it is a tremendous feeling of pride. I grew up hoping I could play for Tennessee. I try my very best not to be boastful around people, but inwardly there is a lot of pride and happiness. I've gotten a big kick out of watching the teams down through the years, as much as when I was a kid. It's my school, still today.

I have been grateful that the Vols have stayed up there among the elite programs for most of these years and have maintained the program's status.

Robert Reese Neyland came to Knoxville in 1925 from West Point as an ROTC instructor and captain. Neyland served three different times as Tennessee coach—1926–1934, 1936–1940, and 1946–1952—and left as a brigadier general. Each time he left Tennessee, it was to take time off to perform military service for his country. Neyland's 21-year record was 173–31–12. His 1939 team is the last team in college football to shut out all of its regular season opponents. Tennessee shut out 112 of 216 opponents under Neyland, and the school still holds the record for shutting out opponents in consecutive quarters (71). General Neyland's teams won four national championships.

HACK, MACK, & DODD
BACKFIELD
1920s

IT WAS AS SUDDEN and uncomplicated a start as a dynasty can have. Gene McEver took a kickoff and raced 98 yards for a touchdown. It was captured on grainy, black-and-white film, but it should have been in living color and plastered all over billboards in the South because the historical significance of the return was immense.

McEver's return was in Tuscaloosa, Alabama, on Saturday, October 20, 1928, and it ignited a 15–13 upset of the Crimson Tide, which was the Southern powerhouse.

Jim Haslam, who played guard for Tennessee's 1951 national championship team, said General Neyland always referred to McEver's kick return and the victory over Alabama as the most vital moment in Tennessee's football history.

Neyland, who was in his third season as Tennessee coach in 1928 and still just a major, had taken down a Southern power. What's more, McEver burst on the national scene and gave the program a hero, its first All-American.

Sure, Tennessee was 8–0–1 in 1927, but the 1928 team with McEver, Bobby Dodd, and Buddy Hackman—the Flaming Sophomores—ignited a passion in the program. In the six-year stretch from 1927 to 1932, Tennessee was 53–1–5.

The victory over Alabama in 1928 cast Tennessee in a different light. For the first time, the Vols were looked upon as a juggernaut, a team that would earn respect down through the years even when it had a modest record.

There was a paradox to McEver's burst for points, because Tennessee football was more about keeping points off the scoreboard then putting them on. In Neyland's career, 112 of 216 Tennessee opponents failed to score.

In the six-year run (1927–1932), Tennessee held opponents scoreless in 38 games. Granted, this was in the day before long field-goal kickers could manage to get points for a desperate offense, but the Vols had a legitimate reputation of being a stone wall.

The '28 team did not seem like a squad that would be a benchmark for the program. After all, there were just three starters returning from the 1927 team and the fabulous freshmen, McEver, Hackman, and Dodd, were just sophomores.

Shouldn't they need more seasoning?

"The Rats," as they were nicknamed, considered themselves seasoned enough. They won all five games as freshmen in 1927 and outscored opponents 165–14, so they were brimming with confidence entering the 1928 season.

The team came together quite by accident, according to former *Knoxville Journal* sports editor Russ Bebb.

In his book, *The Big Orange: A Story of Tennessee Football*, Bebb said that McEver entered Wake Forest in the fall of 1927. "The Bristol Blizzard" had become friends with a Baptist minister, Bebb wrote, and turned down scholarship offers from Tennessee and Alabama to go to Wake. McEver was on the Wake Forest campus a week when Neyland sent one of his assistants to Winston-Salem, North Carolina, and lured McEver back to Tennessee.

The running back joined the freshman class with Bobby Dodd, the quarterback out of Kingsport, Tennessee, and Hackman, who was from Nashville. Bebb wrote that Neyland also hijacked Dodd and Hackman, who were ready to play for rival Vanderbilt.

The three players, who could have played college football somewhere else if not for Neyland's persistence, all have been named to the College Football Hall of Fame. McEver still holds the UT record for career touchdowns (44, from 1928 to 1931).

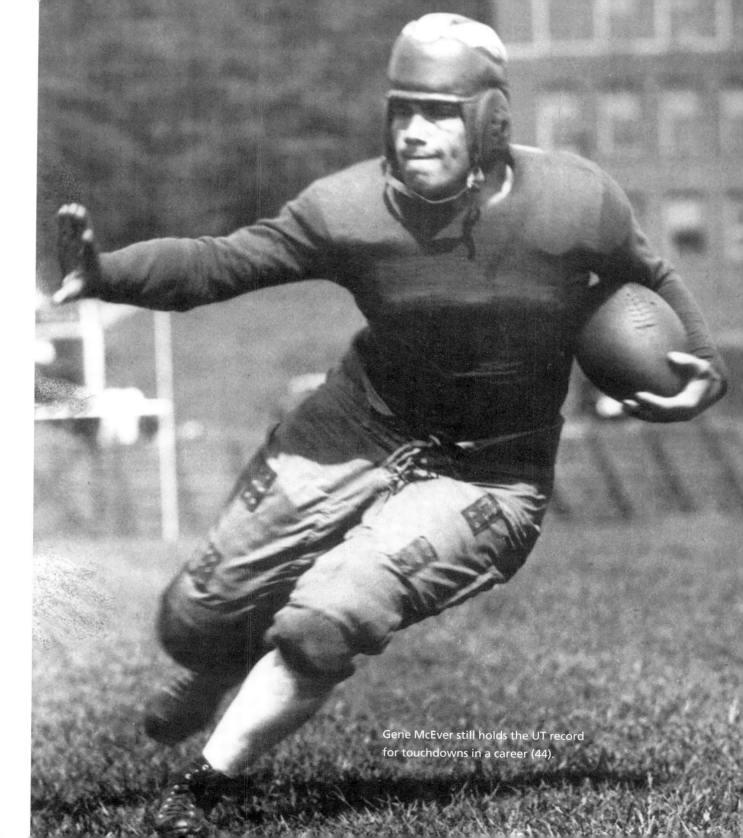

Gene McEver still holds the UT record for touchdowns in a career (44).

Dodd's and Hackman's only loss came in 1930 as seniors—an 18–6 defeat to Alabama. McEver did not play that season after tearing a knee ligament playing baseball.

In 1931, McEver finally played his senior season with a heavy steel brace on the repaired knee. He was joined in the backfield by the next star in line, Beattie Feathers, a sensational runner in his own right.

If McEver's return for a touchdown against Alabama in 1928 was the powder keg, then the arrival of Feathers showed how the program could sustain itself by reloading. Feathers was the star of the 1932 team that went 9–0–1 and won the Southern Conference championship.

It was almost Neyland's last hurrah as Tennessee coach. Bebb wrote in his book that Neyland nearly accepted an offer from Fordham to move to New York and coach that powerhouse program. He turned down Fordham, but in 1935 Neyland could not—and did not want to—turn down the Army as he received orders for a three-year tour of duty to Panama.

It turned out to be just a one-year stint, and when Neyland returned, so did Tennessee's dominance. The Vols suffered through a 4–5 season in 1935 without their legendary coach, and when Neyland returned, it took two seasons to get things right again. Tennessee then roared back with a 31–2 record from 1938 to 1940.

The 1939 team did not give up a point in the regular season, the last team in college football to accomplish that feat. Neyland went off to the military, this time in World War II, and returned to coach Tennessee again in 1946.

When Neyland retired following the 1952 season, he had compiled a record of 173–31–12. It was quite a record for a coach whose only orders when he was hired were, "Do something about the Vanderbilt series."

The FORTIES AND FIFTIES

JOHN MICHELS

GUARD

1949–1952

THERE WERE MANY TIMES when I was coaching in the NFL that I found myself mouthing the words of General Neyland, the words he used in practice with us when I was at Tennessee. I said, "My God, he must be here looking over my shoulder."

I posted the maxims that General Neyland used with us in my office and used them my entire career. I wanted the players who came in to see them over and over. He was very disciplined in that regard; he had a set of principles and he followed them.

There were many times he told us, if it at first you don't succeed, try, try again. The team with the fewest mistakes wins, and so forth. He lives on in each of the coaches that came out of the program. I adhere to those maxims, and I learned from him.

My best memory is running the "10" play in practice over and over and over again. I can walk it right now. I can't run it—I'm too old—but I can walk it. You took five steps, planted your right foot, and turned upfield on the "10" play. The two guards went upfield shoulder to shoulder, the fullback and blocking back kicked the defensive end outside, and the tailback went up in there. Coach Neyland would not let you deviate from how you ran that play.

We had so much confidence in that play, it was unbelievable. We probably ran that play 20 percent of the time. We didn't throw the ball much; we ran, and when we ran, it was the "10" play.

Tennessee football was different back then. We didn't throw the ball as much and we were all about defense. Defensive football was the General's big thing.

I wanted to play defense, but he said, you are a guard, and that was the end of the discussion. I weighed 190 pounds, and I was a guard, but even that put me on the Fat Table.

He wanted me 185 pounds, so those of us who were not at his prescribed weight sat off to the side at a different table, and they served you un-fattening food. It took me about a week to get off the Fat Table. The trouble was I was sneaking food on the side. My wife, who I met at Tennessee, would get me a hot dog or a hamburger. We didn't have much money, but she would get some food for me.

The other thing that was different back then was everybody came dressed up to the games. I was from Philadelphia, and we didn't see that up there. Down here, it was like a ball or a dance because men were in coats and ties. Nobody was shabbily dressed, but they were vocal.

They were smaller crowds, but they made a lot of noise. I found out what football was all about at Tennessee.

Now, I played before 50,000 in the city championship game when I was at West Catholic High School. High school football was bigger than any college football in Philadelphia at that time. So when I came to Tennessee, I was ready for some of the crowds.

Under Neyland, everything was done by the numbers. When they taught the blocking, they taught you to step with your right foot, head up and eyes open. That is the way you practiced. He had the idea that if you didn't run a play at least 100 times in practice, you weren't going to be very good at it.

General Neyland adhered to that, and I found myself doing the same thing when I was coaching the Vikings' offensive line in the NFL. Run it over and over and over. You have no idea how regimented you had to be to play for the General.

It was an extremely strong bond back then because we lived together, we ate together, we did almost everything together. We all lived in the stadium. It was very much like a family. We slept there. It was home.

We had bed check, too. I didn't drink at all, so I never tried to sneak out and I was always worried about getting nailed by something like that with the General. I was chicken.

John Michels was an All-American guard at Tennessee and a successful coach in the NFL.

If you broke down with your grades, it was General Neyland who arranged the study halls, and you had to be there.

I remember three of the toughest games we played were against Alabama each of my three seasons because Neyland emphasized Alabama. The week we played Alabama, he was constantly talking about them. They were always bloodbaths and some of the best football I ever played. The crowds were incredible.

Our fans started appearing at the stadium hours and hours before the game to get themselves revved up just as they do now. None of that has changed. I have season tickets now that we moved back here and I don't miss any games, especially Alabama.

Being from the North, I didn't understand the rivalry between Tennessee and Alabama at first. But after a while, I did. It was the biggest game of the year.

Other than the Alabama games and beating Texas in the Cotton Bowl to end the 1950 season, the one other game I remember was losing to Maryland in the Sugar Bowl. We were 10–0 and had clinched the national championship for 1951, but that loss—well, I can't describe how bad it was. We were at the top of the world and our legs were knocked out from underneath us.

It still bothers me, even after all these years. That game was in New Orleans, and I haven't liked New Orleans since then. It took me a long time to swallow it, let alone put up with it. They ran a gap-eight defense, which loaded up the defensive line and choked off the running game. They had a man on the center, a man on both guards, and then a man playing on the inside shoulder of the tight end and a man outside of that. They choked us off pretty good.

We didn't throw the ball the next year even after that happened to us. His philosophy was, bad things happened when you threw the ball. General Neyland would not throw the football.

The best thing to ever happen to me was coming to Tennessee. I met my wife, and it was a great place to go to school. The guys I played with are still my friends. We meet now, and it is like old-home week.

I'm very fortunate to have gone here because I had some other offers. I was in prep school to go to the Naval Academy when Tennessee was recruiting me. Navy football was big back then. There were about 12 schools that recruited me. Penn State, Notre Dame, the University of Pennsylvania, and

Villanova. I was all-city in Philadelphia two years in a row and had a chance to play elsewhere.

The big thing when I decided to go to Tennessee was people would come up to me and say, "Why are you going down to Tennessee?" They didn't understand it.

I lived eight blocks from the University of Pennsylvania, and people wanted me to go there. But the line coach at Tennessee, a guy named Hodges "Burr" West, did a great job recruiting. He wouldn't let me alone. He kept after me and after me. I will never forget him.

I kept telling him I wasn't going down to Tennessee because I was thinking about Navy or Notre Dame. He said, "Why don't you come down one time and look at the place?"

So I went down on a football weekend and saw Tennessee play, and I liked what I saw. I watched practice one day and just became part of the program. You could see the program was about discipline and you could see the coaching and what football was all about.

When the local schools found out about it, they started calling me and saying, "Why would you go down there with those people?" They were bad-mouthing Tennessee and had no idea about Knoxville or the university. They were trying to scare me by saying, "You don't know what those Southern schools are like."

It turned out to be a great place, which is what I figured when I decided to go there. A lot of things went right for me at Tennessee, though I got a surprise when I returned for my sophomore year. I walked in for the first meeting of camp and the offensive line coach said to me, "Did you get the notebook?" I said no and asked him what he was talking about. He said, you are a guard now.

I had left after my freshman year for summer, thinking I was going to be a defensive player when I came back as a sophomore. If you knew the General, there was no asking; they were telling me. They said, you are moved to guard, and that was it.

That coach handed me a notebook with all the plays in it. I didn't have a few minutes to even think about it. I could take a deep breath, and that was the time I had to think about it. I said okay, and that was the end of the story. General Neyland never explained anything to you, and I understood that.

We knew who the boss was. General Neyland was aloof from us and didn't speak to us in public. He spoke to me just once off the field, and it was after we beat a very good Texas team in the Cotton Bowl. We bumped into each other on the plane, and I said, "Excuse me, General." And he said, "You missed that block on the nine play."

I thought, *My God, we won the game.* He was right, of course, and that's the way he thought and that is what made him a great coach.

He was constantly in that mode of getting things right. I said back to him, "I got the guy the next time." And he said, "That doesn't count." We were all happy and elated, but his mind was on what you had done wrong and how he was going to correct it.

He let the assistant coaches do all the yelling in practice and if he ever stepped in, you knew it was the Voice of God speaking. I remember one time coming up to see him later after I left school, and it was the same way. I sat down and thought we were relaxing, but he hadn't changed a bit. He was the greatest football coach who ever lived.

So what does it mean to be a Vol? Playing for the greatest coach who ever lived. That's what it means.

John Michels was a three-year starter at guard for Tennessee and was part of the 1951 national championship team. He was a consensus All-American in 1952 and won the Jacobs Blocking Trophy given annually to the best blocker in the Southeastern Conference, as voted by the coaches. Michels was All-SEC in 1951 and 1952. He coached the offensive line for the Minnesota Vikings from 1967 to 1993, and the Vikings appeared in four Super Bowls. He is retired and living near Knoxville and regularly attends games at Neyland Stadium.

HANK LAURICELLA

TAILBACK

1949–1952

WE HAD A RUN DIDN'T WE? It was our national championship run, and it was quite a time for Tennessee football.

We lost to Mississippi State in 1950 in the second game of the season, and we didn't lose again until we lost to Maryland in New Orleans in the Sugar Bowl at the end of the 1951 season. We won 20 games in a row. We played and beat some good football teams during that stretch.

The Bear [Bryant] was at Kentucky, and in every game we played against them, they were a formidable team, but we still managed to beat them. That's what I mean when I say we had a good run, because back then we were beating teams like Kentucky and Alabama, and the program was one of the best in the country.

My freshman year, Kentucky tied Tennessee 0–0, and in the following three years, we shut out Kentucky each year. Counting 1948, when I didn't play as a freshman, Bear Bryant never scored a point against Tennessee in four games. Can you imagine that? The Bear's teams did not score one touchdown against Tennessee in four years. That's pretty strong. His Kentucky teams were something good, but we had great defense. That's what we were known for back in the day and what we built our reputation around.

Babe Parilli was his quarterback, and they had very good offensive teams at Kentucky. But as good as he was, he never scored against us in those years.

You could see the national championship team coming together and getting experience in 1949 when we were sophomores. We lost to Georgia Tech and to Duke, and we tied Alabama. We were 7–2–1, but the General wouldn't take us to a bowl game because he said we weren't ready.

Single-wing tailback Hank Lauricella (No. 27), the offensive star of Neyland's last teams at Tennessee, turns the corner on a run.

They didn't have as many bowl games back then, but we still could've gone to a bowl game with that record. Neyland said we were a young team; we shouldn't go, and that was that. We had a lot of sophomore starters on the 1949 team, so that's what he meant about us being not ready and being too young for the bowl game. There were a bunch of sophomore starters on defense, too, so I guess he had a point because we were very young.

In those days, there was no limit on the number of recruits you could sign. We had 100 recruits show up September 1, 1948, for the first day of practice. A whole bunch of them left, of course. It doesn't take long when you get into a big group like that and you start competing to find out who's good enough to stay around. Guys figured out that they needed to go somewhere else or go back home to mama or the girlfriend they left at home.

Neyland had a rule and he stuck by it. He would tell guys, "Young man, if you come here, we want to offer you a scholarship. If you do your work, and we don't have any problems with you, and you follow the rules, your scholarship is good, whether you play or not."

We had some guys in that 1948 group who hardly ever played football but stayed there for four years and got their degrees. They did what they were supposed to do on the field, they did their academic work, and the General kept them on, so they had their education paid for.

That promise was always there by General Neyland. He did not run people off. Today, they run kids off if they can't make it, and that was one of the great things about the General—he kept his word about their scholarships if he recruited them. There were some who just flat-out got in trouble, who did not adhere to the rules and were told to leave, but the guys who followed the rules had their education paid for, whether they played a lot or not.

I know an attorney who is in Knoxville now, who only got to play a few downs in his career. But he stayed and worked in the training room and helped in the equipment room, and he finished, got his degree, and went to law school.

Neyland was the most unusual person in that he was extremely organized, extremely disciplined, and didn't do a lot of talking. I guess it was his military training that enabled him to go at the game and look at it a little bit differently than a regular coach, which is what made him so special.

Games were almost battles to him. Maybe it was in his military background, but defense was his main part of the game. This philosophy was:

I will give you the ball any time in your part of the field. What he meant, of course, was in those days when we did not have the wide-open offenses, he didn't mind for teams to have the ball on their side of the 50. His game was field position and defense.

You had to understand that there were some long plays back in the day, but mostly it was short yardage plays on offense. Football was played in the middle of the line, and you did not spread teams out one sideline to the next. There were 22 guys in the middle of the field all bunched up, so for you to go 75 yards against his defense, which historically would not let you go two or three yards per play, was tough.

That was Tennessee football. The General figured you were going to fumble the ball or you were going to make some mistake that would allow Tennessee to get the ball and be in field position to score. His theory was that he would trade possession of the ball for position on the field. To him that was instrumental.

He always kicked off to start the game. He believed so much in defense, field position, and the kicking game that he would punt on first down deep in our territory. We didn't want the ball backed up in our end because the General didn't want to make the mistake that would give an opponent a short field. Those were mistakes other teams made, not his teams.

21

I punted the ball numerous times on first down because, in those days as the tailback in a single-wing, I would call the plays. I was taught that way, which is that we did not want the ball deep in our territory.

Our bread-and-butter play was the "10" play with two running guards pulling out, the fullback and the blocking back blocking on the defensive end. It was a lot of two-on-one blocking that was concentrated off the right tackle. My high school coach told me before I went to Tennessee that we would run the "10" play until I was blue in the face, and sure enough, we ran it a lot.

We went to a two-platoon system my sophomore season. General Neyland told us, "Men"—he always called us "men"—"the 11 best players are going to be put on defense." That was his philosophy, take our most talented players and win with defense.

After we got the first 11, then we would start creating our offense and our backup teams. If there was a guy who was a good blocker, but also a good defensive lineman, he played defense. The two-platoon gave a lot of kids a lot of opportunities in football that they would not have been able to have in the old, single-platoon system.

I finished my sophomore year as the starting tailback, but I started that season as the number-one defensive safety man and the fourth-string tailback. I got my break when some guys got hurt and others were unable to play against Ole Miss in 1949 and I had a big game. I threw three touchdown passes and did some running and kicked relatively well. After that Ole Miss game, I started every game for the rest of my days at Tennessee.

The Ole Miss game was big because they were hoping to beat us for the third year in a row, and no one had ever beaten Neyland three years in a row. Johnny Vaught was the coach at Ole Miss, and he had a quarterback by the name of Charlie Conerly and some other great players. They had beaten us two years in a row.

The three years I played, we had a great offensive line and we had a great defense, too. We just had so much talent in our class—I would sit on the sideline when we did not have the ball, and it was so amazing to watch our defense.

We played Vanderbilt my sophomore year, and they had a wonderful football team back then. In the second quarter, we were beating them 19–0 and did not even have a first down. That's because our defense was dominating. We blocked a punt, picked it up, and ran it for a touchdown. We intercepted a pass and ran it for a touchdown. We recovered a fumble, and on the first play after the fumble recovery, I threw a touchdown pass. That's what kind of defense we had.

Neyland was able to get good talent to Tennessee because so many of his former players went into coaching on the high school level, and they were spread out in different regions around the South, Midwest, and Northeast. He had former players in Kentucky and Ohio and Pennsylvania, so he was able to recruit very effectively up there. They were strategically located in the hotbeds of high school football, and they were loyal to the General and would send him names of players they thought could play for him.

My junior season, 10 out of the 11 offensive players were not from the state of Tennessee, and something like nine out of the 11 defensive players were not from Tennessee. Just look at the map. From Knoxville, you can easily reach Ohio, Pennsylvania, West Virginia, North Carolina, South Carolina, Alabama, and Georgia. He even got some players out of New York and the New England area because of his former players.

The General did not have a particularly good season in 1947 and was catching a lot of heat, so he got out of Knoxville when the season was over and went to New Orleans. He was fond of New Orleans, having brought two or three of his teams down here to play in the Sugar Bowl.

Over one of the weekends General Neyland was here, I happened to be playing a city championship game and he had a friend down here, an SEC official by the name of Johnny Lynch. Lynch said there was a big game on a Sunday afternoon, and the General might want to go see that game, which was the one I was playing in.

We won, and I had a good game, and the middle of the next week they called me out of the classroom and detailed me down to the main office. They said General Neyland of the University of Tennessee was calling and wanted to speak to me. He said he was coming back to New Orleans for the Sugar Bowl game and wanted to meet me and have breakfast. So I met him for breakfast, and we agreed I would make a trip to Knoxville. I visited and fell in love with the place, and that is how I ended up a Volunteer.

I became a single-wing tailback. It is a lot different than the T formation, where you needed some blazing speed. The single-wing was very deliberate because you waited for the play to open up. That was the reason I went to Tennessee—most other teams had converted from the single-wing to the T formation, but I wanted to take the snaps and make some plays. I was a good runner, maybe an above-average passer, and a very good punter. There were guys who could run better than I could and pass better than I could, but none of them could do all three relatively well.

23

I called all the plays back then. I can think of one game when I got a hand signal from the sideline to run a particular play, and that was when we were playing Texas in the Cotton Bowl. Harvey Robinson gave a me a signal to run the "10" play in a left formation from their 11-yard line. I just put my hand on Johnny Michels's back and followed him to the 1-yard line, and we scored on the next play. That was in the fourth quarter when we trailed 14–13. That was a memorable play. Every time I see John, I remind him about it.

That was a big strong University of Texas football team. General Neyland said we would win this game in the fourth quarter because of our conditioning and our speed. Sure enough, we went up 7–0, but they led us 14–7 going into the fourth quarter.

I remember sitting in the locker room at halftime, and the Texas band marched past our locker room playing "The Eyes of Texas are Upon You," and General Neyland said, "Boys, by the end of this game, they will be playing the Tennessee Waltz."

That was my most enjoyable win at Tennessee and the most important because it brought us back into contention nationally. We were considered a national powerhouse then, and it made believers out of a lot of the young players. That 1950 team was probably better than the 1951 team, which won the national championship.

Hank Lauricella was a consensus All-American in 1951 as a tailback in Tennessee's single-wing. He was All-SEC in 1950 and 1951, and led the Vols in total offense both seasons. He finished second in the Heisman Trophy balloting in 1951 and was named by the Birmingham Touchdown Club as the Most Outstanding Back in the SEC in 1951. He became a successful businessman in Louisiana.

DOUG ATKINS

DEFENSIVE END

1950–1952

WHEN DOUG ATKINS ARRIVED at the University of Tennessee as a freshman in 1949, he marveled over the eight-man blocking sled used for practice. Back home in Humboldt, Tennessee, the practice equipment consisted of a worn tackling dummy, so he wasn't accustomed to such a convenience in football.

He didn't get accustomed to the sled in Knoxville, either. Not right away, at least.

The sled sure looked impressive, but Atkins wasn't going to use it right away. That first practice, *he* was the blocking sled.

Even if General Neyland, the head coach, had known Atkins was going to be one of the greatest players in the history of the school—in the history of football, really—he wasn't going to let the freshman have it easy.

"Neyland was using me as a blocking dummy during practice," Atkins said. "Andy Kozar and Jimmy Hahn kept coming at me, two against one, and knocking me out of the park. Then somebody would scream, 'Touchdown!' and it started again. I was taking a beating."

Neyland didn't feel sorry for Atkins. The kid was there on a basketball scholarship, and that seemed blasphemous to Neyland, for such a mountain of a player like Atkins to run around in shorts. He was 6'5", 240 pounds as a freshman and would grow to 6'8", 250 pounds.

Doug Atkins is regarded as one of the finest defensive lineman to play the college and pro game.

While Neyland didn't feel sorry for Atkins that day in practice, Harold Johnson did.

"Harold Johnson leaned over and whispered some advice," Atkins said. "He told me to lower my shoulder and hit one of those guys. He told me to defend myself. He told me to stop trying to take on both blockers.

"I'd had enough, so I did what he said. I finally got around to popping both of them on the same play. Before long, I hit the blockers and the runners on the same play. That's the day I learned to play football as good as I played basketball."

Paul Hornung, the Green Bay Packers running back and Heisman Trophy winner from Notre Dame, wished that day had never come. A lot of others wished that day had never come. They wanted Atkins to stick with basketball, because he turned into a fearsome player.

"I came face to face with Atkins 30 times in 10 years," Hornung said. "I blocked him twice."

Atkins, No. 91, evolved from that freshman defensive end in 1949 to an All-American in 1952 for the Vols. In 1975, in a poll of sportswriters across the South conducted by the Birmingham Touchdown Club, Atkins was voted the best player of the quarter century (1950–1975) in the Southeastern Conference.

27

Not best defensive player. The best player. Atkins was the only player who was a unanimous pick of the voters.

Tennessee was 29–4–1 when Atkins played varsity football. The Vols won a national championship in 1951, and the strength of the team was defense. It pitched five shutouts and finished the regular season 10–0.

Atkins went on to a 17-year career in the NFL with the Cleveland Browns, Chicago Bears, and New Orleans Saints. He played in the Pro Bowl eight times and helped the Bears win the NFL title in 1963.

His No. 91 was retired in a ceremony at Neyland Stadium in 2005. Peyton Manning and Reggie White also had their jersey numbers retired.

Many people in football would recognize George Halas's name before General Neyland's name. Atkins said there was no comparison. He seemed to despise Halas; Neyland he revered.

"He made it possible for me to play in the NFL," Atkins said of Neyland. "He knew the fundamentals up and down. He taught you the simple things that made a difference. He showed you how to get ahead.

"I learned to play at Tennessee. Neyland showed us a lot of things that players don't do today. He taught me the right angle of pursuit and things like that. He worked us hard, but not too hard. We had something left for the games."

Atkins always seemed ready to play in the games. If he wasn't ready, well, he went looking for help.

"I was on the sideline at the start of one game when Doug Atkins ran up to me," Jimmy Goostree, a former assistant trainer at Tennessee, said. "He told me he was having trouble getting into the action. Then he pulled off his helmet and told me to belt him in the face. I knocked the devil out of him, right across the chops, and he went back onto the field and played great."

"Yeah, that sounds like something I might have done," Atkins said. "I've always thought you had to get your guts rattled before you can get into a game. It's always been a one-on-one war with me. It was better when I got hit and looked bad early in a game. Then I could spend the rest of the game getting even."

Sometimes opponents said the wrong thing, and Atkins would do more than get even.

"Doug had a broken hand, and it was thought he might not play against North Carolina," said Mack Franklin, the left defensive end and captain of the Vols from Madisonville. "Somebody on the Carolina side remarked that it didn't matter, Atkins wasn't too good, anyway. I guess Doug was in on three-fourths of the tackles that day."

Atkins had size, but he also had uncommon athleticism and agility. There were news reports of how he could drop into pass coverage from his defensive end position, much like the flex defenses of today and bat down balls or snare them for interceptions.

"He had all the physical attributes," Andy Kozar, a teammate, said. "He was strong and could run like the wind. He could run step for step with Hank Lauricella and anybody on the team for 70 or 80 yards.

"What I enjoyed doing was watching Doug high-jump. It was fascinating watching a guy as big as he was clearing 6'5" and 6'8", which was a pretty good jump back then."

The Tennessee basketball coach Emmett Lowery said Atkins could have been one of the NBA greats if he had devoted himself to the game. Following his sophomore season in football, Atkins went to play basketball for the Vol cagers and, in just a week, was in the starting lineup.

Mickey O'Brien, the legendary Vol trainer, said Atkins had trouble with the continued fast pace of the Vols basketball team. Atkins was being treated for asthma and had to take doses of antihistamines to keep up.

"And he had it pretty bad, too," O'Brien said. "It was very difficult for him in the late summer and early fall when the flowers were still in bloom. He had to go through some pretty hard times and he didn't complain about it.

"Doug just couldn't take that constant running up and down the length of the floor at full speed because of his asthma. If we had been playing the slower style of game, he could have managed it."

Finally, Atkins gave up basketball following his sophomore season. That was just fine with Neyland.

"He didn't think much of basketball," Atkins said of Neyland. "After I played two seasons of basketball at UT, he told me I would be better off playing football. He told me there wasn't much stature involved in playing basketball at a football school. The General was pretty good figuring out what a man should do with his life."

What Atkins eventually did with his football life has been duplicated by no one else.

29

Material for this narrative was pulled from the Atkins archive at the University of Tennessee, which included articles by Wirt Gammon Jr. of the *Chattanooga Times*, Ben Byrd of *The Knoxville Journal*, Al Browning, Paul McAfee, and Dave Hooker of the *Knoxville News Sentinel*, and John Bibb of the *Tennessean* in Nashville. Atkins is 78 years old. He was too ill to be interviewed for this book.

JIM HASLAM

TACKLE

1950–1952

WHATEVER SUCCESS I HAVE ACHIEVED in life can be attributed to what I learned under General Neyland and playing football at the University of Tennessee.

What he taught in football enabled you to be successful in most anything you did in life. The game maxims, such as, "The team that makes the fewest mistakes wins," are among the things we should always talk about when we talk about Tennessee football.

He doesn't say the team that makes no mistakes wins. It's whoever makes the fewest mistakes wins. You are going to make mistakes in life, and he taught us that you just have to make fewer mistakes to succeed.

Then he said, "Play for and make the breaks, and when one comes your way, score." So think about it. There are opportunities in life. You have opportunities, I have opportunities, and what we have to do is be ready to take advantage of those opportunities. If you recover a fumble on the 8-yard line and don't score, it hasn't helped you any. Those are the kinds of things he talked about with us.

The next maxim was, "If the breaks go against you, don't get rattled and get down, put on more steam." That's what happens in life, too. You can't get discouraged, you have to get going. It's what life is all about.

The first thing a coach has to do is go out and coach players, and the second thing he does is he puts players in the right position to succeed. Then he

Jim Haslam played on the offensive line in the single-wing and was captain of the 1952 team, which was General Neyland's last team at Tennessee.

establishes a game plan and asks the players to execute. That's what you do in business. You get the right people, you put them in the right positions, and then you have some discipline to follow the game plan and execute.

What General Neyland wanted in addition to those things was discipline and accountability. Tennessee has always had a winning tradition because of the discipline and accountability that General Neyland established in the program years ago.

We played in bowl games every year, so Tennessee football back then was like it is now, very respected nationally. It was one of the top five or 10 programs in the country. A Tennessee football player was something special, just like he is now, and we were expected to win, just like they are now.

Back then, there were just four bowl games, Rose, Sugar, Cotton, and Orange, and we still went to a bowl game every year. Tennessee was a powerhouse, and even with so few postseason games, you could still find the Vols playing after most everyone else was finished.

Once I came up here from Florida to go to school, I never left. Coming to Tennessee to play football was like going to Kentucky to play basketball. It was a big deal. Playing for Neyland was like playing for Adolph Rupp at Kentucky in basketball.

General Neyland liked to go fishing in Florida, in Sarasota, and he came and watched me play basketball. The line coach at Tennessee had told General Neyland about me, so he came to watch. When he asked me to come play for him, I said, "I can go to Tennessee? Why would I want to turn that down?"

General Neyland and Tennessee were national names, so it was an easy choice for me. There was a little downtime in the program when General Neyland came back from the war in 1946, but then we got it back going again. There were no limits on recruits and scholarships back then, so the class I came in with in 1949 had about 80 of us.

Florida wasn't that good, they were something like 0–9 when I was a senior in high school. I looked at Duke. I looked at Alabama and Auburn. Tennessee was just a step above everybody, so I wanted to go there.

We really had a good team in 1950 when we finished the regular season fourth in the poll. We lost the second game of that season to Mississippi State, then we came back and actually won 20 games in a row before we lost to Maryland in the Sugar Bowl at the end of the 1951 season.

The game that sticks out in 1950 was beating Alabama 14–9, when Andy Kozar dove over for the winning touchdown. Before the game, General Neyland said, "Alabama is bigger than you and faster than you, but you have it right here," and he pointed to his heart. He told us we were going to win it in the fourth quarter, and we sure enough did.

I remember General Neyland, gathering us around him after a practice when I was a freshman and telling us, "Men, you have never lived until you have beaten Alabama," and then he paused and said, "…in Tuscaloosa."

He would remind us during preseason drills when it was hot that it was hotter in Tuscaloosa. Everything was aimed at Alabama. Florida has become a key rival and so has Georgia, but Alabama is still the biggest to me.

When we were in school, the Kentucky rivalry was big because Bear Bryant was there. Back then, we played Duke and North Carolina every year, and they were rivals because they were so good and we could ride a train over there.

We played Texas in the Cotton Bowl, and General Neyland said the same thing about having the heart to finish, and we beat them in the fourth quarter. We had some games like that where we outplayed teams like Kentucky that had some great players. Babe Parilli, the quarterback for Kentucky, was the Brady Quinn of Notre Dame back in our day, and we beat them 28–0. The year before in Knoxville, in 1950, we beat them 7–0 in the snow.

The game that sticks out was the 1951 Cotton Bowl at the end of the 1950 season when we came back to beat Texas. On the first play of the game, Hank Lauricella made this great run and we got down to the 5-yard line and scored to lead 7–0.

Hank was my favorite player because he was my buddy and a guy everybody admired and led a great life. In more recent times, my favorite is Peyton Manning because, even if he didn't play football, he would be a guy who you could admire by the life he leads.

Back to Texas and the Cotton Bowl. They score twice, and it was 14–7 at halftime. We scored early in the fourth quarter, but Pat Shires missed the extra point to tie the game. Pat came off the field, and General Neyland said, "Don't worry, son, we didn't come down here to tie."

We got the ball and drove it down. Kozar scored with a minute or two to go, and we went ahead 20–14. Texas came back and went down the field. Jimmy Hill, he was a defensive back from Maryville, intercepted a pass. Bill

33

Stern, who was the premier radio announcer at the time, said they ought to build a statue for Jimmy Hill in Maryville for that play. We always gave him a hard time over that.

We ran the single-wing and didn't throw the football much. The basic Tennessee play was the "10" play, which was tailback off tackle. That was our play, and General Neyland would run it and run it.

Sports is all about winning, and we won at Tennessee. I think Tennessee has historically won in the right way. I think we had coaches who won in the right way. We had a lot of outstanding players, too. You hear about kids making bad decisions, but that's a very small percentage.

This has been a very good program over the years. There was a down time from 1959 until Doug Dickey got it going again, but it has been mostly a great program. It is a credit to Phil Fulmer and Tennessee football tradition that people think 8–4 is a down year.

Tennessee could play Slippery Rock, or somebody like that, and draw 100,000 people. That's a measure of your tradition.

Now, it was different back when I played because you didn't have all those people coming to games, and you didn't have all the orange. People wore ties and coats to the game, and you didn't have television. But it was just as big in a different kind of way. The players were not as readily recognizable, but the whole thing of Tennessee football was big. It was the biggest thing in the state, just as it is now.

It got that way under General Neyland and started, specifically, when they beat Alabama in 1928. General Neyland always said that was the key date in the history of the program. Until then, Vanderbilt beat us regularly. In fact, Neyland was hired to beat Vanderbilt.

The checkerboard end zone, the Vol Walk, and "Rocky Top" are the big traditions, but none of them could have become as noticed as they are without the winning. The tradition of the program is winning.

It bugged everybody that Alabama had won a lot of national titles, so it meant a lot when we won in 1998 after 47 years of going without one. It did a lot for the state. I remember reading that when the Yankees lose, they don't sell a lot of Derek Jeter shirts, and nobody is in the bars. Tennessee is the same way. When you lose in this town, everybody is upset, nobody goes out. The people eating dinner out don't give decent tips. It's a morass around here.

That's why somebody like Philip Fulmer will say, "It's great to coach Tennessee, but there is a lot of pressure because they are used to winning around here."

Where Tennessee's tradition comes in is when the recruits come in on a Saturday and they see all this. We recruit from around the country, and if you don't have that tradition, that presence on game day that has been built over the years, you couldn't have a national recruiting base like we do.

It started with General Neyland, continued with Bowden Wyatt, then Doug Dickey, and on to Johnny Majors and on to Phillip. It is a national appeal that started 80 years ago and still thrives.

Jim Haslam was a starting offensive lineman and the captain of the 1952 team. The 1951 team, with Haslam as a starting lineman, still holds the single-season record for rushing yards in a season (3,068). He is the founder and chairman of the board of the Pilot Travel Centers, LLC, and chairman of the board and president of Pilot Corp., which is headquartered in Knoxville. In November 2007, Haslam and his wife, Natalie, gave the University of Tennessee $32.5 million, the largest gift ever to the university from individuals.

JOHNNY MAJORS

TAILBACK

1954–1956

I HAVE ALWAYS BEEN A WORRIER. Before I went into the first grade, I worried; before I went to Tennessee to play football, I worried; before I got my first coaching job, I worried. I have always been a worrier. Ninety percent of what I have worried about hasn't been worth worrying about as I look back on it.

But if you think about it, the worry probably helped me get prepared and be a decent player and a good coach. The worry got me ready.

So, naturally, the first week I was at Tennessee in 1953, I was worried. The first week I was there, I was concerned about my first scrimmage and the first encounter with the varsity.

My freshmen buddies and I were the "T" team, and I was running as Jackie Parker, imitating the T formation quarterback of Mississippi State, who was a sensational player. My first time on the field was as the quarterback for this scout team, and I was plenty nervous because this was the varsity of Bowden Wyatt I was up against.

It was a controlled scrimmage, and even the guys from the big high schools were scared. Here I was from this little high school in Huntland, Tennessee, so you can imagine what was going through my head.

It didn't go as bad as I thought it would. On one play, I broke open inside and ran eight yards. I was relieved somebody missed me on a tackle. A kid from Huntland getting eight yards, that was something. Then I made 17 yards

Johnny Majors was an All-American in 1956 and runner-up in the Heisman Trophy balloting.

on a run, and three people missed me. Then I made a run of 25 yards, and three or four people missed me.

General Neyland had moved to athletic director, and he would come watch practice every day. He was sitting there in the stands with no shirt on and in his army khaki shorts and a coaching hat. He boomed out from 15 rows up on the west side, "Who is that No. 15?"

"That's Majors from Huntland, General," Farmer Johnson called back.

When that scrimmage was over, I was not only surprised that I was alive, but I was able to walk. The closest phone was up on the main street through campus, Cumberland, at Ellis and Ernst drug store, and I ran up that hill to that phone. I weighed in at 144 pounds after that scrimmage—the players used to call me "Spider" because I didn't have much meat—and then ran up the hill and called my folks. My dad answered the phone, and I said, "Daddy, they miss tackles in college just like they do in high school." They were greatly relieved to hear me say that.

It meant a lot to play at Tennessee because of the tradition, and even though I never got a chance to play for General Neyland, he was still around, and his presence added something to the experience.

In my day, it was single-platoon football, where you played both ways. We played the wide-tackle-6—6-2-2-1—and I was a safety. I was the tailback on offense, and I think my favorite play was to sprint out passing and look over the field. We did a lot of option-run passes. If the receivers were open, you hit one of them. If they were covered, you ran.

Buddy Cruze was what they called the "weak end," and he was an outstanding receiver, an All-American. Bill Anderson was a very good receiver as a wingback. We had a good tight end who could catch the ball, Roger Urbano.

In 1956, Tennessee and Oklahoma were the only two teams to finish the regular season untied and undefeated. We beat Georgia Tech that season in Atlanta, 6–0, when they were No. 2 and we were No. 3.

Sports Illustrated, in its 100th anniversary of college football issue in 1969, picked that Georgia Tech–Tennessee game as the number-two game of all time.

We knew after the 1955 game in Knoxville, when we tied Georgia Tech 7–7, that we could be two of the top teams in the country in 1956. We were both basically junior and sophomore teams with a smattering of seniors. Georgia Tech won the conference a year before and played Pittsburgh in the Sugar Bowl, and they had 90 percent of their team back. We were going to be playing for some high stakes.

Back then, you could sell your game tickets if you were a player, and it helped if you were particularly well-known. A lot of big schools around the country did that, particularly in the South, and you could make good money. So I bought some extra tickets in the summer before the 1956 season to that Georgia Tech game because I knew it was going to be a big game. I sold them for $100 each.

It ended up being one of the biggest games in the history of Southern football. I know the fans ended up crashing one or two gates trying to get in—that's how much interest there was in it.

I knew going into the game that any small break could turn it around for one team or the other. Any minor mistake would be a factor. There was a lot of anticipation, a lot of excitement, and we had a tremendous following of Tennessee fans down in Atlanta.

It was a very tightly played game. You had two General Neyland advocates coaching the game, Tennessee's Bowden Wyatt and Georgia Tech's Bobby Dodd, who were both in the Hall of Fame as players and as coaches. Also, Frank Broyles was the backfield coach at Georgia Tech. Dodd played for the General.

I remember how much our coaches and General Neyland wanted to beat Bobby Dodd. It was a very competitive type of thing. I'm sure he would take great pride in beating Tennessee, which was his alma mater. I heard our coaches always talking about how much they wanted to beat that Bobby Dodd. There was a history and a rivalry between the two schools.

The kicking game was the biggest factor in the game for both teams, and that was the essence of General Neyland football. Having the ball was not as important as where you had the ball, and the kicking game determined field position. We didn't want the ball backed up. We didn't want to take any chances. I remember I quick-kicked on first down in that game.

We played it close to the vest for the most part, but then we opened it up some and scored the only touchdown. I faked a draw to the fullback and hit Cruze on an out-cut in front of our bench for about 17 yards. On the next play, we faked the draw and hit him on the post pattern, what we called the weak-end inside, for 31 yards to the 1-yard line.

Tommy Bronson, a great inside runner, scored on the next play. We missed the extra point, and that was the game, the only points scored all day.

The freshman group I came in with graduated from high school in 1953, and that was the last group that signed with General Neyland before he retired. His last season was 1952, so he was still coach when we signed in December.

He was bigger than life, and I was real disappointed I did not get a chance to play for him. He was a large human being, a big handsome man, and walked with a great, erect walk. He didn't spend any time talking to players, though he might acknowledge you walking into lunch.

39

I did like Alabama, and I liked Georgia Tech, and I was a fan of Tennessee. But, really, my favorite team was the Army 1944 team. I can still recall most of the players. In 1944, 1945, 1946, I knew all the players from Alabama, Vanderbilt, Tennessee, Army, Georgia Tech, and Auburn. I was a fan of more than one.

So when I got into my senior season, I did not know where I wanted to go to school. I listened to all those games on the radio. Even Arkansas started to write me, and Wyoming, and I had a lot of choices. I finally narrowed my choices down to Tennessee and Auburn.

We had 32 in my graduating class in high school, and we had a very good football program. We used a single-wing, and my dad's teams were 71–1 in seven seasons. My dad started the first football team they ever had there in 1949, which was my freshman year. I was the oldest of seven boys, and the next three boys were two years apart, so we all were single-wing tailbacks, and two of us even played together in the same backfield.

I was a small-town boy from Huntland, Tennessee, and I felt very comfortable at Auburn when I went to visit. It was a small-town atmosphere with a small stadium. I thought I was better suited there because I didn't have the confidence to be a major-college player as a high school senior. I couldn't imagine myself playing for Tennessee.

It came down to making a decision between Auburn and Tennessee, and I just felt more comfortable at Auburn. My mother told me she knew I was having a hard time making a decision. My dad was more confident in my ability than I was and said to me one day very plainly, "John, I think you can play at Tennessee."

My mother said she would like to see me stay close to home and play at Tennessee. It taught me a lesson as a coach when I went out recruiting. Always recruit the mother first.

Farmer Johnson, who was the defensive line coach under Neyland, came down our way to visit his folks before one of our spring practices. He was in a poolroom in Winchester, the county seat, and someone told him he ought to go to Huntland to see this Majors boy. He came over and asked my dad to run some plays, so he could see me in a single-wing. That's when Tennessee started to recruit me.

I didn't visit but three schools—Tennessee, Auburn, and I took a train to visit the University of Georgia. Auburn had a couple of poolrooms and a movie house, and Huntland had a poolroom but no movie house. I was evaluating all kinds of things.

So I made up my mind to go to Tennessee, and I had nightmares the summer before enrolling in school. The summer before I worked on a county road, repairing wood bridges, and I kept thinking about what it was going to be like. I couldn't imagine anyone missing me on a tackle.

After I finished playing there, I went back and got my degree because I lacked one quarter. Bowden Wyatt told me, "If you want to coach, I have a job for you." So I coached there for two years as assistant freshman coach. I would go back and ask General Neyland questions, and he would always find time for me. He was very nice to me, and it was a great experience to be around him.

I remember when I was a student there, walking past the big pictures of the All-Americans, like McEver and Feathers and Dodd, and how many times I looked at the pictures of the 1926 team and the 1951 team. I knew a lot about the history of Tennessee football and the people who played there.

When I went back to be the head coach at Tennessee in 1977, it was quite a challenge. It was more of a challenge than I really thought it would be when I took the job. I had great support, and we finally broke a little bit of the ice in the third year when we went to the Bluebonnet Bowl and finished with seven wins. It was a breakthrough that year because we beat Auburn early in the season.

We started off with a better team in 1980 and had Georgia 15–0. We lost that game 16–15, and they went on to win the national championship. We lost to Southern Cal by three points in the next game. We ended up with a lot of injuries that year and did not have a winning record, which was disappointing because we had been making progress.

In 1983, that was the first real good team. We won nine games and won the Citrus Bowl over Maryland, and we beat Alabama again.

In 1985, we cracked the big ice. We won the SEC championship and had the big upset of Miami in the Sugar Bowl. That team was nicknamed the Sugar Vols. That set us up for a good run, which included my best three years in a row, 1989, 1990, and 1991, when we won 29 games. We went to the Sugar Bowl, Cotton Bowl, and Fiesta Bowl and won two of three. Then came my ignominious demise following my heart surgery, and I was not the Tennessee coach. They moved me out.

Playing under the Neyland protégés was very important to my coaching career. I learned the fundamentals, the techniques, and conditioning. Nobody was better at conditioning than the staff of Bowden Wyatt, which was a great staff. They were disciplined and great builders. Bowden Wyatt took us from being mediocre into being a great program in the mid- to late '50s.

Johnny Majors was an All-American in 1956 and the Heisman Trophy runner-up to Notre Dame's Paul Hornung. Majors was All-SEC in 1955 and 1956 and led the Vols in total offense both seasons. Majors was the SEC Player of the Year in 1955 and 1956. In 1976, Majors coached the University of Pittsburgh to the national title and the next season returned to his alma mater as head coach. He compiled a 116–62–8 record in 16 seasons and was SEC Coach of the Year in 1985. Majors is retired and lives outside Knoxville.

BILL JOHNSON
RIGHT GUARD
1955–1957

I DON'T KNOW IF I WANT TO admit this or not, but my senior class can probably say that we were the ones that had a lot to do with getting Bear Bryant hired at Alabama. We were big rivals with 'Bama, of course, and we did something regarding Alabama that no other class can say. In the three years I played against Alabama, in 1955, 1956, and 1957, they did not score on us. Not one point. We beat them 20–0, 24–0, and 14–0.

Bart Starr, who was a great quarterback with the Green Bay Packers, played at Alabama back then, but just in the 1955 season, so we had to contend with him for one season. Honestly, though, Alabama was down a little bit. But that's okay, we still enjoyed the wins whether they were down or not.

In 1957, I was named All-American. I had a chance to appear on *The Perry Como Show* with John David Crow of Texas A&M, who won the Heisman Trophy, and we were all set to play A&M in the Gator Bowl that year.

We beat them 3–0, and that was Bear Bryant's last game at Texas A&M. He went to Alabama the next year, and you know what happened with that. He really brought Alabama back.

I remember that Gator Bowl as a tough, knock-'em, sock-'em game. They had a really tough running team with John David. It's funny because he and I became friends after that game, even as hard-fought as it was, and we took a trip overseas to Spain and Portugal, and we stayed friends through the years.

Bill Johnson was an All-American lineman at Tennessee in 1957 and later a member of the board of trustees.

We played a 6-2-2-1 defense, basically, and just ganged up at the line of scrimmage and hit old Crow as many times as we could. That was one of the toughest games I remember playing at Tennessee, and we upset them. They were ranked in the top 10 and we were No. 13.

That was my last game, and we ended on a good note with that win. It was much different than when I started school in 1954. We didn't play as freshmen that year, and Tennessee did not have a very good team. We won four games and lost six, and that was Harvey Robinson's last year as head coach, so my class was part of a transition at Tennessee.

Bowden Wyatt came in to coach and brought the program back. There was some urgency to get it back to where it was under General Neyland in the late '40s and '50s when Tennessee football was in its heyday, and Wyatt was one of the General's men.

Coach Wyatt came in spring practice in 1955, and it was as intense as it could get. We were as conditioned as you can be because we played both ways in those seasons after the rule changes got rid of the two-platoon system. I played offensive guard in the single-wing and played defensive tackle and weighed 190 pounds.

My position coach was a guy named Dick Hitt, who I dearly loved. He knew more football than anybody could imagine. He took a little 190-pound guy—me—and taught me enough tricks to survive on the line. To play football at 190 pounds, you had to play close to the ground because people you were playing against were a lot bigger and a lot stronger.

The single-platoon system was to my advantage because a little fast guy could stay on the field longer than a big guy who played both ways. We won a lot of fourth quarters back then because of the conditioning under Coach Wyatt. At 190 pounds, you had to keep your belly on the ground for leverage against the big guys or you would get knocked out of there. I probably averaged 50 minutes a game in my senior year.

That 1955 season, my sophomore year, marked a changing of the discipline around the program. We said, "Yes sir," and, "No sir," and did exactly what we were told. We felt everything coming back that season, just the way it was under General Neyland, and then we had it all together the next year in 1956 when we were undefeated in the regular season. We won the SEC championship and then went down and lost to Baylor in the Sugar Bowl, which was disappointing.

We won 10 games and lost one in that 1956 season. We had good depth, and we had speed. The thing about our teams with Coach Wyatt is that we were well-conditioned and fundamentally sound, and that's how we won a lot of games. Coach Wyatt carried over the game maxims that General Neyland had started when he was the head coach. That is a true Tennessee tradition.

Our best play out of the single-wing, what we call the "number one," was the run-and-pass with Johnny Majors, who was the tailback. He would take the ball and sprint out to his right, and the wing back would be out in the flat, the blocking back would flare out to the flat, the strong side end would go down and out, and the weak-side end would come across. Majors would make the right decisions on where to go with the ball; he was a terrific player, an All-American.

We would out-formation people a lot of times. In this single-wing, you were overloaded to the strong side, so the defense would try and match up and overload to the strong side. That allowed you to get a lot of things done to the weak side. We would start flow one way and go back the other way. That was a key to our success.

The game I remember most from my career was when we played Georgia Tech in 1956 in Atlanta. We were No. 3 in the country, and they were No. 2. The fans wanted to get into that game so badly they knocked down the gates and stormed into the stadium before kickoff. We were getting ready to come out for the kickoff, and the fans were pushing through the gates to get in. It was a dramatic atmosphere that day.

45

Bobby Dodd, the Georgia Tech coach, played at Tennessee and was now coaching Tech, which added to the excitement of the game. It was one General Neyland's stars playing against his alma mater.

They were favored because they were No. 2 in the country, but we won 6–0. It was all about the kicking game, and I think we punted 12 or 14 times. That's the way you played back then; field-position football, and get yourself set up for the short field to go in and score.

Coach Wyatt had a phobia about flying. He took us on the train whenever he could. My senior year we were going on the train to Memphis, which is where we played Ole Miss. The train went down to Chattanooga and then started west. At about 2:00 or 3:00 in the morning, we were somewhere in West Tennessee and there was an accident at an intersection, and it stopped the train for seven or eight hours.

We did not get to Memphis until 12:00 for the 1:00 kickoff. We barely had enough time to warm up and have the coin toss before we started playing. Coach Wyatt was not too keen on going by train to games after that because we lost that game 14–7. They were No. 8 in the country, but we still should not have lost that game. We were No. 7 and were playing in Tennessee, so we should not have lost that game.

We lived in the east end of the stadium. It was a three-man room, but I stayed in the same room on the second floor of the stadium for three years while my roommates went off and got married. You went right up the hill to your classes. The dressing rooms and cafeteria were right there on the bottom of the stadium; your whole life revolved around that circle there.

I still have a Tennessee connection because of Tommy Bronson, who was a fullback and one of my roommates while I was there. His son married my daughter, and we have five grandchildren between us.

I am lucky enough to have a locker named for me in the current locker room. My number was 66, and that number pervades in that locker year-to-year. I cannot be prouder.

I owe the University of Tennessee a debt I can never repay. I got a quality education and the university paid for an athletic scholarship, which some people forget about as they go through school and go through life. That experience enabled me to make friends and connections that helped me throughout my business career. It was such a wonderful experience and privilege to wear the orange, and I will forever be grateful to the University of Tennessee for what it did for me in structuring my life.

Bill Johnson was an All-SEC and All-American guard in 1957. Johnson was a trustee at the University of Tennessee for 21 years and a successful banker in Sparta, Tennessee. In 1996, Johnson and his wife Rena gave $100,000 to establish an endowment fund for students and faculty. The Johnsons designated their gift to the library, the history department, and the football program.

The

SIXTIES

STEVE DeLONG

GUARD

1962–1964

WE JUST PLAYED FOOTBALL THEN. There were not a lot of the extra things that surround the game today. It was all football, just rock 'em, sock 'em. The one thing I did well in my three years was that I stayed consistent and brought the same effort to each game. Some games I made a lot of tackles, some games I didn't, but I had some discipline, and I think I played well every game.

We had three different head coaches in my three varsity seasons, Bowden Wyatt, Jim McDonald, and Doug Dickey. Knowing that, I might have gone somewhere else to play college football, because things were always so uncertain around the program. We had finally gotten rid of the single-wing and gone to the T formation in my time there, which also added to the uncertainty around the program, because it was a transition.

General Neyland had been the athletic director, and he didn't want Wyatt to change the offense. He thought Tennessee could still win with it; but we were one of the last, if not the last, to finally get rid of it.

I had a lot of scholarship offers and almost went to North Carolina, but Tennessee was running the single-wing, which we ran in high school, so I knew the offense. There was also a guy named Ed Beard who was from my high school, and he played at Tennessee and got me down there. Then he got kicked out of school, and there I was. He was a tackle, and a very talented

49

Steve DeLong is one of just two Tennessee players to win the Outland Trophy, which goes to the top interior lineman in college football.

athlete. Bowden Wyatt had recruited him, and then Wyatt and Jim McDonald recruited me.

McDonald was there one year and, really, he got screwed. What happened was Bowden Wyatt went down to the coaches convention in Florida and ran into Scrappy Moore, the Chattanooga coach, who had beaten Wyatt and Tennessee in 1958. It was a bad loss for Wyatt. It was like Appalachian State beating Michigan. Well, they were drinking down there, and Wyatt got mad and threw Scrappy in the pool. Tennessee fired Wyatt over that.

It was pretty open that there were other issues in the athletic department besides Wyatt going after Scrappy. When they had that incident, it was in the summer and too late to do a coaching search. They needed somebody to put in there for a year, so they hired McDonald, who was there as an assistant coach under Wyatt.

Bob Woodruff, who was the line coach, moved up to athletic director, and he let McDonald coach just one year before he went out and got Doug Dickey. McDonald was 5–5 and a good guy, but they got rid of him just like that.

One of the problems with the athletic department, and the football coaching staff, really, were on some off-field issues. There were some parties, things like that, and it created some trouble. So there were some things going on that were not good for the program. There was some raising hell, too much for a major program. The turmoil, I think, led to the administration bringing in a new coach to get things back in order.

Vanderbilt had beaten us, which gives you an idea of what it was like. We had trouble with teams that we should have been beating. We were not that good, which was another reason for the change.

I got quite a bit of recognition because I was a good defensive player, but when it came to offense, we didn't have any. Our offense was three-and-out. We couldn't do much because we didn't have the talent. When I say I played both ways, it didn't mean much because we weren't on the field long enough on offense to get tired; it was three and out.

I played single-wing in high school and then played both ways in 1963, guard and middle guard. I also covered punts and covered kicks. I was on the field a lot for Tennessee and played a lot of football.

We were a program in transition. We didn't have a quarterback, were all white, and had no speed. Art Galiffa was all right as a quarterback, really, but there was no speed, no playmakers at wide receiver. I can't remember a time in that season where we made a transition to the T that we made yardage consistently.

One of the big things was the black athlete was coming in, and we didn't have any, so there were two issues for the program. One, I think we couldn't win with the single-wing. Two, we didn't have any of the black athletes, and they were good football players. That was big. We were behind other regions of the country, and the black athlete did not come into our conference until later on…1967, 1968, 1969.

There was a track coach named Chuck Rohe who finally came along and got the black athletes to come to Tennessee. I was gone by then, but while I was in pro football, I saw what was happening then as Tennessee started to catch up to the other regions of the country. Rohe would recruit the black athlete for track, and they would find their way to football.

We did have some good players, especially one guy, Dick Evey, a tackle. He was a horse, a great player. The Bears took him in the first round in 1964, which was a year ahead of me. Dick had a career in the pros because he was that good.

We had some bright moments, it wasn't all down. One game I remember was in 1964 when we tied LSU 3–3 in Baton Rouge. They were ranked No. 7 in the country, and we weren't even on the charts. Again, we played well on defense and struggled on offense. That was the game where we stopped them on the 2-yard line in the third quarter, which helped us tie. They had an All-American guard by the name of Remi Prudhomme. They tried to run right over him and get the touchdown, but we stopped them. I helped stop the line surge, and the linebackers made the tackle. It was louder than I had ever heard that place, just like they say it is today down there.

Dickey was the coach, and he came back and worked us really hard that week after we tied LSU. He said, if we had been in better shape, we would have won the game. The next week, we beat Georgia Tech in Atlanta, 22–14. They were No. 7 that week, and we beat them—so we played well there in the middle of the season in those games with LSU and Georgia Tech.

Some games I made a lot of tackles, some games I didn't. I got sacks, too, not just tackles from the middle guard. There were some games in which I had 15 or 16 tackles and really played well. There was an All-SEC center from Alabama, and I was able to beat him up a little bit and made 12 tackles in a game against them. One of the big things for me was the use of my hands. I was very good with my hands.

I was on the field a lot, but I really didn't take a beating with my knees and legs because I kept moving. Today, these guys are so big that they are constantly getting in pileups and getting caught up in things, which is how you get hurt. The important thing was to keep people off your legs so you could avoid the big injury.

I had some speed and size; I was 6'3" and 235 pounds, and I could move my feet. I didn't lift weights back then, but I did a lot of running, especially on the stadium steps. There were 70 of those steps. I would count them, up and down, up and down. We didn't have a weight program, per se. Tennessee had never done it, so it wasn't the thing to do until LSU started to do it.

It means something to have played at Tennessee and to have gone to school there. I don't live and die by it, like some other people, but it was an honor. I worked hard at it, and if anything, what they taught me over there was to work hard. It helped me to accomplish some things in life.

Steve DeLong is one of the four greatest linemen ever to play at Tennessee, along with Doug Atkins, Reggie White, and John Henderson. DeLong and Henderson are the only Vols to win the prestigious Outland Trophy, which has been handed out since 1946 to the nation's top interior lineman. DeLong won the Outland Trophy in 1964 and was recognized as an All-American in 1963 and 1964, despite playing on Tennessee teams that were a combined 9–10–1. He was also named All-SEC guard in 1963 and 1964. He was voted Defensive Lineman of the Year three times in the Southeastern Conference. In 1993, he was elected to the College Football Foundation Hall of Fame. DeLong was picked in the first round of the 1965 NFL Draft by the Chicago Bears but ended up signing with the San Diego Chargers of the AFL. He suffered a fall six years ago and is partially paralyzed and lives in a nursing home in east Knoxville.

FRANK EMANUEL
LINEBACKER
1963–1965

WHEN PHILLIP FULMER BECAME the head coach at Tennessee—and this will tell you what kind of person he is—I told him he was going to have a hard time as the head coach of this program. He asked me why, and I told him it was because he was not tough enough, that he had to be meaner.

Fulmer was a prospect when I was a player at Tennessee, and I helped recruit him, so I know a little bit about his personality even from the early days. We are still dear friends. He was a great person, solid, and low-key; and that's part of the reason I thought this job would be tough on him.

He was quiet and would keep to himself—a thinker, what I would consider a typical offensive lineman. He was not outgoing, and I just didn't know if a good guy like that could do this job. It turns out he's done an unbelievable job. He has developed into a great coach. I have the greatest respect for him and what he has done there.

As a player, Phillip was Mr. Steady and the kind of person you would be glad to have as your son. He does not waver, and he sticks to his guns. Phillip has responded much better than I thought he would, and that's not degrading him. It's just his personality as a younger person was more laid-back and low-key.

My identity as a player started with a commitment to be a good player. I don't think I was ever the greatest athlete—the biggest, the fastest—but no one studied the game harder than I did. I think, in some respects, I am a lot

Frank Emanuel was an All-American linebacker in 1965 and went on to become a coach in the NFL.

like Peyton Manning, as far as knowing the game. What he knows about quarterbacking his position, I felt like I knew about linebackers. I committed myself to studying each opponent each week and seeing what they were going to do. And I think that helped me get to the ball a lot quicker. I certainly enjoyed hitting, but I would never classify myself as a player who survived simply on athletic ability.

I was 6'3", 215 to 225 pounds, which was decent size in my era for a middle linebacker. I always stayed in the middle.

My era, from the 1962 season to the 1965 season, and that group that I came in with, had an enormous amount to do with putting Tennessee back on the map in college football. When we came there, Tennessee had been down for a few years. They had fallen off in the late '50s and early '60s. In my first year of eligibility, which was my sophomore year, we were 5–5. That was in 1963.

In 1964, my junior year, we were 4–5–1. Then we really turned it around. In 1965, we went 8–1–2. We lost that one game by one point, 14–13, to Mississippi. We finished No. 7 in the country, and I think the program has taken off from there. That group of guys helped Tennessee get back to national prominence.

Of course, the seniors in 1967 might feel like they were the class that turned it around, but they did not go from losing to winning as we did. They did not have a losing season as sophomores and see what the bottom looked like. They carried it on and were a really good group, but they didn't lose like we had lost. The program was reeling for a couple of years then, so I'm proud of what we were able to do.

When Doug Dickey came in as head coach for my junior season, he made some changes in discipline and did some things that all new coaches need to do in structure and organization. I had a lot of respect for Dickey because he gave you the impression that he was so intelligent, and he was. He was also tough and disciplined.

55

In his first year, he dismissed three of us from the team after we got drunk and got in a fight. It was after we lost to Vanderbilt 7–0, and these guys were taunting us. They didn't know we were football players, so we got in a fight.

You had to understand that Dickey was a very structured and disciplined person. If the meeting is at 4:30 and you come in at 4:31, you are off the team, that's what kind of guy he was—and to get drunk and get in a fight as a football player, it didn't matter how good you were, you were gone.

We had to move off campus, and we lived in a boarding home. I worked at Alcoa for several months, and there was no guarantee he was going to let us back on the team. He was making us understand that you can't fool around and jeopardize your college education or your football career.

I mean, they dismissed us from school and we were gone, finished. We had to ask to come back to school and to get back on the team. I think he kept in touch with people who knew what we were doing and that we had stayed around and worked and proved to him we wanted to come back.

We had challenged his rules, and he had thrown us off the team, even though two of us were starters. Harold Stancell was a starting cornerback and a good player for us. Dickey set a great example to the rest of the guys in the program, and I think that was a foundation for our success.

There were other football things about Dickey that were impressive. I remember his talking to us often about statistics, and bend but don't break. There was so much strategy that he was up on, and he would talk about things such as a team that has the ball so many times is due for this many mistakes. You knew that he had a grasp of the game and the details, and guys paid attention.

I think he came to trust us as players, even though he had not recruited us. He did not run us off and gave us a chance to prove ourselves to him. He had a philosophy that he instilled in us, which was don't think, react. We had been coached all week about the game plan, and that is when we did our thinking. He wanted us out there reacting. You are thinking, but you are thinking on the move.

I do think back about the game against Mississippi, the one game we lost, and how close we came to being undefeated. It was a missed extra point. Of course, we tied two other games, so it wasn't like it was a spotless season. We came pretty close to being undefeated with that group, though, which would have been an amazing thing.

We went through three different programs while we were there. We were recruited by Bowden Wyatt and learned his system, then Jim McDonald took over for a year, and then Dickey came in. The weight programs were different back then, and other things, but there were so many things that changed from coach to coach to coach.

We got our noses beat in early and then to go 8–1–2, well, I think we accomplished a lot. I think what we did was influence a lot of the guys who came along in that class of 1967.

One of the things that helped us was that back then freshman did not play varsity, they stayed together as the scout team. So it did not matter how good you were in high school, you all got your butts beat together by the varsity. We grew together as a group of freshmen and stayed together and went through it all the way. Today, that is a lot different because every freshman who goes to college now thinks they are going to start. Staying together and living together built a chemistry.

What we really did well was play defense. We allowed 58 points in the first nine games our senior season, so we were pretty salty on defense. I still remember one terrific player we had on that defense, a linebacker by the name of Tom Fisher, who was a year behind me. He was going to be an NFL star.

He died tragically in a car accident on the way back from spring break. I'm certain he was going to have an NFL career. Potentially, he was going to be a phenomenal player. He had great speed and was the same size as me.

What was interesting about that team was that, at one time, I was the heaviest guy on the team at 218. Our linemen were very light at 210, 215 pounds. We would slant and do all kinds of things to utilize our quickness. We were a fast defense, but we were very small on defense. We never lined up and played you straight ahead. We learned to utilize our personnel.

I don't know if there is a word that describes what it means to be a Vol. I came to Tennessee because of the tradition and the thrill of the orange and the enthusiasm people had throughout the state. I am from the Tidewater area of Virginia, and I am sure there are other programs that have something like this, something that is similarly indescribable.

Your blood really does bleed orange, even after these 40 years since I played for Tennessee. You go out through the community and the state, and people live for the football season. Being a Vol is a great, great experience, and it is something I will always hold dear to my heart. The school and the football program gave me the chance to get a degree and have a career in football, and that is something you do not take lightly.

Frank Emanuel was a first-team All-American linebacker in 1965. He was also first-team All-SEC in 1965 and started two seasons for the Vols. He was selected in the fourth round of the 1966 draft by the Philadelphia Eagles. Emanuel came back to Tennessee as an assistant coach for Johnny Majors before going into the NFL to coach for the Tampa Bay Buccaneers. He is retired from pro football and living in the Tampa area.

RON WIDBY

PUNTER

1964–1967

IREMEMBER READING ONE TIME how they called Tennessee "Wide Receiver U," but if you look back, we had some very good punters at Tennessee. It probably doesn't have the same ring to it—"Punter U"—but you know what I mean. We've had some kickers.

That had a lot to do with Coach George Cafego, who played for General Neyland and stayed there 40-something years. He carried on a tradition as special teams coach because Neyland was all about field position and defense, which meant you needed a good punter.

Just look at all the great punters who came through there. Johnny Majors, Bobby Majors, Herman Weaver, Neil Clabo, and all the Colquitts. I think punting is a solid tradition at Tennessee, something that has carried through the years and has been a hallmark of UT teams. Coach Neyland instilled that tradition of good special teams, and I think it has carried on through the years.

Basketball was really my main sport, but when I was a kid and went to Fulton High School, I used to ride over there on the bus and watch football games, as well as the basketball games. I knew I always wanted to go to the University of Tennessee.

In my eighth game of my senior season in football, I broke my arm and shoulder, and we weren't sure how it was going to affect my basketball because you have to get your arm up over your head to rebound and shoot.

That was about the time Tennessee and Bowden Wyatt offered me a football scholarship. I didn't even hesitate before accepting. I ended up having a good year in basketball and had some inquiries about playing for other schools.

Well, I told coach Ray Mears, who had just come in as varsity coach, that I really didn't want to play football, I wanted to play basketball for UT. I was tall and lanky and got hurt a lot in football. The coaches just said, "We'll keep you on football scholarship, and you can play basketball." So I just skipped all the football practices before the season and got ready to play basketball.

Then the football coaches came to Coach Mears and said they did not have a punter on the freshman team. The season had started, and they wanted me to come out for practice so they would have a punter. So I went out there and, before you know it, I made the freshman team. They liked me enough to ask me to try out for the varsity team as a sophomore.

I ended up making the varsity football team. What I would do is practice football early in the afternoon, walk right back to my room, put my football uniform in the closet, and get dressed to go play basketball. I lettered three years in basketball and three years in football. I also had two letters in baseball and one in golf. I lettered in four sports and made All-American in two.

My favorite sport was basketball, but my senior year I led the nation in punting average and got drafted by the New Orleans Saints in the fourth round. I also got drafted by the New Orleans Buccaneers of the old ABA.

We thought football might be a better way for me to make a living because the money was about the same, and it was less travel. Except when I got to New Orleans to work for the Saints, I wasn't used to that punting every day and that kind of work, so they shipped me off to the Dallas Cowboys.

I stayed on the taxi squad one year and made the Dallas Cowboys the next season. As it turned out, I ended up kicking in two Super Bowls. We lost one and won one.

I have no doubt what was my best and most memorable game at Tennessee. It was when we went down to play Auburn, and they had a great punter named Jon Kilgore. He was the best in the Southeastern Conference, and I remember all week Coach Cafego just kept pumping me up, saying I could kick with this guy. They were ranked No. 8 in the country, and we battled them and lost 3–0.

I think Kilgore kicked 10 times for a 49-yard average. I punted 11 times for a 48-yard average. I had a 90-yard punt, but it was called back because of a roughing-the-kicker penalty, which gave us a first down.

There was an old clipping my mother had that I saw a recently that said it was one of the best punting duels in UT history. There was a defensive coach, I can't remember his name, who pumped me all week along with Cafego. He told me Kilgore was the best in the country, and even though I was a sophomore, I could kick with him.

I think what helped me most in kicking is that I never got nervous; the games never got to me. I had a great snapper, and we covered the punts well. I just kicked it.

Coach Cafego was my tutor all four years there. What he taught me most was how to drop the ball and extend through the ball and get your toe pointed. It's all about how you drop the ball, because it's important how the ball gets placed on your foot before you kick it so you don't shank it or hit it on the end. He was a great coach.

The other thing that helped me was I had a lot of leverage because of my height. If you look back at Reggie Roby, he had tremendous muscle. Jerrel Wilson at Kansas City exploded through the ball. I was more finesse and mechanics. It is like a golf swing; you had to have some form to punt well.

Playing for Tennessee was one of the greatest thrills of my life. We used to do our Vol Walk and we might've seen 100 people. I took my boys to a game last year, and the Vol Walk is amazing. We had to get there an hour early just to see the team.

Neyland Stadium was much smaller back then, but it was always full, and it sent chills through you. I used to go over there when I was a kid and watch all the Majors boys, and to think I was playing on the same field where they once played. It was an honor.

One of my earliest memories of being at a Tennessee game was in 1959. I started to walk through the north end zone during a home game against LSU, and that was the big game that season and, for that matter, one of the biggest games ever in Neyland Stadium. Tennessee put on a goal-line stand and upset LSU. I was right there at the fence with the hot dogs that I was supposed to be selling, but I had to stop and watch.

LSU was No. 1 in the country, and they were going for two in the fourth quarter with their All-American Billy Cannon, and we stopped them. It was Charlie Severance who stopped him at the goal line, and we won that game in a big upset.

I had to get a new job every week when I went over to Neyland Stadium because I wouldn't sell enough to keep the old one. I was watching too much

Ron Widby, a Knoxville native, was a two-sport All-American and lettered in four sports at Tennessee.

football. I would go back the following week after trying to sell hot dogs, and the man would look at me and say, "You didn't sell enough hot dogs last week, you can't have a job."

So I would go find a Coca-Cola man, and I'd sell Cokes. If it was a real hot day, I could sell plenty of Cokes and still get to see some football. I sold peanuts, too. Whatever they had, I would sell just so I could get in the game. My daddy would give me enough to take the bus from north Knoxville, and I would stand in line like all the other kids trying to get picked to be a vendor.

One other game I really remember was when we beat Syracuse in the Gator Bowl in 1966. They had Larry Csonka and Floyd Little and were really a good team. We also beat Tulsa, which had Jerry Rhome, in a bowl game.

There was an LSU game in which I had to kick six or seven times out of the end zone, and that was down in Baton Rouge, where they could get pretty loud. That was my sophomore year, and we tied them 3–3.

I remember my junior year on a Friday night when we played in the first round of a basketball tournament, the Shreveport Classic in Louisiana. I played that game and then flew to Houston for the Bluebonnet Bowl on Saturday, which we won. Right after the game, I flew back to Shreveport. We won the Shreveport Classic, and I was the Most Valuable Player. It was a good weekend.

Nobody plays two sports anymore. College football is like pro football; they don't want anybody to get hurt. They want to keep everybody in their particular sport. I was very fortunate that Coach Dickey and Coach Mears worked it out. I was trying to do my best to help the University of Tennessee win games, and I was a young kid, so I could play all day. People said I must have been tired, but I wasn't tired, I was in good shape.

I loved punting, but I also loved basketball. And next to those two things, the thing I loved most was beating Kentucky. We beat them twice my senior season, at home easily and in Lexington. We won the SEC championship in basketball my senior year, and that had not happened in quite a while. We were picked to be fifth or sixth in the conference, but we won it with just one senior on the team, me.

We were 4–2 against Kentucky in basketball, and I remember it was a madhouse at our place whenever we played them. Coach Mears loved to get under the skin of Coach [Adolph] Rupp. I remember when we would walk down the streets of Lexington wearing our orange blazers. They didn't like that one bit. When we played them, either up there or down in Knoxville, you couldn't hear a thing on the floor it got so loud. It was a real rivalry. I wish we had the three-point line back then because I liked to make them from the corner in the 1-3-1 offense we ran.

I have a lot of pride in being a Tennessee Volunteer. I'm 62 years old, and tomorrow is Saturday. My wife wants to know what we're going to do. Well, at 7:00 PM, Tennessee is on TV, so I am going to watch football. She's very good about that and will let me watch in the den. I played in the NFL and I will watch the NFL games every once in a while, but I will watch the

Tennessee games all the time. I was born and raised in Tennessee and am proud to be a Volunteer.

Living here in Texas, you see that other orange from the University of Texas, but my son has a No. 11 Tennessee jersey, and my grandson has his own Tennessee jersey. When they talk about UT down here, I tell them I went to UT, the real UT. We support the bright orange, not the burnt orange.

> Ron Widby was the last four-sport lettermen at Tennessee. He earned three varsity letters in football, three in basketball, two in baseball, and one in golf. Widby led the nation in punting in 1966 and was named an All-American. He was SEC Player of the Year in basketball in 1966–1967 and an All-American. Widby scored 50 points in his final home game as a UT basketball player. He punted in two Super Bowls for the Dallas Cowboys and had a six-year career in the NFL.

BOB JOHNSON
CENTER
1965–1967

G O BACK AND TAKE A LOOK at that roster and starting lineup from 1967, the team that lost its first game of the season to UCLA and then won nine in a row. We had guys like wingback Richmond Flowers, linebackers Steve Kiner and Jack Reynolds, and defensive halfback Albert Dorsey. But there was not a more talented unit than our offensive line.

I know I am starting an argument here because that '67 team had a lot of talent. We were named national champions [by Litkenhous, one of several polling organizations] and we won the SEC championship, so there was talent all over the field that year.

But I'll tell you how good that offensive line was. We played Tulane and won 35–14, and we ran the same two plays all day. It was fullback up the middle and tailback off-tackle, and we scored 21 points in the first quarter. We ate some people up with that offensive line.

We had an offensive tackle named John Boynton, whom the Dolphins drafted. He wasn't as quick, but he was a very good player. We had a converted defensive tackle named Joe Graham, who played left guard and had hurt his knee, but was still a very good player.

Then we had Charlie Rosenfelder, who was the right guard. We had a guy at left tackle named Elliott Gammage, who, I swear, could have been an All-American tight end. They just never got him out there. We had an athletic offensive line that could run and block.

Bob Johnson is a member of the College Football Foundation and Hall of Fame and the most decorated Vol offensive lineman.

You have to say I was a good run blocker. I also snapped for punts and got drafted in the first round, the second pick overall, in 1968. I think Coach [Paul] Brown was looking for people who were good in the locker room. I was a captain at Tennessee, and I was a captain with the Bengals. I think he wanted a reasonable person in the locker room.

I played at 235 pounds my senior year in college, and I'm about 6′5″, which means I was big in college for back then. We weren't allowed to hold like they are now, and it has changed the whole dynamics of how you run-block. You can stand up now and push with your hands. The smaller defensive tackles could not play in today's game because the big guards in today's game can just stick a hand out and push you away.

That turned out to be a very good team in 1967, but we did not start out very well. We read our press clippings, went out to UCLA, and got beat 20–16. They had Gary Beban, who went on to win the Heisman Trophy, and we had a young defense. Overall, we did not play very well.

It was our only loss in the regular season. In the rest of the regular season, we played very well and would win by 10, 11, 12 points or more in a very competitive conference. It was a tough schedule, but we managed with a solid offense and good defense. There was one close game when we were ranked No. 4, and we beat LSU 17–14.

Ray Trail was our offensive line coach that season, and he was there after the tragedy when three of our assistant coaches were killed at the railroad crossing in 1965, which was my sophomore season. Bill Majors, Bob Jones, and Charlie Rash died in that crash. They were crossing the railroad tracks, coming to work in one car. It was still dark, early in the morning, and a train hit them. Coach Trail came in the middle of the season. He was just 24 years old when he had to step into that situation, and he did very well, considering the circumstances.

You have never seen a sadder day when they had the funeral for those three young coaches. They had young wives, and they each had two or three kids. Looking at those toddlers who had just lost their fathers, you forget how young coaches were back then. It was awful.

During my junior year, we had two players killed in a car crash coming back from spring break. So we had two incredible tragedies back to back, which says a lot about how Coach Dickey held the program and the team together.

I do remember Coach Dickey breaking down a couple of times in front of the team when he was trying to tell us that these coaches and players who died would want us to go on. He handled it appropriately, with dignity and class. He confronted each tragedy and did not try to sweep it under the table and pretend it wasn't there.

Coach Dickey had a lot in common with Coach Brown, who is a Hall of Fame coach in the NFL. They both had backbones made of granite, just steel. If they thought something was right, there was no bending. They did not have unrealistic rules, and they didn't care who broke them—everybody was dealt with the same way.

Coach Dickey was very consistent and did not waver when it came to his rules, which is why there was so much respect for him. We had a couple of better players get in trouble, and he threw them off the team. That got everybody's attention.

The highlight of the 1967 season was beating Alabama 24–13 in Birmingham. The year before, in 1966, we missed a short field goal and lost 11–10 to 'Bama, and they went on to win the national championship, so to come back and beat them was great. There are a lot of us who think that kick was good, that it went right over, or just inside the upright. They called it wide, but I'm not sure it was.

The play before the field-goal attempt, there was a gaping hole in the line off right guard, and our fullback thought he could take a dive and make it, but he didn't make it. Bear Bryant called that the best team he ever had, and we should've beaten them.

So in 1967, when we got another crack at them, we had a great game and won. My wife and all of her family are from Alabama, so that was a big deal to go down to Birmingham and beat them. We didn't make many errors, and I think Kenny Stabler threw three interceptions. We ran the ball pretty darn well and controlled the line of scrimmage.

67

We had three quarterbacks that season [1967] and had to use the third-string quarterback in the middle of the season. Bubba Wyche had to come in, and he did a good job. That's what was so good about that offensive line. We were playing with a third-string quarterback, a young player who was a good player, but we helped keep it together with solid play.

The only other game we lost my senior season [1967] was the Orange Bowl game in Miami. I think we thought of it as a reward and took it a little lightly. We just didn't play very well, and Oklahoma played pretty darn well and beat us 26–24.

We had been to two bowl games my sophomore and junior seasons, so we were taking it for granted, I think. The other problem was that, back in the '60s, the final polls came out before the bowl games, and it didn't make much difference what happened in the Orange Bowl. We were No. 2 in the country in most polls and were going to stay there. USC was No. 1 in the polls, and they had lost a game. Our chance to be No. 1 in the polls was gone by the time the major polls came out, so I think we lacked some incentive.

Even after 40 years, the allegiance to Tennessee does stay with you. I swear, I get up for my morning workout, and everything I have to wear says "Tennessee" on it. If you grow up there—and I'm from Cleveland, Tennessee—you don't lose that allegiance. I was on the athletics board for several years, and that helps to plug you back into a great place.

We had a reunion in 2007, and I think the guys from this team were most proud that we got the program turned around from where it was in the early '60s. When we came in as freshmen, Tennessee was down, and we ended up going to three bowl games. In 1965, we were 8–1–2 and ended up playing in the Bluebonnet Bowl. We were 8–3 in my junior year and beat Syracuse in the Gator Bowl. We just kept getting better.

I don't think Tennessee has looked back since those three seasons. The program has had a couple of mediocre seasons since then, but when you look back, that is really 40 solid, sometimes spectacular, years of football.

Bob Johnson was such a dominant player on the offensive line for Tennessee, he was sixth in the Heisman Trophy balloting in 1967. He was named an All-American in 1966 by *Football News*, and in 1967 was on 10 different All-America teams chosen by various media outlets. Johnson was named to the All-Time Academic All-America team, which was announced in 1997 by the College Sports Information Directors of America. He is a member of the College Football Foundation Hall of Fame. Johnson had a successful career in the NFL with the Cincinnati Bengals.

RICHMOND FLOWERS
WINGBACK/TAILBACK
1966–1968

I GREW UP WITH THE MOST HATED white man in the state of Alabama, my father, the attorney general of Alabama. When George Wallace was the governor and standing in the schoolhouse doors to keep blacks out, my father was taking the position that segregation was immoral and illegal. He fought the Klan and he fought George Wallace.

The day I broke the national high school record in the 110 high hurdles in Mobile and they asked my dad to present the award, he was booed. That was the straw that broke the camel's back. I said there is no way I could go to Alabama. That's when I decided I needed to go to Tennessee.

It was hard to turn down Bear Bryant, but it wasn't hard to turn down Alabama because of the issues with my father. Coach Bryant did not do a lot of recruiting, but he was in my house recruiting me, and I don't think he was very happy about all the things happening around my father and the boos and the harassment. I knew that if I went to the University of Alabama, I was going to be hazed from the moment I walked in the door.

A lot of people did not recruit me, because if you were a good player in Alabama, you went on to play for Bear Bryant. No one expected you to ever leave. It just didn't happen. He didn't lose them.

I didn't know the Tennessee program was on its butt and struggling, and that's why Doug Dickey was hired in 1964, to get it fixed. That first real recruiting class, my class, ushered in a new age of Tennessee football. We were more wide open on offense and we threw the ball.

The change in offensive philosophy was big, but so was the change in philosophy regarding black athletes. While I was there, Tennessee started to recruit black players, and one of the benchmarks of my time at Tennessee was the arrival of Lester McClain, the first black football player at UT. He was being recruited because he was supposed to be the roommate for Albert Davis, a great running back from Alcoa, but it turns out Lester was a good player in his own right.

I went to see Albert Davis play in Alcoa. He was averaging 300 yards a game—he was the real deal. I saw him get 300 in the first half that game. The next time I saw him, I was playing for the New York Giants and he was playing for the Philadelphia Eagles in the NFL. He was the same size that he was in high school, same build, same everything. He could've played in the pros in high school, he was that good. He was a big running back who was fast, the first Herschel Walker or Bo Jackson.

The problem was he couldn't pass the entrance exam at Tennessee. He was too hot to handle. Tennessee did not want to get into a recruiting issue with him. He went to Houston, but was too hot to handle down there, too, and he went to an NAIA school. But did you know that he got his Ph.D. in education from the University of Tennessee? He was an example of a black kid who grew up in a segregated school system and was a victim of it. Once he got out of that system, he was a better student.

I went to an all-white high school in Montgomery, Sidney Lanier, and we had 25,000 people come to our last game of the year against a crosstown rival. High school football for me was big-time. I was recruited by more than 100 schools. I remember being recruited by Missouri, and I went out there and watched them play Kansas in Gayle Sayers's last year. It was freezing cold.

I still remember how our track coach arranged that trip for me to Missouri. They put us in the locker room, and it was the first time I had ever seen a black athlete. I was in there with all the Missouri recruits; we are all lined up, and Dan Devine, who went on to coach at Notre Dame, came to me—he didn't know who I was—and said, "Good to have you here, son," and passed right by me. The track coach at Missouri crumbled right there because Devine didn't know I was pretty good in track. A month later, I ran a 9.5-second 100, and Devine called. I didn't care that he didn't remember me; I did care that it was freezing cold, and I wasn't going there.

Richmond Flowers decided not to go to Alabama, his home-state school, after his father was booed presenting him with a trophy. Although an injury kept Flowers out of the Olympics, he had a good career with the Vols and later in the NFL.

Tennessee recruited me because of track. Chuck Rohe, the track coach, a Hall of Famer, brought me up there. He had a way of making things fun for you. So I really enjoyed my visit because they took me to Gatlinburg and the mountains, and there were girls, and I thought this was great. Coach Rohe also handled recruiting for football. But Doug Dickey, who was the coach, thought there was no way I was leaving Alabama and Bear Bryant, and that I would go there to play football.

I remember Coach Dickey came up to the dorm room where we stayed and asked if I had a good time, and I said, yes, thank you. The only reason I was there was they were recruiting a kid from my high school who I didn't like. When I heard he was going up there, I asked the recruiter if I could go for a visit, too, up to Knoxville with this kid. I didn't want him getting a scholarship offer and not me. The recruiter, who was this Tennessee alum from Birmingham, said, "You want to go?" He couldn't believe it. That's when Chuck Rohe got involved with my visit. He was a prominent track-and-field coach.

So when Doug Dickey came to see us near the end of our visit, he asked me, "Would you go here?" And I said, "Yes."

He made me repeat it because he couldn't believe it. We went to get in the car to go to the stadium, because that's where the offices were, and he got in the back seat and I went to get in the back seat, and he said, "No, you get in the front." I won't forget it, because whenever I rode with Coach Bryant in his state patrol car, I rode in the back, and Coach Bryant rode in the front, which is the way it should have been. Coach Dickey's humility really impressed me; it was a remarkable contrast from being in Alabama. I deserved to be the in back seat.

I went to run track, too, even though the track team was running in a tobacco barn. They told me they were going to build a track, and I believed them. When I was a freshman in college, I ran second in the national AAU 60-yard dash. That's when I was on the cover of *Sports Illustrated*. When I was still in high school, I beat the silver medalist from the 1964 Olympics.

One of my highlights in track was the NCAA race in Cobo Hall in Detroit in the NCAA Championships in 1968. I have the video that shows Earl McCullough sitting against the wall, being bored about being there. This was right before the race, and he thought he was going to blow everyone away, including me. They introduced him as the world-record-holder, and he was sitting there against the wall like he was just going to walk away with this thing.

I won that race by diving at the finish line. I almost ran into a pole and broke my neck. He got the lead on me—you can see in the clip he'd got me by a half of a step—but I didn't give up. We came off the last hurdle, and he had me by a step-and-a-half. How do you win a race when you are a step-and-a-half behind coming to the wire? I won that race because, back then, it was the first part of your body going across the finish line. Today it is your chest. That was the closest I came to losing in college.

The first year I was eligible to play was 1966, and I was a wingback. Well, that position had not been totally converted to a skill position; it had been manned by a fierce blocker named Hal Wantland, who would crush defensive players to make way for the running back. I couldn't crush a pecan. I was 162 pounds and just a fast guy. After Coach Dickey realized I was not an effective blocker, he moved the position out, and we went to a two-receiver scheme.

Dewey Warren, the "Swamp Rat," had a lot to do with the evolution of the wingback from blocker to receiver. I'm sure everyone remembers how he used to say, "I like to hum that tater." He was a passer. He could throw it. He didn't run much, but he didn't have to run because he could throw.

In 1966, my sophomore year, Charlie Fulton, who had been the starting quarterback in 1965, was moved to wingback. Well, we went to Auburn for the first game of the year, and it was hot. At halftime, he was blown away because it was so hot. Other players had trouble, too. I got to play the second half. I'll never forget the fourth quarter and how hot it was. I was ready for Charlie to come back in. We won 28–0.

I don't feel like there was a defining moment for me at Tennessee. I know the moment, or game, that stands out was beating Alabama my senior year. I was the tailback then, and Doug Dickey gave me the ball three times going in for a score. It was the opening drive of the game and our only touchdown in a 10–9 win over 'Bama.

I gave a dimension to the team in that linebackers didn't hang around in the middle very long because I could go outside. But I was only a part of the team; there was no defining, "Michael Jordan" moment of a game-winning play because I played on some great teams with a lot of good players.

One of the fun things I did was cover punts when Kentucky had a terrific punt returner, Dicky Lyons. He was as good as anyone. I didn't get to do it all the time, but against Kentucky they would let me cover punts because I was fast and could get down there to cover Dicky as he caught the ball.

Dicky led the country in punt returns, and we had great punters, like "Thunderfoot," Herman Weaver. He was so strong he could out-kick coverage, but he couldn't out-kick me. So I would run all-out for 50 yards, and if Dicky caught it and tried to run, I would have killed him.

I guess one of the biggest moments of my Tennessee career came in 1968 as I was getting prepared for the 1968 Olympics in Mexico City.

I had a very good chance to make it, and then I tore my hamstring in the spring. It was a big disappointment because I missed the Olympic trials. The U.S. Olympic Committee then decided to have a second trials because I was hurt and so was the great distance runner, Jim Ryun. I just wasn't in shape and ready to go, and I didn't make it again.

The day of the second trials was in mid-September. It happened to be the first day of the 1968 college football season, and Tennessee was playing Georgia.

I was in Los Angeles, and Coach Rohe put me on the phone with Coach Dickey, and he knew I was disappointed. He told me if I came back I could play tailback—he knew that's where my heart was. I should have taken a red-shirt year, but he knew I wanted to play running back, and they needed a back. Walter Chadwick had been the tailback when I got to Tennessee, and he was really, really good. So they had moved me to wingback, and that's where I stayed.

Well, Walter was gone to the NFL in 1968, and I had a chance to play tailback, and I jumped at it. It helped me get my mind off the Olympics.

That was the year we beat Alabama in Knoxville, and Dickey gave the ball to me two or three times near the goal line. I got stuffed the first time, just hammered. I was in the huddle, wondering what we were going to call next, and they called the same play. I thought, "Oh, my God." The first time I ran it, Mike Hull, their middle linebacker, stuffed me. This time, the word came from the sideline for me to jump. When Dickey sent the play in, they told them to tell me to jump. Walter Chadwick was a jumper, and it had worked for him.

Alabama got fooled. They thought I was going to go wide, but I jumped. There is a picture of me jumping over Mike Hull, and he is looking up at me.

When I got into the NFL, writers in New York kept asking why I didn't play for Coach Bryant. One day, I guess, I was feeling my oats and I never, ever should have said this, but I told them, "I would rather beat him than play for him."

That was not good. I had a brain cramp and got a lot of hate mail over that. But if you say, who would you rather beat, Muhammad Ali or his sparring partner, you say Ali. I wish I could have played for Coach Bryant, he was an amazing man. That's not to say I regret going to Tennessee. I would do it the same way again.

It was Coach Bryant who got me into the University of Alabama Law School. I had been turned down by Tennessee because I didn't do well on the LSAT. I was dyslexic and didn't test well. But Coach Bryant got me in at Alabama. He had connections and took care of it, which shows you what kind of man he was.

If I had to do it over again, absolutely, I would go to Tennessee. Even though people tell me it was a spiritual experience to play for Coach Bryant, I'm a Vol. I think the biggest thing I can say about it is that Alabama was about Bear Bryant. That's the tradition there.

Tennessee is about great teams over history. It wasn't about Doug Dickey, it wasn't about Richmond Flowers, it was about the players. They made the tradition at Tennessee. That's what it means to be a Vol.

Richmond Flowers was an All-American wingback in 1967 and All-American hurdler in track and field. He was a world-class hurdler, even as a high school athlete in Alabama. A favorite to make the 1968 U.S. Olympic team, Flowers tore a hamstring before the U.S. trials, which ruined his chances to compete in Mexico City. His father was the attorney general of Alabama (1962–1966) and challenged Governor George Wallace over segregation, which was a big reason Flowers chose Tennessee over Alabama. Flowers was drafted in the second round of the 1969 draft by the Dallas Cowboys and played defensive back for the Cowboys in the 1971 Super Bowl.

CHARLES ROSENFELDER

GUARD

1966–1968

WHEN I WAS TRYING TO PICK a college to go to, Ken Donahue was the line coach at Alabama under Bear Bryant, and he was recruiting me for Alabama. What made it odd was that he was a star player at Tennessee under General Neyland. I still remember the note he wrote me that said, "You need to come to the land of the rising sun."

Donahue recruited me pretty hard, and Bill Anderson was the recruiter for Tennessee. When it came time to decide, I went to bed at night after telling my dad I was going to Alabama. The next morning I woke up, I wasn't comfortable with it and told my dad I was going to Tennessee. I never regretted it.

One of the reasons I went to Tennessee was that I thought the new coach, Doug Dickey, was going to turn things around. Alabama had just won a national championship in 1964, but Tennessee was my state university, and I thought if I had a good career, maybe it would help me later with business dealings. That thought, plus Dickey's character, were a couple of the reasons I didn't go to Alabama and stayed home.

I got ready for college football in my senior year in high school in Humboldt, Tennessee, because we practiced two or three times a day in the preseason in extremely hot weather. We started with 35 players in camp and were down to 27 when the season started. It helped me get in shape and show people what I was made of. I also moved around and played a lot of different positions.

Kentucky, Vanderbilt, Alabama, Memphis State, and Tennessee really recruited me. I got offers from all those schools, but I felt pulled by Tennessee because Coach Dickey had a very talented coaching staff, and I liked the way he went about doing things.

There was a change of eras going on at Tennessee when I came in, not only to Coach Dickey, but also in our offense. Tennessee had finally moved away from the single-wing to the T formation, and then to the I formation. I came in as one of 40 guys in that recruiting class of 1964. I think 30 of us graduated, and we take great pride in being part of the turnaround of the program in the mid-1960s. We have always been a close-knit group and like to get together with each other.

I still remember Section X in the old part of the stadium where we did our winter workouts. It was an old boiler room, a real sweatbox, sort of like Marine duty. You learned a lot about yourself and your buddy in there. You did a lot of wrestling and pull-ups, and there were a lot of endurance drills that helped our team and made us better. To this day, if you mention Section X, you will get an immediate response from Tennessee football players.

When you got on the practice field after a winter of working out in Section X, you knew where you were as a player. We had some great guys on the offensive line when I was there. Elliott Gammage was a very good tackle. A Miami Dolphins coach said John Boynton was one of the best one-on-one blockers he had ever seen in college football. John just didn't have the speed to get out and block the defensive end coming off the edge.

I played with two Hall of Fame centers in Bob Johnson and Chip Kell. Joe Graham was Sophomore of the Year in the SEC and then had major knee injury. So we had a lot of talent on that offensive line, and that was a real strength of our team.

I was one of the quicker guards, and people used to say I was offside all the time. I was in the defensive lineman's lap before he knew it, and that came from playing basketball all through junior high and into high school.

My first game with the varsity was against Auburn, and Coach [Ray] Trail came up to me after the game and said, "Rosenfelder, you were the fastest man off line, but you didn't hit anybody the whole game."

That's what I was known for, getting off the ball quick. I guess my trademark was the whip-kick, which is illegal now. You used that to take care of defensive players who tried to run around your block. Cecil Dickerson was my line coach in high school, and he said to just whip-kick those guys, sort

Charlie Rosenfelder was a unanimous All-American as an offensive guard in 1968.

of like a donkey hitting you in the head. I would fire off and then whip-kick around with my legs. I came around so hard I would break the defensive lineman's headgear. It is a wicked block and considered a trip, and like I said, it is illegal now.

Opponents hated it. I played in the All-America game in Atlanta one year, and I made the mistake of trying to whip-kick this big lineman from Syracuse. On the next play, he came around and just unloaded on me. It will wear you out. Guys didn't like it, but they learned not to go around you.

We also did a lot of scramble blocking, which is illegal now also. You would fire off and put your head right in the guy's gut—right in his middle—and that guy wouldn't know which way you were going, so you had an extra moment to block him. I had a Riddell helmet with a band in the middle, and I hit so many people with it that first week of practice, I looked like a unicorn with the size of the bump coming out of the top of my head. I wasn't too pretty of a sight. Today, there's not enough firing off. It is zone blocking and letting the back find the hole.

One of the games I won't forget was my senior year in 1967 against LSU when we did so much trap blocking and hitting people I was punch drunk after the game. LSU was among the most physical teams we ever played. We ended up winning 17–14 in what was our toughest game of the regular season.

The one thing I will never forget from my days at Tennessee was the death of Tom Fisher, one of our linebackers, in 1966. He and Tom Crumbacher were on their way back from spring break, and they were hit head-on by an 18-wheeler. They died, and there was a third player in the car who survived. My first date with my wife was with Tom and his girlfriend, so we had become good friends. It was devastating to lose him like that.

Tom was going to be an All-American linebacker. He was fast, and he could play the game. His death inspired me to want to be an All-American. I told myself I would dedicate my life, if the Lord would allow me, and I would honor his name and be a witness for him the rest of my life.

I was number four on the depth chart that spring, my sophomore year, and there were two players who were good friends of Crumbacher who came back and were not in good shape after what had happened, and Coach Trail ran them off. Another player, who was a senior, hurt his ankle, and just like that, I was the starter. I was All-SEC sophomore team, then All-SEC varsity my junior year, and consensus All-American my senior year. The Lord really honored me.

Coach Dickey was super in the way he handled the different tragedies that hit the team. Three of our assistant coaches were killed at a railroad crossing, and then we lost two of our teammates. Coach Dickey always managed to say the right thing at the right moment, and it drew us together.

The tragedies were an opportunity for the Fellowship of Christian Athletes to help support the people on the team. I remember Richmond Flowers coming up to me some years later, and he was one of the stars, and he said, "Charlie, I thought you were kooky and crazy because of your witness, but now I am one of ya."

There were some memorable games. I remember my sophomore year we had the short field goal that missed, and we lost to Alabama 11–10. I swear it went right over the upright. They called it "Wide Wright" because our kicker was Gary Wright. I still think that kick was good. That game bothered us so much our motto all through Section X workouts in the offseason was "Beat 'Bama."

When we played them the next season, we scored on the first drive and beat them pretty good, 24–13. There was no doubt we were going to beat those guys. That was the game Albert Dorsey became an All-American because he intercepted two or three passes and returned two for touchdowns.

Bob Johnson and I picked Dickey up, and they got a big picture of us taking him out to midfield after the game to meet Bear Bryant. I would rather beat 'Bama than anybody. We beat them two out of three years I played.

I remember a few years later I had to travel through Tuscaloosa, so I spent the night there and then got up early because I figured Coach Donahue would be there watching film. Sure enough, when I went over there, he had a coat and tie on and he had already been through the film twice. They did not have a good game against Southern Miss, and there he was studying the film, twice, before breakfast.

Then there were some not-so-memorable games—not many, but some. We had a good season in 1968 when we lost just one game in the regular season and then we went down to the Cotton Bowl. Texas just wore us out with that wishbone and won 36–13. They had that down pat and the next year they won the national championship.

There were a lot of special moments for me at Tennessee. I feel very honored to have played there and traveled and met people. I still hurt when they lose and rejoice when they win. I know it is a different game than when I played, but it is something special to be in the Tennessee family. We have a very close relationship among players, which includes passing on the jersey number and remembering the guy who had it before you.

Phil Fulmer got my No. 65 after I graduated. I got the number from Steve DeLong, who was a great player and Outland Trophy winner. It creates a bond, a connection, and that is something you do not lose, even 40 years after you took off the jersey for the last time.

80

Charlie Rosenfelder received an industrial engineering degree from the University of Tennessee and lives in Knoxville. He works in sales for Rogers Petroleum. He was a consensus All-American in 1968 and was named to nine All-America teams. Rosenfelder was twice named All-SEC as a right guard. He was a three-year starter for the Vols. Rosenfelder's No. 65 was also worn by UT great Steve DeLong. The number was passed on by Rosenfelder to Phillip Fulmer, an offensive lineman and future Tennessee head coach.

STEVE KINER

LINEBACKER

1967–1969

I LOVED BEAR BRYANT. One of my high school coaches in Tampa played for Alabama, so I had an understanding of what it meant to play against the Crimson Tide. It was special.

That's why, when Tennessee played Alabama in 1967 when I was a sophomore, I knew I had arrived as a player. That game was in Birmingham, and we were highly ranked [No. 7], and so were they [No. 6].

It was a beautiful day in Legion Field, and I played very well. We all had a good game against Alabama and beat them 24–13. Ken Stabler was their senior quarterback, and you know what kind of player he was, an All-Pro in the NFL. It was quite a feeling to be lined up against Alabama because, three years before, I was sitting in my living room watching Alabama and Joe Namath play Nebraska in the Orange Bowl.

I always seemed to play well against them. My senior year, I had a very good game against them with an interception or two, a sack, and a bunch of tackles. I think I was the AP national defensive player of the week.

There is a picture of me walking off the field with Bear Bryant, and he has his arm around me. Bear Bryant was like God to me because I was avid about football, and he defined Southeastern Conference football. He always said nice things about me in the paper. After we played them my sophomore year, he told the Alabama papers it was pretty hard for Kenny Stabler to throw the football when he had Kiner hanging on his neck the whole game.

He picked me out as a thorn in his side, and I thought that was incredible, especially since we had so many good players.

As that picture was being taken, I said to him, and I was not trying to be disrespectful, "Coach Bryant, it doesn't seem like your guys are proud to be wearing those Crimson jerseys."

He said, "I noticed that, Steve, and I'm going to fix that. I appreciate your saying something."

That was in 1969, and I think Alabama beat us the next 11 years in a row.

I was a quarterback and linebacker in high school, and Tennessee recruited me as a defensive back, so they knew I could run. At first, they thought I wasn't big enough to play linebacker because I was 6'1", 175 pounds in high school.

But I got in the weight room and got bigger and stronger—I gained 30 pounds between my freshman and sophomore year in college. I could still run, though, so I could cover those backs.

I moved around to three different linebacker positions in three years. The first year, 1967, we played a 3-2, and I played inside with Jack Reynolds. The next year, we went to a 4-3, and I played the weak side, on air. The third year, I played over the tight end. I could run; that was my identity as a player, playing "on air," or what they call playing "in space" these days. I could run and I could tackle in the open field.

The first two years, the coach played me on air a lot because I could get to the sideline. A back has got to block you or a guard has to pick you up. The tackle is not quick enough to get to you.

One of the things I'll remember about playing with Jack Reynolds was watching him take on the run. He took on the run as well as anybody. I wasn't as big as him, but I learned how to take on the run. His advantage was when he was in traffic in the middle. He was strong and big.

My advantage was playing on air, or in space, but I could also play inside if I had to. I remember my sophomore year, playing inside with Jack against LSU, and they had this fullback named Eddie Ray, who was 6'4", 265 pounds, and they ran that son of a bitch between the guard and tackle all day long. I thought, if they run that guy one more time, I'm going to throw my helmet on the ground and walk off. He beat the crap out of me and Reynolds.

That guy was bigger than any of our defensive lineman. We played Steve Owens of Oklahoma, who won the Heisman, and let me tell you, I would tackle Owens all day before Eddie Ray. We beat LSU 17–14 when Karl

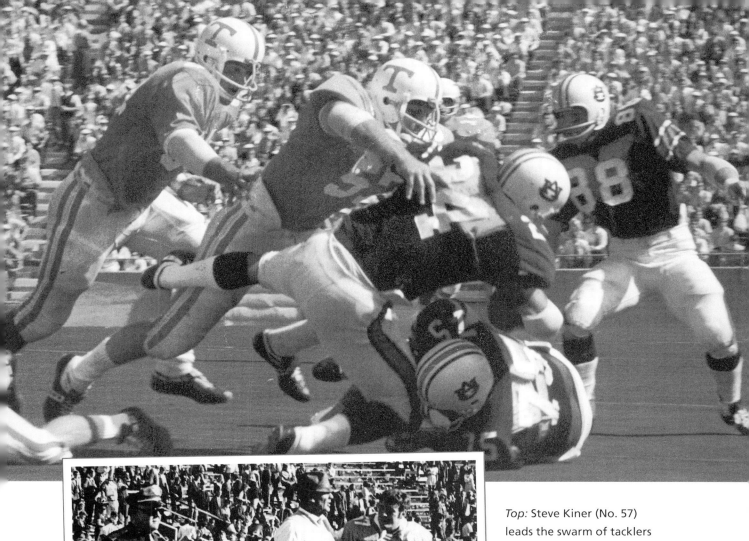

Top: Steve Kiner (No. 57) leads the swarm of tacklers against Auburn. Kiner was part of an era when Tennessee was called "Linebacker U."

Left: Kiner tells it like it is to Alabama coach Paul "Bear" Bryant after Tennessee's 1969 win.
Photo courtesy of Steve Kiner

Kremser kicked a field goal with a minute left. That made the pounding easier to take, let me tell you.

There are maybe a handful of guys in my life who I respect as much and who mentored me as much as my father, and Doug Dickey, my college football coach, is one of them. My dad handed me off to him when I went up to Tennessee.

Dickey was the one that turned the program around and got it going back in the direction it had been going in the early '50s with General Neyland. That 1967 team, my sophomore year, was an important team in Tennessee football because things were really starting to go in the right direction. Dickey did that without a bunch of superstars. He did it with a bunch of kids who did what he asked them to do. I don't know that we were extremely talented. I remember playing Auburn, and I thought they had twice as much talent as we did.

Dickey was never overbearing. To me, he was one of the greats, like Tom Landry and Bum Phillips. Now, I had a coach, P.W. Underwood, who would grab me by the face mask, jerk my head around, and forearm me in the head—that was his way of communicating. Dickey just exuded confidence. He came from Arkansas, where he was a graduate assistant. That's where he learned his football, under Frank Broyles. Then he brought two or three guys from Arkansas, Ray Trail and Kenny Hatfield, who were very good assistant coaches.

Now, a couple of those years we had some great players, and one of them was Chip Kell, one of our offensive lineman. I remember Alabama had this nose tackle named Sammy Gellerstedt, who was considered a very good player, and Kell owned him. You have to understand that, before Kell hurt his knees, he could really run. They had him pulling from center to go out and block a defensive back on the corner. Are you kidding me? You are out there, 185 pounds, and here comes this 285-pound guy, and you can't get away from him, he just eats you up.

That was Kell's coming out, when he played Sammy Gellerstedt. He was a little guy and quick, but Kell was just as quick as he was and two times stronger. He slapped him around down there when we beat the hell out of them, 41–14 [1969].

These guys today have it better than we did. Back then, they could sign 50 kids in a class, something like that, then have maybe 20 or 30 walk-ons, and then they would see how tough you were. They ran off a lot of players.

Today, they might be able to do 10 days of two-a-days, but back then if they wanted to do four weeks of two-a-days, they could get away with it. We had 22 guys left in the class that I came in with. The guys who were left may not have been the best athletes, but they were the guys who were not going to quit. Georgia had the same kind of kids. You go down to Athens and beat them, and that was a battle. That was doing something.

I thought I was a tough guy, and Reynolds thought he was a tough guy, too. And he was. He was the prototype middle linebacker. He was the same size as All-Pros like Willie Lanier and Mike Curtis. He would stand you up in the hole. He had short legs, so he had tremendous leverage, and he would explode into guys. He could plug the hole.

I still remember those offseason workouts in the stadium in the middle of the winter at 5:00 A.M. They would get us in the room and have the heat on, and it would get up to 90 degrees. We had to do heavy calisthenics and then get in a big circle and wrestle. If you won, you could leave. If you lost, you stayed. It was "anything goes." People were vomiting all over the place. They had these stools, and you had to jump over them rapid fire, which is hard to do 20 times.

People say to me, it must have been tough. It wasn't tough. My father had it tough. He was captured by the Japanese in World War II and made the Bataan Death March. Guys died all around him. It was awful. After the bomb dropped on Nagasaki, he was still a prisoner of war, and the Japanese made him pick up corpses for three days. That was tough. I'm 60 years old and I have never had a day as bad as my father had.

When you go through all the rigorous stuff that we went through, it makes a real tight community. When we had a reunion in 2007, there were more than 40 guys there, and this was from 40 years ago. It is like a fraternity, but stronger. You go through the fire and come out the other end.

Steve Kiner was an All-American linebacker in 1968 and 1969. He was named All-SEC in 1968 and 1969. He lives in Carrollton, Georgia, and manages emergency psychiatric services for Emory Healthcare. He played in the NFL for nine years and retired in 1979.

CHIP KELL
GUARD
1968–1970

WHEN IT CAME TIME for me to play my sophomore year, I knew I was in a big-time place and at a big-time school. Standing on our sideline one day at practice was Vince Lombardi, the legendary Green Bay Packers coach. This was in 1968, and there he is, the Super Bowl coach, on our sideline. He was a friend of our head coach, Doug Dickey.

Coach Lombardi spoke to the team, and we were all looking around at each other like, "Our coach knows what he's doing...his mentor is Vince Lombardi." How cool was that?

Needless to say, we ran a lot of the Packers' offense.

That was the thing about Tennessee: there were always people around to look up to and watch and learn from. I think that's what it means to be a Vol. The coaches were on top of things, and you had upperclassmen who were good players and knew how to win.

That's why that 1968 season, my sophomore season, was very fulfilling for me. We were 8–2–1, and we played a lot of sophomores. We had won a national championship the year before with a veteran team, and we were in a little bit of a transition, but we still won eight games.

Coach Dickey hired good people to be around him on his staff, and that had a lot to do with our success those last two years I played for him in 1968 and 1969. He had Ray Trail as the offensive line coach and Bill Battle, who was the receivers coach, and went on to be named head coach when Dickey

Decatur, Georgia, native Chip Kell was recruited nationally by schools such as Southern Cal, but chose to go to Tennessee.

left for Florida. Vince Gibson was an assistant coach, and he was good enough to be named head coach at Kansas State. I am a high school coach, and I can tell you, you are only as good as the guys around you.

I have always said one of the reasons I was successful was I had one of the best offensive line coaches in the country in Ray Trail. He was an all-conference guard at Arkansas, and he demanded the best out of you and then some.

You know what the expectations were at Tennessee? The coaches expected you to play over your head every game. You learned that from the competitors on that squad and the upperclassmen like Richmond Flowers and Charlie Rosenfelder, who was a guard. There was enough senior leadership sprinkled in there that rubbed off on the underclassmen, and we got better because of it.

Think about it. Here I am, an offensive lineman playing my first year, and I am lined up next to an All-American, Charlie Rosenfelder. That rubs off on you. It has to. You line up next to a guy like that and you are going to play the best you can. It was that way all over the team, position to position. That was the essence of Tennessee football, what it meant to play for the Vols. It was pride all over the field.

I moved to guard from center my junior year, and the coaches' explanation was that teams were going more to an even front than an odd-man front, so they wanted me nose-up on somebody. The center on an even front is basically going after a linebacker, whereas in an odd-man front, you have the nose guard on your nose and you have to take care of him. Some guys might hesitate, but by that time I trusted our coaches to put us in the best position to succeed.

Our offense required a lot of pulling, and Trail wanted me at guard to be the lead guy on the pull for the sweep and to be the lead trap guy. We ran the veer and the Green Bay sweep where both guards pull and the lead guard, which was I, kicks on the safety coming up. My junior year, I was 255 pounds, and I could run.

What helped me the most was that my dad started me early in strength training, so I was ahead of my time compared to a lot of players coming out of high school into college. I was also pretty quick on my feet. I ran a 4.7-second 40-yard dash. In that day, that was considered fast.

It was the strength and speed that got me noticed. Southern Cal even recruited me because they ran those student-body sweeps and liked the guards who could get out there and plow. The SEC schools recruited me, and being from the Atlanta area, I wanted to stay closer to home.

My senior year in high school was 1966–1967. When I went through Avondale High School, there was only one recorded loss in that stadium, so I was accustomed to being with a winning program. Tennessee was coming on strong in football under Coach Dickey, and they were also one of the leaders in the Southeastern Conference in track. I threw the shot put, so I got a dual scholarship, which was like Richmond Flowers, who was a very good receiver. During that era, they had won nine SEC championships in track, and in my freshman year, I set the SEC record in shot.

We could have played for the national championship my senior year in 1970, which was Coach Bill Battle's first season, but we lost to Auburn and finished 10–1 in the regular season and then beat Air Force in the Sugar Bowl. Auburn had that Pat Sullivan–to–Terry Beasley deal going and hit a couple of bombs on us. Sullivan was just a junior and won the Heisman Trophy the next year.

We should've won that game. We had more than 500 yards of offense and also had a touchdown called back; but basically time ran out on us, and we lost 36–23. Their scores were kind of quick, and we went up and down the field.

We won comfortably in a lot of games that season. UCLA gave us a test, and South Carolina hung around because of mistakes before we pulled it out. The thing about that Tennessee team was we played together for three years; we had a lot of closeness. That had a lot to do with that 11–1 season. All Coach Battle had to do was discipline us and get us in shape. We knew what to do because it was a veteran team.

We were a run-first team in 1970. The quarterback was Bobby Scott, and he wasn't what you'd call a Peyton Manning–type quarterback who could make all the throws, but he was a very good leader on the field, and he got it done. We won 11 of 12 games, and we had a lot of leadership from Bobby. You have seen these guys before. They get things done, maybe not with all the great passing statistics, but they make the right calls, they don't make mistakes, and they lead.

We could run the ball, and there was one game in particular in which Curt Watson ran for 197 yards against Georgia, which was my home state team. That was one of my better games and one of my favorite games because we beat them 17–3 down there.

It was a rainy day in Athens, and Curt was one of those guys who ran low to the ground, which really helped him. He had a low center of gravity, so he was hard to bring down. They were pretty quick on the defensive line, so we did reach-blocking instead of trying to block them head-on. It's the same thing as what they call zone blocking today, and the running back just runs to daylight. They did a lot of stunts, so we did some trapping and popped some long gains.

We had some success against Alabama, too. I also remember my senior year against Alabama where we beat them 24–0.

We also beat them 41–14 my junior year. Steve Kiner, who was a linebacker for us in that game [1969], made one of the famous comments of the Bear Bryant era following that game.

Back then, everybody shook hands with the legendary Bear Bryant after the game. We were lined up to shake hands and Kiner said to Coach Bryant, and with a lot of respect, "Coach, your players have lost pride in that maroon jersey."

Coach Bryant didn't get angry, but right after that they got powerful again. Some of it had to do with recruiting black players, but he said he remembered Kiner's comment and said Steve was right to say that, and it motivated him and woke him up. Not long after we beat them 24–0 my senior season, Alabama got going again, and Tennessee—and a lot of other programs—started having trouble with Alabama again.

I got to play for two coaches at Tennessee, and I think they both did a good job. Coach Battle made a difference for me when he took over before my senior season because he made me lose 15 pounds, which made me a lot quicker and faster. I was also in better condition. He was a disciplinarian, and he took it to the limit in what he expected from players.

I played for Coach Dickey for two years, and he built the program back to some prominence starting in 1964. It is still going strong. He left in 1970 and went to Florida and then he came back as athletic director and made sure it kept going. Of course, he caught a lot of static when he left to go to Florida. The fans didn't like that.

Being a football man like I am, the game is the foundation of my life, so it means everything to have played at a place like Tennessee. They say it is something that is in your blood, and I can believe that. Your blood flows orange. You are orange all the way when you have been in the trenches in Neyland Stadium. That's where your heart is and that's where it stays.

My favorite tradition is running through the T; it sends a chill up you, and you will never forget it. Once I retire from coaching, one of my priorities is to go back up there and spend more time because they did so much for me at that school and I will be forever grateful.

Chip Kell won the Jacobs Blocking Trophy twice as the best blocker in the SEC and was All-SEC for three seasons and a two-time All-American. Kell is one of only four Vols to be named All-SEC three times. Kell also won the SEC title in the shot put in track and field. He is a high school football coach in Chattanooga, Tennessee.

LESTER McCLAIN
WIDE RECEIVER
1968–1970

AFTER I GOT TO A CERTAIN AGE, I realized it was not all my doing to be the first black player at the University of Tennessee. There were a lot of people who made some serious decisions that allowed me to come through the doors. You have to remember that, a few years before, George Wallace, the governor of Alabama, stood in the doorways and said blacks were not going to go to school at the University of Alabama. The governor of Tennessee, members of the board of trustees, the athletic boosters, did not stand in the door and block my entrance to one of the premier football programs in the South. Kentucky, I think, had black players, but as far as a major school in the Deep South, Tennessee was first, and I was blessed.

Here is the bottom line. There must have been a meeting, somewhere on that Tennessee campus, where someone stood up and argued passionately that black players should be allowed to play. Somebody stuck their neck out for me where, in Alabama, nobody stuck their neck out for Bear Bryant.

It's funny, but I was not supposed to be the first black football player at Tennessee. When I was a senior in high school, Tennessee was recruiting more talented players than myself, and one of those was Albert Davis. He was the Herschel Walker of our era—big, fast, would run over you. He was black and he was the one Tennessee wanted.

Albert was the 39th recruit in a class of 40, and I was number 40. I was recruited to be Albert Davis's roommate. He needed a roommate. And, then, he decided he was going to go to Tennessee State, which was a historically black college. That left me by myself.

As a kid, I had no idea what I was walking into. All I wanted to do was play major-college football, and this was my shot. My options, in reality, were limited, but I had some delusions of grandeur and thought my classmates and I were going to bust through and have a great opportunity to succeed and achieve things others before us had not achieved.

I went to an all-black county high school, Haynes High School, for three years, though the system was starting to change with the classes coming up two years behind me. You were going to be able to go to schools close to where you lived, rather than get bussed to the black school. Haynes was changing, but I didn't stay around, I went to Antioch High School my senior year because I thought that was the one chance to get a shot to play college football.

I had a gentleman by the name of Bill Garrett, who was a prominent pharmacist in the area, support me. Bill was the guy who ran the kids into shape in the summertime at 6:00 in the morning before the coaches were allowed to practice. He was also a very prominent guy in doing recruiting for Tennessee at the time. When the season started, I was playing cornerback and receiver. We ended up having a pretty good year, 8–3, and I think I had a pretty good year. I ended up playing some running back, too.

Middle Tennessee had a lot of prospects at that time, and Mr. Garrett had a lot to do with those talented players going to Tennessee. Bill Garrett constantly kept pushing me before Tennessee, but there were better players than I. They were looking at other players, which included Albert Davis. He was a man. A real football player. He signed in the late spring and then, after some others went elsewhere, they offered me the 40th and last scholarship. Albert did not go to Tennessee, so I was the lone black recruit. I could have gone to Tennessee State, but I did not choose to do so.

Like I said, as a kid, you don't realize what you are walking into and have that fear. I just wanted to live and play football. Thinking back on it, I was not very concerned about my position until the day my father and brother dropped me off at school. As I saw them drive away, I realized what was happening.

The first few weeks were a little interesting, and a little intimidating. I worked hard every day in practice, tried to do my job, and did what I needed to do. I wanted to do well. My freshman year, my roommate ended up being

93

Lester McClain, the first black player for UT, ended up a Vol by accident. He never thought about being a pioneer, he just wanted to play major-college football.

a gentleman from middle Tennessee named Jim Maxwell, who was a quarterback. Jim was good, and he was okay with the situation. The situation was probably tougher on Jim than on me. I don't know that anyone volunteered to be my roommate, as much as they were drafted.

There was a respect for players who came out, showed great effort, and did what needed to be done for the team to win. I did my part, and the team respected that, so some of the other stuff, and being the first black football player at Tennessee, had less of an impact. I don't know all that the players thought or said, but as long as I did my part, I was okay. Who I was, or what I represented was secondary to being a teammate because I worked.

Probably the most frightening thing I heard my freshman year was the word *redshirt*. It sounded like the most awful thing, almost like failure. There was a fear in me that if I was redshirted that black players would be set back. I ended up having a very good year my freshman year, and I think I worked harder so they wouldn't redshirt me. It was almost like total failure. There was a responsibility to the black players who would come after me to work hard and succeed.

As far as how much I felt the responsibility, let me answer it this way. I remember my first big game. It was my sophomore year and we came to Atlanta to play Georgia Tech. It was my first start. I will never forget the first pass thrown to me: I dropped it.

It was a third-down play, and I remember coming to the sideline and looking at Coach Dickey and almost pleading with my eyes to give me another chance and throw me the ball. I was really frightened that they were going to think I couldn't be depended on. And, of course, the fraternity guys in the Georgia Tech section were really getting on me with harassment. I didn't necessarily hear all of it, but I knew what was going on. I'd wanted to do well.

Bubba Wyche, our quarterback, was going to be fair with me. I should have understood that. He was an exceptionally good guy, so I got another chance. What helped me was that I played two positions, split end and wingback. I remember Gary Kreis bringing a play in from the sideline and replacing me at split end, but it was so hot that Bill Baker was vomiting because he was trying to play sick. Baker was the wingback, and Kreis wanted to know if I should stay at split end, and he would just stay in and play wingback for Baker.

I said, "No, I am going to move to wingback for Baker because you are supposed to be coming in for me at split end." The play ended up being my first touchdown. I ran over a couple of guys, in fact. Later on in the game, Bubba threw a deep pass against man-to-man coverage, and I got a chance to make my first exceptionally great catch, and it went for a touchdown. Someone told me there was a story in the Atlanta paper the next day saying something to the effect that there had been integration of the field before, but not such that it had affected the scoreboard.

One of the highlights, besides the Georgia Tech game, was that we beat Alabama all four years I was there. Three years for the varsity and one year as a freshman.

One of the key things for me was the coaching of Bill Battle, who was the receivers coach under Coach Dickey. He was outstanding because he worked on the little things. If you were right-handed and lined up on the right side, you put your right hand down. If you lined up on the left side, you put your left hand down because that gave you a chance to take the same number of steps on either side of the ball. He was the kind of coach who pushed you to run with precision. We also worked hard on making the difficult catch. We would work on that after practice. He would always tell us the majority of balls are hard to catch, and that is what we need to work on. I was about 6'2", 190 pounds, and probably a little bit of a speed guy and possession receiver. I had a long stride, but was not particularly fast.

I enjoyed my time in Knoxville, and I really didn't run into any trouble. In fact, I remember my first game in Neyland Stadium. It was a nationally televised game with Georgia, and it was the first game with artificial turf. Sometime late in first quarter, or early second quarter, I ran onto the field and got a standing ovation. It was wonderful to have that; it could have been different. I have always been given respect from people. I know several years earlier, a visiting team came with a black player, and there were some issues with things being thrown at him, and I did not have those ugly situations. Things changed.

I take great pride in having attended Tennessee, and when the Vols lose, I ache all over, just like any Tennessee fan. The pain is unbelievable because I want them to win so badly. I had a chance to go to the national championship game in 1998, but I was so afraid we would lose that I decided not to go. I think that emotional attachment is what it means to be a Vol.

Lester McClain was the first black football player at the University of Tennessee. He was a wide receiver for the Vols from 1968 to 1970. The East Tennessee chapter of the National Football Foundation and College Hall of Fame honored McClain with the chapter's Distinguished American Award in April 2007. McClain is a lawyer and lives in Nashville.

The
SEVENTIES

BOBBY MAJORS
DEFENSIVE BACK
1969–1971

I'M IN THE RECORD BOOK at Tennessee for a few things. The all-time leader in punt returns (117), return yards in a season (457), and punt-return yards in a career (1,163). I'm also in there for the most interceptions in a season. I had 10 in 1970.

Now, I will have to say that the punt-return records are still in the record book because of the defense we had. We stopped their offense; they had to kick. People punted a lot against us.

The interceptions were the result of the scheme, a three-deep zone, and the players around me. I think I was a good player, but quarterbacks were always under pressure from our linemen and had to throw it.

So what we did on defense was we either stopped you or took the ball away. In 1970, we led the nation in the number of takeaways with 36 interceptions and 21 fumble recoveries. That was the season I led the nation in interceptions with 10.

We had a defensive backs coach named Buddy Bennett who got us in good shape and had us breaking on the ball so well, we didn't think anybody could complete a pass against us. We thought we would knock it down and intercept every pass; that was our belief.

We played 99 percent zone; we played man-to-man maybe four plays a game. That's it.

Bobby Majors holds the
Tennessee single-season
record of 10
interceptions.

We played a three-deep zone. We didn't play any of that two-deep zone they play so much of today. That is the worst defense going. It was created primarily to stop the run so the corners could come up in run-support. Well, somebody developed a pass attack that took that defense apart. We tried to play it, and from a safety standpoint, it was too hard to cover the field. You had to cover one-half of the field. There was too much gap between you and the cornerback.

We played three-deep with me in the middle and the two corners outside. The strong safety had curl area. The linebackers had the short flat. We could get seven people into pass coverage, and that's why we intercepted so many passes and why our record is safe as long as they play this two-deep zone and have defensive backs running with their back to the ball.

I played defense, returned kicks, and punted—and I also did some kicking off. I would have liked to have done more, but they didn't allow me to play offense, which would have been some fun.

I played wide receiver as a sophomore and was a backup to Lester McClain. I wanted to be a running back, but they had some really good ones there at the time, so I just returned kicks. I didn't make the grade as a running back, but as it turns out, I'm glad they moved me to defense.

We were five brothers and one sister. John played up there, I played up there, and Bill played up there. Bill was one of the guys who stopped LSU's Billy Cannon at the goal line in 1959 when they were No. 1 in the country. We won the game 14–13, and it was one of the biggest wins in Tennessee football history. He was a safety, who just came up to help make the stop. They were going for a two-point conversion, we stopped them, and it was a huge win.

I was the heaviest of all the brothers, 190 pounds. John was light, and Larry was 138 pounds soaking wet and played for Daddy at Sewanee. Joe played at Florida State. He went to Alabama, but found himself behind Bart Starr, so he thought he better get out of there and go somewhere else, because Bart Starr was going to be pretty good.

All of my brothers played single-wing for my dad at Huntland High School, but when I came along, Daddy had become head coach at Sewanee. I wasn't smart enough to go there, or else I would have played for my daddy. I considered Georgia and Alabama. The family was okay with that; it didn't matter to them, just as long as I was happy. Nobody put any pressure on me to go to Tennessee.

I considered the other schools, Georgia and Alabama, because when Bill played at Tennessee, the teams had some horrible records and the fans booed my brother. Once I got old enough to understand that those things happened when you have a losing record, I softened up for Tennessee. Besides, John had played there and had a good experience by the time I came in the fall of 1968.

When I was a freshman in 1968, they used me as the safety man against the number-one offense because freshmen could not play. In 1969, I was a wide receiver.

When Bill Battle took over in 1970, which was my junior year, he moved me back over to defense and away from wide receiver. After I had 10 interceptions as a junior, they wouldn't throw close to me, and I had only three that senior season [1971]. They didn't go down the middle at all with the ball.

My technique was to watch the quarterback the whole time as I was backing up in pass defense. I just read the quarterback and broke on the ball. When I was young and played against my older brothers, my daddy taught me football, and I knew where the ball was going and the routes.

When I was 12 or 14 years old, they had taught me so much and I was punting the ball so well, I was kicking the ball further than the first-string kicker at the University of the South where Daddy was coaching. I had to be halfway decent with all that good coaching.

I think the success I had returning punts had to do with being able to feel people as they approached. It was that old saying about having eyes in the back of your head. I had a knack of feeling those people from the blind side and making them miss me. I wasn't fast, but I wasn't slow.

The one punt return that stands out was against Alabama. I have a picture of me running toward the end zone, and there is Bear Bryant, standing on the sideline watching the play. It's a priceless picture for me. I returned another one in that game that was called back because of a clip. That game was a highlight of my career at Tennessee.

There was another punt return against Penn State, my last home game in 1971, when I was a senior. They came in ranked No. 5 in the country, and we wore them out, 31–11. It was a return of about 42 to 44 yards; we got into the top 10 with that win, went on to play Arkansas in the Liberty Bowl, and beat them.

Everything went our way in that game with Penn State. I returned kick-offs that day and had something like 216 yards in returns. I was named Offensive Player of the Game even though I was a defensive player. The game was on national TV. As far as I know, being Offensive Player of the Game as a defensive back has never been done since.

We played against some great backs, like Penn State's Franco Harris and Lydell Mitchell. Harris was not a bruiser or a tough person to hit, but the guy who was tough to hit was Alabama's Johnny Musso. I hated to see that guy coming. He was the hardest guy I had to tackle in my college and pro career. He would hurt you. He ran with his knees high and had a good body angle and good forward body lean. Musso was the only back I didn't want to tackle.

As far as the best receiver, Auburn's Terry Beasley was by far the best I played against. Our junior year, I went for an interception—it was one of the few times we played that two-deep zone—but I missed the ball and the receiver caught it and ran for a touchdown. That was the only game we lost that season. I didn't do well. I gambled too much.

Their quarterback was Pat Sullivan, and he would win the Heisman Trophy the next year. Beasley was not only fast, but he lifted weights. Terry had to be able to do a 4.3-second 40-yard dash. His upper body strength was very good.

All of us got that thing, "Are you Johnny Majors's brother?" because John had established his name by doing so well at Tennessee and almost winning the Heisman Trophy. Daddy had also established our family name in Hunt-land, but I felt like I also had an identity as a player and human being.

I was 15 years old when Bill died in that train accident in Knoxville that morning in 1965. He was 27 and had played safety and tailback in the single-wing at Tennessee. I was always bugging my brothers to play with me; I was the youngest, and he would take the time to play with me. I was closer to him than any of my other brothers. He was loyal, matter-of-fact, and a reliable individual. It tore me up.

It has been hard for me to go back to games at Neyland Stadium. At first, in the '90s, it was what happened to John when he was removed as coach. I was loyal to him, and it meant I couldn't go back for games. I think it happened for a reason; I think John will live longer because he got out from under that pressure. I also don't like the crowds; I didn't like the crowds even when John was there, so I don't go to games. I've been once when they honored me as being a Legend of Tennessee football, which was very nice of them to do.

Tennessee football is all about the rivalries with Alabama, Georgia Tech, and Auburn. We grew up in the days of Bowden Wyatt, and my brothers saw the last of General Neyland's great teams. Those teams created the mystique about Tennessee football for my family.

What it meant to be part of Tennessee football was you didn't think you were going to get beat. It didn't hit me until I was 40 years old that what it meant to be a Vol was that you expected yourself to win. That feeling is for life, just like all the friends that you made there.

The Bible says we are not supposed to be prideful people, but I have a lot of pride to have been a Vol.

Bobby Majors was a consensus All-American in 1971. He set a school record with 10 interceptions in a season in 1970. He was All-SEC as a defensive back in 1970 and 1971. Majors was part of a defense that forced a school-record 57 turnovers in 1970. He lives in Ooltewah, Tennessee, and owns a chemical manufacturing company.

JAMIE ROTELLA
LINEBACKER
1970–1972

WHERE DID ALL THE LINEBACKERS come from in that era of the late '60s and '70s? We had some great ones, didn't we?

Steve Kiner, Jack Reynolds, Jackie Walker. Three All-Americans. When I was there, it was coaching from Coach Lon Herzbrun that made such a difference. He was a great Tennessee player and a great coach. At that time, the wishbone was a great offensive attack, and we pretty much shut down the wishbone because of his coaching.

Teams did not have a lot of success against us using that offense. That 1972 defense gave up just 83 points in the regular season, which would be amazing by today's standards. Teams could bust 83 points in two games now.

We had some shutouts [two] and played well together, and you have to credit the coaching and the chemistry. We definitely had a good approach on defense. I do remember the coaches talking, and they said when they recruited the top athletes, they would move them over to defense. For example, Steve Kiner played quarterback in high school and was moved to linebacker. He gained weight and strength and looked like a natural fit.

So, during that time, to answer the question how we attracted so many linebackers, I would have to say it was because we were defense-oriented and were willing to put quality athletes on defense. Jackie Walker would have played offense for most teams. He was like today's ballplayers, just fast and gifted. Jackie played strong-side linebacker at 188 pounds, and he was a big hitter.

What he lacked in size, he made up for in hits. Coach Herzbrun was all about leverage and having the proper technique. He would talk about Henry Aaron, that Aaron was not a big guy, but when it was time to strike, he knew how, and he would explode at the moment of contact. That's what he instilled in us, and Jackie personified that.

When I made the starting team, it was a thrill for me because I didn't have to be Jackie's tackling dummy anymore. He would explode right under your chin, and it didn't feel very good. He could run and had skill. He scored from the linebacker position I don't know how many times.

Back then, if there was a fumble, you had to curl up on it; you couldn't return it. There were a couple of times where he actually caught the lateral in the backfield from the quarterback to the back—the pitch—and took it for a touchdown. His reads were so good, no false steps, that he could grab the pitch and score. He returned interceptions for touchdowns, too.

Athletically, he was comparable to today's athletes, and that was 35 years ago. He was a leader. I believe he was the first African American captain in the SEC. He was the man. He was right on the cusp of the African American player coming into the SEC. The captain position had a lot of respect from us, because it was voted on by the team, so you knew what we thought about him.

My dad played at Tennessee and was a coach in Tennessee before he got a coaching job in New Jersey and we moved in the seventh grade. But even though we moved, I was a Tennessee boy all the way. We lived in LaFollette and Irwin. I played high school ball in New Jersey, and I was telling somebody that Joe Paterno is so old, he recruited me. That's pretty old.

I didn't go to Penn State because, as it turns out, I got the last scholarship Tennessee was offering my senior year in high school. The person that was getting that scholarship backed out, and they had one left over, and I got it. They said, "Let's give it to Al Rotella's boy." A hot prospect signed with another school instead of Tennessee. I got his scholarship and was overjoyed. I didn't mind at all that I was considered a leftover. I was in the door.

My dad had brought me to games when I was a kid; I was in the locker room about the time I could walk. The first time I took the field at Neyland Stadium as a player, I don't think I felt my legs hit the ground. I was sky high.

I played at about 215 pounds, 220 tops, which was big back then. I was a plodder, and I liked it when it rained because it brought everybody down to my speed. I was a mudder. I made an All-America team, but we had 10

Jamie Rotella was an All-American linebacker in 1972.

defensive linemen who rotated in and out of the game—you couldn't tell the difference in their talent level—and they made a difference for me.

I don't want this to sound like false modesty, but we really were well coached and we had a great defensive scheme that shut down teams. Our defensive staff worked really hard and got the most out of us.

I think the evidence for what I'm saying about the coaching is that none of the guys on our defensive team went on to have a distinguished NFL career even though we were playing against John Hannah of Alabama. We played against guys who had terrific NFL careers and did well against the teams they played on. But none of us were All-Pro.

We were pretty average guys who made up a great team. That is what's so cool about football; it is the ultimate team sport. It is 45 pieces and coaches and the chemistry that goes into that. We had a great team without crazy talent. Bobby Majors, who was a year ahead of me, was the closest thing we had to a superstar. He could have played in the NFL, but he lost a step or two when he tore his knee up. Bobby was very elusive; he would give them the leg and take it away—that's how he scored his touchdowns—but the knee injury hurt him.

Coach Herzbrun got all he could out of my talent. I am 6'2″ and 220, so I was considered big, but I didn't run. I lined up over the offensive tackle, and at that time, we had somewhat of a unique scheme because we had three linebackers in a stand-up position and pulled back off the line, a little bit more than normal, over the strong guard, the center, and the weak tackle. Everybody lined up on the man in front of them. The weak-side linebacker did not walk up on the line of scrimmage like he does today.

We tried to get as deep as the running backs. Another thing that was different was that we read the running backs rather than the linemen. The backs were our keys, and if we got the same depth, the worst we could do was meet them at the line of scrimmage. It really made it tough on linemen to pursue us. We took a forcing angle. It was fun playing against the running game. I was in on a lot of tackles.

The game that stands out is Alabama in 1972 because they had a superior team and were just blowing people out. It was the second year they had gone to big linemen, and it was the second year of their wishbone attack. They were huge, led by John Hannah. We had shut them down in that game and were winning 10–3. They didn't even have 100 yards rushing by the fourth quarter, and this was when Alabama was getting 300 yards rushing and rolling over teams.

And then we lost it. We let it get away and it still rips at my gut. There was a game this season [2007] when Boston College scored twice very, very late and beat Virginia Tech, and I got sick all over again. It reminded me so much of that Alabama game we lost 17–10 in the last two minutes in Neyland Stadium.

We had them. They were No. 3 and one of the best teams in the country. They were bending linebackers over backwards with those big linemen and crushing folks, and we had a good scheme and handled them.

Still, it was a very good season for us, 10–2, in 1972. We ended up playing LSU in the Astro Bluebonnet Bowl when they had Bert Jones. He was a terrific quarterback, but we won 24–17. We finished No. 8 in the country.

The games we lost that season were very close. For average ballplayers, we were just a notch away from the big-time and a chance to be No. 1. We lost to Auburn by four points [10–6] and to Alabama in a close game.

In my sophomore year, in 1970, that was our best chance to make a run at a national title because our offense was very strong. What I remember about my sophomore year was that we had played four games and got to the week of the Alabama game. The older players looked at me and said that it was time to start playing football. They said you had not played in a football game yet until you played against Alabama.

107

I found out what they meant. After the game, my forearms were black and blue from the shock of the hits. They had Johnny Musso that year, and he ran at you as hard as any back.

We had a good run when I was there from 1970 to 1972. They were pretty darn good before I got there, and we kept it going with a lot of wins [31 in three seasons].

Bill Battle was awful young to be leading a program like that. There are a lot of aspects to being a head coach, and it is a tough role. He is a very good man, and I just can't imagine being a major college coach at 28 years old.

What happened to the program his last three years? The talent fell off. If you look at somebody's record, like Coach Fulmer, and you can sustain that kind of record over such a long period of time with all the various aspects of coaching, I think it is a great accomplishment. You have to be a salesman, too, and do it all; and I think our talent level fell off after 1972.

It is pretty typical of any ballplayer that they will tell you the thing they miss most is the camaraderie with teammates and the coaches. They miss the closeness throughout the ups and the downs of a season. You do lay it on the line, not 12 games, but every day of the year. Every program has that, I think, but what makes a difference for Tennessee are the fans.

You have to accept the bad and the good. They overreact sometimes, but they overreact in a positive way, too. There is a lot of pride in Tennessee, and we expect to win in Tennessee. The fans talk about Tennessee football all year long, and I think that adds to the prestige.

That is one of the reasons I stayed in Knoxville for almost 12 years after I left school. It was the football and the atmosphere around town with the program. I was in the explosives business and in the coal mining business with surface blasting, and that helped me stay in Knoxville.

The fans talk about it before, during, and after the season. You can't be sensitive to criticism, but they are great fans. I think part of what it means to be a Vol is to feel the passion generated by those fans.

Jamie Rotella was an All-American linebacker in 1972. He was also named All-SEC in 1972. He got a degree in business and transportation and was on the SEC Academic Honor Roll in 1972. Rotella currently sells real estate in Panama City, Florida.

CONDREDGE HOLLOWAY

QUARTERBACK

1972–1974

WHEN I WAS TRYING TO decide where to go to school, Coach Bear Bryant told me I could not play quarterback at the University of Alabama, but I could play another position. So, the truth is, other schools helped me make up my mind about where I would go to school because they wouldn't let me play quarterback. And I wanted to play quarterback.

Now, Tennessee did a good job recruiting, too. It's all about who gets you here, who believes in you, gives you that chance. In my case, it was Coach Battle, and assistant coaches Ray Trail and Jim Wright. There was a strong relationship with the person directly recruiting me, which was Ray Trail.

My dilemma did not turn out to be choosing between two schools and who would let me play quarterback, but between playing baseball for the Montreal Expos or playing football for Tennessee. My parents wanted me to go to school. Bill Battle, the head coach at Tennessee, told me if I was good enough, I could play quarterback, so the rest was really up to me.

Coach Battle told me that, once I established myself on the football team, I could go out for baseball. Once he told me he would let me try out as the quarterback—and he made no promises—I decided to go to college rather than try and play professional baseball. I think my mom made the right decision for me.

I remember the scout with the Expos telling me that if I signed with Montreal, I could be up in the big leagues early because they were already out of

109

Condredge Holloway was the first black quarterback at Tennessee, but became known more for his elusiveness than for his color.

the pennant race. That was the good news. The bad news, he said, was that Bob Gibson was going to be pitching when I got up there, and he would hit his mother with a pitch, so I would have to stay loose in the batter's box.

Seriously, though, I did want to play baseball, but the football opportunity from Tennessee was a full scholarship and a chance to get an education. So I signed with Tennessee, even though I was this kid from Huntsville, Alabama.

I have a lot of respect for Coach Bryant because he told me the truth about not being able to play quarterback at Alabama because I was black. He sat me down and said, "We're not ready for this." George Wallace was still the governor of Alabama, and I'm sure it was a unified effort not to let a black play quarterback at Alabama.

Coach Bryant could've told me, "Sure, kid, you can play quarterback"—and then I'd get down there and be put in the defensive backfield, and what am I going to say? Am I going to call a legendary coach a liar, me, a 17-year-old kid? They are not going to believe me. What Coach Bryant did was big in my book.

You look back at it and you see that Bill Battle played for Coach Bryant at Alabama and was on one of his national championship teams, so there had to be, I think, some like-minded values with Coach Battle and Coach Bryant. Coach Battle let me play quarterback, so he had to have learned those values someplace, which makes me think Coach Bryant was teaching the right things, and that it was somebody over him—though I don't know who that would have been in Alabama—who kept me from playing quarterback at Alabama.

Now, I did not like being called "the Artful Dodger." That wasn't flattering to me because I did not want to run around back there for my life. I wanted to be comfortable like Peyton Manning and go through reads and find the receiver, not run for my life.

My freshman year was Coach Fulmer's senior year, and he was part of a veteran offensive line. Then all those guys left when I came to play quarterback, and we had a brand new offensive line, a bunch of sophomores in a very tough league, and I was the starting quarterback. We started over on offense.

I wouldn't trade my teammates for the world, but we had to find a way to get it done because we were so young. I went through the same thing in the Canadian Football League. Two wins, 14 losses, and a hundred-something sacks. The next year we won the Grey Cup. We got better at Tennessee, too. We won 25 ballgames and two bowl games, so we got better together.

I remember one season, we ran the veer offense. Somebody on the defense takes the dive to the back, all the other defenders crash into the backfield to see how tough the quarterback is with the ball after he pulls the ball and runs.

That was me. I think my freshman year I weighed 149 pounds, so as an upperclassman I might have been 165 running the veer, which is not a healthy weight for that offense, but that was part of it, so you went with it.

I think a memorable game for me was my senior year when we played UCLA. We were both ranked in the top 20, and we tied 17–17. I remember it because I hurt my knee and my shoulder, and it was the first game of the year. No way I was going to sit out, so I kept playing that season. Coach Battle asked me if I wanted to stop, heal up, and just get ready to play baseball in the spring. You don't do that to teammates, at least back then you didn't do it.

There was no selfishness back in our day, you had to play, you didn't take an easy way out and think about what was best for you. I did not take that offer from Coach Battle. I couldn't.

Back in that time, too, a lot of my football teammates were baseball players. Can you imagine me laying out of football and then trying to go back and play baseball with them in the spring? I had to continue to practice, because I can't function if I don't practice.

It was very important for me to succeed. My dad told me something that means more to me now because he is not here. After I won the starting job as the quarterback and we were going to play Georgia Tech in Atlanta and they had a black quarterback, too, there were a lot of questions about the significance of that. My dad said there will be somebody that keeps the stats and measures you, but your job is to make sure the next young black man has a chance to play quarterback.

That stuck with me. My dad said that I needed to do the position justice, and do it in such a manner that the next black kid that comes along will have the opportunity. That meant a lot to me. I never forgot that and I never will. In fact, I have a picture on the wall here in my office with Tee Martin, who was also a black quarterback at Tennessee and is from Alabama, and it says, "To Condredge, Thanks for opening the door for me."

I think the biggest play I ever made was actually making a tackle, not completing a pass. It was my first game as the starting quarterback, and it was against Georgia Tech. I threw an interception early in the game—an out pattern to the field, which was a sophomore mistake—and then I had to run down the guy and caught him at the 3-yard line. Our defense held them to a field goal on that possession and then we routed them 34–3. I remember Jamie Rotella, one of our linebackers, telling me not to worry, that we were going to stop them, and that meant a lot because the team didn't hold it against me and rallied.

There was another memorable game, the time I fumbled against Alabama and let them win. They scored 14 points in 90 seconds. We had them 10–3 and we lost 17–10. They won the national title that year. We had played perfect football on both sides of the ball, and I cost us the game. You remember those games, and you don't let it happen again. And it didn't. Coach Battle was very comforting to me during that time because that was really hard on me.

That's what kind of man he was. I will never forget we had a fake punt blow up on us against Georgia at home, and he took all the blame. We lost 35–31. We were going to try a fake punt from our 25-yard line, then it was called off. The only person who did not hear the check-off was the center, Mike Overton. He snapped the ball to the up-back, Steve Chancey, and everybody else was running downfield to cover the punt. Chancey got swarmed, Georgia got the ball in our territory in the third quarter, and the game turned around. Coach Battle took all the blame.

That was a bad loss for us. We were ranked No. 11 in the country. But Coach Battle would not tell people what happened. He said he made a bad call, and it was all his fault. Coach Battle never told the real story. That was the kind of man I was playing for. They were all saying, "What a dumb coach you are, Bill Battle. You have the best punter in the country, Neil Clabo, Georgia is having trouble running the ball, and you call a fake punt." He wouldn't defend himself at the expense of one of his players.

So I will tell you *that* is what it means to be a Vol. It is the people. It is the people who told you the truth when you got there and told you the truth four years later when you left. It is the people who tried to make you a better football player and a better man.

Condredge Holloway, the Artful Dodger, led Tennessee in total offense for three seasons (1972–1974) and is heralded as one of the most exciting players in UT football history because of his ability to escape tacklers. He ranks ninth all-time in total offense at UT. Holloway played 13 seasons in the Canadian Football League and is a member of the Canadian Football League Hall of Fame, the Tennessee Sports Hall of Fame, and the UT Baseball Hall of Fame. Holloway is UT's assistant athletic director in charge of player relations.

MICKEY MARVIN

GUARD

1973–1976

No one gets to a level of success, however you define success, by himself. Like the Bible says, we do not live and die to ourselves. It is the people who take an interest in you that make a difference, and Don Slaughter, my high school coach at West Henderson, North Carolina, took an interest in me.

He was the one who introduced me to the Big Orange.

Coach Slaughter recognized I had some God-given ability, so one Saturday he took me to a UT scrimmage game, which was in the spring of 1970. It was the first time I had ever been over there to Knoxville. I was amazed at how big the stadium was as I sat up there watching the great All-American linebacker Jackie Walker, and I thought, *This is where I want to play*.

And that's when he said something to me that stayed with me all my life. He wanted me to realize that, at the time, I had rare size and athletic ability. I was 293 pounds, and I was one of the first truly big offensive linemen coming along in football. I had won a state wrestling championship in North Carolina, so I was blessed with a lot of athletic talent. I had country strength, not weight-room strength, but natural strength.

So he told me, "Mickey, if you ever get the feeling you're too big for your britches and the team can't go on without you, just go out and get a bucket, fill it with water, and put your foot in it. Then take your foot out of the water and the hole that is left behind will be how much you will be missed."

Mickey Marvin said he wanted to attend Tennessee the first time he set foot in Neyland Stadium as a high school senior.

There is no hole left in the water, and you will not be missed because the team will move on without you. That's how he wanted me to play at Tennessee.

And that's what it means to be a Vol.

Be part of the team and be part of the big picture. He wanted me to stay humble and be appreciative of the people who touched my life.

There has been a steady stream of players from this area of western North Carolina that have gone on to Tennessee—myself, Jimmy Streater, Leonard Little, Heath Shuler, Benjie Shuler, Carl Pickens, and Jonathan Crompton, who is going to be a fine quarterback there in the next couple of seasons. I was probably the first, but there have been some very good ones after me.

I was offered scholarships by most schools in the SEC. Alabama called me the week I was supposed to sign with Tennessee. Ken Donahue, who was Bear Bryant's defensive line coach and coordinator, wanted me to come visit Alabama, but I told him I was keeping my word to Tennessee. He told me, "Well, you are going to the second-best school in the SEC."

Lou Holtz, who was at North Carolina State, recruited me hard and made me laugh when he said N.C. State would change its colors to orange and white if I signed. People were flattering, but I didn't string anybody along. I got close to Paul Deitzel at South Carolina. They pushed hard for me.

When I got to Knoxville, they had changed the rules allowing freshman to play varsity football. I was just 17 years old when I walked on campus, but I was big and I could run. I was there a couple of weeks when we had a scrimmage, and Coach Battle and Coach Ray Trail put me out there as a starter as a true freshman at right guard.

The bullets were flying. I just about panicked, and they realized a 17-year-old did not need to be out there that fast as a starter. I remember the scrimmage started late on a Saturday night because of a problem with the lights. We warmed up with individual drills, and I was knocking people all over the place because I was so much bigger and I had natural explosion. Well, I got out there and—you've heard about the deer in the headlights?—that was old Mick. I panicked big time and fell apart.

I finally became a starter, near the end of my freshman season against Kentucky in Lexington. We won that game, and once I got in there, and I was comfortable, I started playing well. I made the *Sporting News* All-Freshman team.

I wanted to play defense at UT when I got there. There is an All-Star game for high school players in North Carolina, and I had 10 unassisted tackles, and I just knew I wanted to play defense for the Vols. Coach Trail sat down with my mom, Inez, and my dad, Gordon, and I came up in an age where you respected authority, so I didn't get too disappointed. I just accepted that they needed me as an offensive lineman. This was Ray Trail, who coached some great offensive linemen at Tennessee, so you accepted it. He was the guy who helped Bob Johnson, who played in the NFL, and Chip Kell, who was an All-American. These were the guys you were measured against if you were an offensive lineman at UT. You see guys like Charlie Rosenfelder in a picture on the wall in Coach Trail's office, and you understood the tradition.

I look back on it, and I probably had too much success early on at Tennessee. I broke my arm between my sophomore and junior year when I fell off a horse skipping out of Sunday school and church. I missed all of spring practice, and my weight got up, and I didn't have the kind of junior season I envisioned, or that my coaches envisioned.

I'm not sure how deserving I was of making All-SEC my junior year. It was one of those life lessons, and I rededicated myself going into my senior year and lost about 50 pounds. It was very humbling because I had not played up to the standards I set as a freshman and sophomore. Those two seasons, if you put a guy on my nose and, to God be the Glory, I could steamroll him off. We ran an unbalanced line where I would not have to chase linebackers, and that was a good formation for me.

117

I had professional scouts come up to me even when I was a freshman at Tennessee and tell me I was going to be a number-one draft pick. That is pretty heady stuff to be putting on a kid, 17 or 18 years old. That is hard to handle.

In professional football, I was 310 pounds in Super Bowl XV; and in Super Bowl XVIII, I was 270. I have always been able to run and could consistently run 4.8 seconds in the 40. I played in the NFL from 1977 to 1988, which was with John Madden for two years and with Tom Flores for nine. I have to give credit to my coaches at Tennessee for helping me achieve that.

When I went there, Tennessee was one of the premier programs in the country with a rich tradition. There were some marvelous players like Condredge Holloway, Andy Spiva, Stanley Morgan, Larry Seivers, and many more.

Condredge Holloway, who I played with for two years, was as fine a college quarterback as I've ever seen, and I have been scouting college football for 20 years. He was the Artful Dodger and a folk hero. He was like Barry Sanders; that was the type of runner he was. His height was the issue that kept him out of the NFL, but he had a terrific career in the Canadian Football

League. He was one of the best college football players I've ever watched. He could make you miss in a telephone booth.

There are some really great openings—where the team comes out onto the field—in college football, and I've seen a lot of them as a scout. But nothing beats running through the T at Tennessee. I cried the first time I did it and the last time I did it. It was a gift that God put in my hands. Can you imagine a 17-year-old kid running through that T? There are a lot of people who remember me when I go back, and I am humbled by that.

What does it mean to be a Vol? It means being around people like Coach Trail and Coach Battle, and teammates like Condredge Holloway. Life is all about relationships, and that is what you build at Tennessee.

I love Bill Battle and what he did for me. I hated to see what he went through when the fans were running him off. It was a tough year for him that last year in 1976. His father collapsed and died in the stands in the Liberty Bowl after one season, and then they sent the moving vans to his house and put up "For Sale" signs in his yard his last season. He was the epitome of class and grace and dignity under pressure.

I still remember the quote from Coach Battle when he resigned. He said, "Fellas, if you ever get to a place in life where they want to run you out of town on a rail, make sure you are at the front of the line so it looks like you are leading the parade."

He resigned after the Kentucky game my senior year, and we had one more game to play, which was against Vanderbilt. I'll never forget what he told all those fans who wanted him fired. He said, "If all you people up here on Gay Street knew as much about your business as I know about my business, you would be on Wall Street instead of Gay Street." He was getting his jabs in.

It was a very emotional week, and practices were closed that last week because he wanted to share all that time with his players. The guys lifted him up on their shoulders and carried him off the field after that last game. That's what it means to be Vol.

Mickey Marvin is one of only four Vols to be named All-SEC first-team three times. He played for the Oakland Raiders from 1977 to 1988 and is currently a college scout for the Raiders.

STANLEY MORGAN
RUNNING BACK/WINGBACK
1973–1976

I PLAYED 13 YEARS FOR THE New England Patriots, but when I go out in public and people hear my name, or when they recognize me, they always associate me as a player for the University of Tennessee. I played a lot more games in the NFL than I did in Knoxville, so it's amazing what people remember and their loyalty to the program. I had a nice pro career, but they hear my name, and I'm not a New England Patriot, I'm a Tennessee Vol.

There are two games that stand out for me—both of them were against Clemson, one in 1974 and another in 1976—and we won both of them. They were very exciting games, but what made them special for me was that I grew up 15 minutes from the Clemson campus in Easley, South Carolina. I was able to go back home and say I made the right decision about where to play college football, which was at Tennessee.

Both Clemson and the University of South Carolina recruited me heavily, so when I chose to go to Tennessee, it upset a lot of people. For me to play against Clemson and for us to beat them, it made it easier to go home.

I don't know if many people understand that I signed with South Carolina right after my senior season in football in high school. A week later, the decision did not feel right, and I changed my mind.

You have to understand that, back then, Clemson and South Carolina were both known as basketball schools because they played in a basketball conference, the ACC. Clemson did have some football tradition, but in those two

Stanley Morgan would have preferred to play wide receiver for the Vols, but was used mostly as a running back while at Tennessee.

or three years in the mid-'70s, they seemed to be better at basketball, and I wanted to go to a big-time football school like Tennessee.

I never would have been able to go to Tennessee if South Carolina had not declared itself independent that December of my senior year in high school. I had signed with South Carolina in December, which you could do then, but then I called Coach Battle at Tennessee and asked him if I could still come there, and he said absolutely. He sent someone down to sign me, and that was that.

So when South Carolina went independent, I was able to withdraw my commitment. There was some kind of rule, or agreement, that if a player had signed with a school in another conference, even an ACC school, that they could not jump right to an SEC school. The SEC honored those things. But South Carolina was an independent. If not for that, I might've played for South Carolina. I caught some flak for that because a lot of people wanted to see me stay in state.

My aspirations at that time were to get into the NFL, and I felt like if I could play at a big-time football program like Tennessee, and make it there, that would give me an indication that I could play at the next level. Tennessee just had an edge at that point over South Carolina and Clemson, who were in the ACC, but I didn't think their football was where it should have been.

The key point of my Tennessee football career came early in the 1974 season. I had started the season as a wide receiver, and then they put me in the backfield as a tailback. Well, I was up in arms with Coach Battle over that because I felt like I was too small to be a tailback in major-college football, and if I was going to play at the next level, it was going to be as a receiver. I was more comfortable as a receiver, even though I played running back in high school.

I was pretty adamant about it, but Coach Battle said I was the new tailback, and that was that. I have heard the argument that they wanted me to get as many touches of the ball as possible, and the best way to do that is to put me at tailback, but I think there are other ways to make that happen.

I still think to this day that, with Condredge Holloway at quarterback, Larry Seivers on one side of the field at wide receiver, and me on the other side as a wide receiver, we would have had one heck of a passing game. Condredge was very good, and you know about Larry, he was an All-American. If it came near him, he was going to catch it.

I guess that's the one real disappointment of my college career, not seeing us together in that passing game and how we could've run up some points on people with an awesome passing attack. Back in those days, people thought you always had to run the football. It is not like today, when people are confident with the passing game.

Finally, in my senior year, we went to a veer offense, which is an option game, and I went to wingback. I was pretty adamant with Coach Battle that I wanted to play some receiver, and I got a chance to catch some balls as a wingback.

I don't think I made it over 170 pounds, so I thought I was pretty light. There were a lot of times after games where I would go straight to my room and just fall into the bed because I was so tired. I didn't have enough energy to go out to parties on Saturday nights. But I think the only time I was really hurt was my junior year, and I didn't get 100 percent healthy until late in the season.

I got better just in time for our game in Hawaii. That was a great trip, and I had a good game, 201 yards, and we won pretty easily [28–6]. That made me the first running back in Tennessee history to rush for 200 yards in a game, so that was a fun thing.

Even though I was upset that I didn't play more wide receiver, there were more highs than lows. Beating Clemson was big for a kid from South Carolina. I had a good game against them the first time, scoring two touchdowns as a running back. We beat them 29–28 when Larry Seivers caught a two-point conversion at the end of the game. We had another close game we won with them when I was a senior [21–19].

That senior season I lined up as a wingback, and we would run some counter plays up inside. I wanted to take that wingback and split outside and do some things downfield, but that never really happened. My idea was to have Larry Seivers controlling things underneath, Condredge running to the edge, sprinting out, scrambling, and me going down the field and stretching out the defense.

When I knew that wasn't going to happen, I appreciated Condredge's patience with me as they made me a running back. He went over plays constantly with me and talked about different things, and I learned a lot from him that helped me. He was one heck of an athlete.

They finally used me and Larry as receivers in the same game against Georgia Tech. I remember our lining up in a slot formation, and we were able to do some things to hurt them. But that was the only game I can remember getting in the slot outside with Larry. I would have loved to have seen what I would have done for four years at receiver.

You know, it wasn't that bad playing running back, but I think we could have been better as a team. If we would have had a great line, we could've been 11–2. We could have been one of those teams in the top 10, but I think we were inexperienced on the line.

I'm still surprised, really shocked, that I am still the all-time leader in all-purpose yards at Tennessee. Just think about all the athletes that have come through there, and that record is still there. I can't believe it.

In this day and time, it just shocks me I have a record that is 30 years old. The key to my success, I think, as a wingback, tailback, and return man was seeing an opening and hitting it quickly. It was all about speed and making that decision to go. I think returning punts helped me as a running back because I learned how to make guys miss.

That experience at Tennessee is something you just never forget. Even after 30 years, playing football for the Vols still holds a special place for me. Maybe things didn't go exactly as I wanted them to—I wish I would've stayed in one position—but it was still a very valuable time of my life. I think that shows how strong the pull is of being part of the Big Orange. It's something you continue to think about.

123

Stanley Morgan is still the all-time leader at Tennessee in all-purpose yards with 4,642 from 1973 to 1976. He is the only Vol to achieve 1,000 yards rushing and receiving in his career. Morgan was an All-SEC receiver in 1976 as a wingback in the veer. He played in the NFL from 1977 to 1989 with the New England Patriots and in 1990 with the Indianapolis Colts. Morgan and his wife, Rholedia, have chaired the Alex Haley Golf Tournament in Knoxville the third weekend in May the last five years. The tournament helps raise money for African American scholarships. He is an engineer with Homeland Solutions, which handles government contracts building infrastructures.

LARRY SEIVERS

SPLIT END

1974–1976

NOW, PEOPLE MIGHT REMEMBER ME as a possession receiver, but I wasn't really slow. I could run the 40 in 4.45 to 4.6 seconds, and that's not bad, but the problem was I was lining up next to Stanley Morgan, and he could run a 4.2 or 4-point-whatever he wanted to run. He was fast, so when you lined up next to him, you looked slow. If they had not moved him to running back, I would have been second team behind Stanley and maybe not have had a successful career, or even stayed at Tennessee.

The problem was Stanley. He is a guy who could hurt your confidence. I saw him doing some things on the football field, and the next thing I know I called my dad and asked him if he thought I could still go to Middle Tennessee or UT-Chattanooga. I mean, you watched that guy and wondered if you belonged or not. That's how good he was.

I was real close to leaving. I was on that green team my freshman year. It was not fun and, I thought, a waste of time. They redshirted me my sophomore year, and back then, they would redshirt you if they thought they had made a mistake recruiting and thought you could not play.

All indications were I was not going to do anything at Tennessee. The problem was they had trouble getting the ball into Stanley's hands enough times because of all the attention he was getting. Then I caught a few passes when I had the opportunity, Stanley was moved to running back, and things worked out. I always say, Stanley was the greatest receiver who played tail-back at Tennessee.

We did run twin receivers on the same side against Georgia Tech in one game—I was getting double-teamed by then. Stanley tore them up, and we won 42–7. There was no way three of them could cover two of us. We did that twin-formation just that one time, unfortunately.

Larry Seivers celebrates a dramatic win over Clemson. He almost left Tennessee when coaches redshirted him, but went on to become a two-time All-American.

Catching the two-point pass against Clemson my sophomore year [1974] that beat them 29–28 helped get me going in my career at Tennessee. All of a sudden, I had reporters around my locker for the first time, and I was getting phone calls from all my buddies from high school. That's when I first thought to myself, *I can do this*.

The touchdown catch in the Liberty Bowl my sophomore season against Maryland was also a big thing for me, personally, as well as for the program. We were down 3–0, and Randy White, their All-American defensive tackle, had knocked Condredge Holloway out of the game. Randy Wallace came in at quarterback and he threw the pass for the touchdown to me, and we won. I never did see the film of that game.

That was the game that Coach Battle's father died, and we never saw him after that. They just pulled him into the stands to be with his family. We had all driven to Memphis on our own, and we just all left and went home. It was a bittersweet night.

That next year, my junior season, I proved myself again and proved I belonged. I was named All-American, which probably never would have happened in this day, because I caught something like 50 passes, and that is nothing compared to the numbers they put up today. I was named All-American again my senior year, and that would be a real oddity today, a two-time All-American. Today, if a guy is named All-American, he is immediately gone to the NFL and doesn't even think about being an All-American a second season.

Coach Battle was a class act, and when we weren't winning enough, he would move coaches to different responsibilities rather than fire them. Maybe he should have done things differently and he could've saved his job, but that wasn't his style. Some people did leave when they saw the ship going down, but he wouldn't just lay it off on others.

I think the other issue that contributed to Coach Battle's being fired in 1976 was that Johnny Majors was having a lot of success at Pittsburgh, and people saw a chance to get him here as head coach. Just think about it, Coach Battle, who came up as a receivers coach, who played at the University of Alabama, which is our rival, up against Johnny Majors, a legend who played at the University of Tennessee, who was about to win a national championship at Pitt.

I'm glad Bill Battle got his chance. Tennessee benefited from having him around, I will tell you that. Today, he never would have been hired. He was just 28, 29 years old, and they don't give coaches that young a chance at a major-college program.

He kept his poise the whole time they were trying to get him fired. We were right in the middle of it, and he tried to shield us from it and keep us focused on football.

One of the sad parts about his tenure at Tennessee was that, when we upset Maryland, which was in the top 10 and had All-American Randy White, in that Liberty Bowl, he couldn't even celebrate it with us. He went right into the stands because his father had had a heart attack and died. His mom had passed away 30 days earlier.

Things worked out for the best for Coach Battle because he got into collegiate licensing and made a lot of money. He deserved it. Some of us have spent a weekend with him the last couple of years, and it is great to be around him. He still is a class act.

We finished with a 6–5 record my senior season in 1976 and it was over, just like that. Coach Battle was out, and we went home.

I do remember that Coach Majors treated us well when he came in. He let us come back and get degrees and finish up. Stanley Morgan and I actually played for Coach Majors that January in the Hula Bowl. They didn't turn their backs on us after the Battle regime left, and we appreciated that. I tried pro football a little bit and didn't finish up my class work until the following year, and, again, they took care of it and let me come back.

127

My game was as a possession receiver and learning to catch in a crowd. I was not going to run away from anybody. I learned to catch the ball in the crowd the year I redshirted because, if you caught the ball against the first-team defensive guys, they made us run the play again. I was 6′4″, 200 pounds, so my game was to go up and get the ball.

We didn't throw the ball much, probably less than 20 times a game. We ran a pro-set offense the first couple of years I was there and then the veer my senior year, but we never passed the ball much.

I think the game I remember most was my sophomore year in 1974 when we beat Clemson 29–28 on a last-second play, a two-point conversion. Condredge Holloway did most of the work; I just caught the pass for the win. He was awesome and a lot of fun that senior year.

Condredge had this patented dive where he would roll out and dive into the end zone. In the Clemson game, he told me in the huddle, if he couldn't make it, he was going to fumble the ball into the end zone, and I had to be ready to jump on it. Clemson knew we were going to run that dive play, too, and they sent 11 players after him. He dodged three of them and yelled my name. I was coming through the end zone in the direction he was scrambling and he threw the pass and I caught it. It was supposed to be a running play, and I'm sure we had a lineman illegally downfield, but we made the play and won. With Condredge, you never knew what to expect.

I've lived in the Knoxville area ever since I got out of school, but I'm not one of those guys who hangs around the program all the time. I think I've been to one practice, but I talk to Condredge and I keep up with what is happening. I root like heck for them, but it's hard to go to games when I'm going to watch my own kids play. If I'm on the road and it is Saturday, then I will find a TV to watch Tennessee.

The best part of being a Vol is getting together with the guys I played with and telling war stories about the games we went through. I still enjoy sitting around with Condredge and the others, talking about our days at Tennessee. I don't have much in the way of memorabilia. In fact, the first time I saw some of my old pictures was when my wife pulled them out and framed them when we redid our basement. I'm glad I have those pictures because it was great being part of the program.

Larry Seivers led Tennessee in receiving three straight years in 1974, 1975, and 1976, and ranks ninth all-time in receptions. He was an All-American in 1975 and 1976. Seivers was first-team All-SEC in 1975 and 1976 and was named SEC Athlete of the Year in 1976–1977. He is a successful businessman in east Tennessee.

CRAIG COLQUITT

PUNTER

1975–1977

GEORGE CAFEGO TAUGHT ME what the Big Orange was all about. It was a patriotism. Once you are here, and once you have the bug, it is your obligation. It is a game, but you should take huge pride in playing it for Tennessee. He would do the motivational speeches before the Vanderbilt game. He hated Vanderbilt, and I think it was the haves versus the have-nots (which was us), and it was an interstate rivalry. They had good teams when Coach Cafego played, and he didn't like them one bit.

Then, when Coach Majors came, it became even more patriotic wearing that Orange. I tell Coach Majors that he and Cafego were the reasons I made it to the NFL. It is one thing to be a walk-on at that university and kick in front of that large crowd, but it is another thing to play in the NFL for an organization like the Steelers. I never thought I could make a living doing that; they had a lot to do with it.

Coach Cafego was so good at picking out the different parts of your kicking that if you varied, that is when you heard the wrath of Cafego. He didn't try and change everything you did, but he wanted you to be consistent. He was a tremendous athlete, and what Coach Cafego passed on to us came from General Neyland himself. Jim Haslam, who played line at Tennessee in the early '50s, told me his hero was Coach Cafego. He said Cafego had the original moves, the jukes, as a runner. No wonder he coached there for 40 years. He knew the game and he could play it.

I was two years out of high school before I decided that I wanted to go to Tennessee and be a punter. I worked at Miller's department store in the china shop. Tennessee was advertising in the newspaper that they needed a punter. Neil Clabo was in his senior year, and they needed to find a punter, so I wrote Coach Cafego a letter and he said to come on down. I tried out, and they kept me around.

My parents were elated. My mother had lived in a boarding house on Circle Park Drive, which was part of the campus years ago. My father worked as a security guard at Neyland Stadium, and they loved Tennessee football. My father was a police officer, and he tried to get as close to Bear Bryant as he could to try and be part of his security detail, just to be around a legend.

My mother's family would go down and watch practices, so she was bitten early by the Orange bug. My parents ran away to get married—on bicycles—when they were 16 and 17. Everybody was upset with them, but they ended up being married 54 years.

I punted in high school, was a kicker, a starting running back, and starting defensive end. I never left the field playing football. It was the old South Knoxville High School across the Henley Street Bridge. I got offers to go to college, Wofford, which was a full scholarship, and Lees-McRae, which was a junior college. I went to visit Wofford, but it was an all-male school, and I didn't want to go there. It was disappointing to me.

When I went to Lees-McRae, which is in Banner Elk, North Carolina, there was so much fog, you couldn't see out the window. Destiny is an awesome thing. If it had been a beautiful day, maybe I would have stayed there with the snow bunnies, gotten credit for skiing, and maybe there would have been one less Colquitt kicking for Tennessee.

Jimmy, my nephew, was 12 years old when he said, "Uncle Craig, please teach me how to punt." We were in the backyard, and I told him that, when he could kick it over that big tree, I would teach him. About a year later, he kicked it over that tree.

The best part of working with Jimmy was that Coach Cafego was going to retire, so I asked him to come watch Jimmy, that he needed to see this kid punt. He said his knee hurt, his back hurt, he'd had enough, and he was going to retire. I told him, "Coach, if I bring you a punter and all you have to do is sit in a chair, watch him, and yell at him when he makes a mistake, you promise me you won't retire."

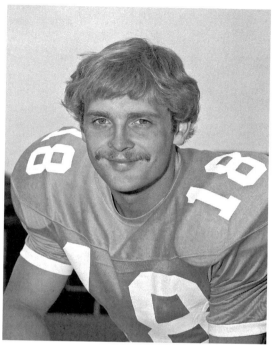

Craig Colquitt got the Colquitt punting dynasty started as a walk-on and then lettered three years (1975–1977).

He said, "JC, you show me that punter, and I won't retire." A few days later, he sent a couple of coaches out there to see Jimmy and he called me and said, "JC, I guess I'm not retiring." That's how much potential Jimmy had.

Coach Cafego would always call you by the wrong name. He called me "Peter," "Sam," all kinds of things. I guess it was his way of getting your attention. I finally said he could call me "JC," and that stuck. It's what everybody calls me down there now. He stayed on because Fuad Reveiz came in at the same time and became an All-American kicker, and Jimmy an All-American punter.

When I first walked on in the spring of 1975, and I will never forget Cafego walking up to me and saying, "The objective of punting is kicking the ball down the field." My style was unorthodox—I think I had mishit a few—and he would needle me. I would kick 200 times a day with Cafego, and he would sit there and watch. He was a dedicated person who enjoyed being around athletes and coaching.

Then there was one day—and I remember the old saying, when the pupil is ready, the teacher appears—I kicked the ball 15 times, and Cafego said, "JC, that's enough." I usually kicked the ball 200 times, but that day there were just 15 kicks, and he told me to go in. It was his way of saying I was starting to get it. That was in 1976, and in 1977 I made All-SEC. It came together for me, I started feeling comfortable, and he saw it.

I had come a long way since my first punt attempt in college in 1975, which had been a disaster. We were playing Maryland on national TV at night in Neyland Stadium, and the first snap to me bounced off my chest and hit my face mask. I was standing in the back of the end zone. I grabbed the ball and was getting ready to punt when one of the Maryland guys smothered me. I was so nervous, and so disappointed. My hands were shaking so bad.

My father had used his connections to get into the game, and he was standing not far away from me in the back of the end zone when this happened. When I got to the sideline, Coach Cafego said, "Way to go, JC." He wasn't being sarcastic or getting on me. He was picking me up for not fumbling and giving them a touchdown. That picked me up emotionally. That was a wake-up time in 1975, which was my sophomore year.

Two games later, after we beat Auburn, I ended up getting a scholarship. Coach Battle walked up behind me while I was waiting for the elevator before dinner at Gibbs Hall. He congratulated me on a good game, and there was a quiet moment, and he said, "By the way, you are on scholarship."

It was tremendous. I couldn't wait to tell my parents; there was a crying moment for them because I had started as a walk-on and had finally made it. They were paying $640 a quarter, and that was pretty tight on them, so to get a scholarship was really a huge deal, not just for the money, but for all the work. What didn't work was thinking I could make it as a walk-on as a running back as well as a punter. Coach Cafego was concerned I would try this, so he followed me over to where they were doing the Oklahoma drill. I think he was trying to keep an eye on me.

Well, that was the year we had the two guys called the Twin Towers, Jesse Turnbow and Phil Clabo, and they were big human beings—6'8", 280 pounds. You had to run between the tackling dummies in this drill, and I was crushed, twice. I gave up on that idea of trying to walk on as a running back at Tennessee.

That 1975 season was the first time I remember how horrified I was at flying in an airplane for the first time. It was out to UCLA. What I remember most about that game was getting off a good kick, 50 yards or something.

The guy returning it got to the 50-yard line, and I tackled him. I hit him so hard he went into the bench. The next week we beat Auburn. I had a consistent game, and that is when Coach Battle gave me the scholarship.

My breakout game, the game where I thought I was pretty good, didn't come until 1977 against Oregon State when I had my longest punt, which was 70 yards. I had a 50-yard average in that game. It was one of those games where you just don't think about it, you go out there and perform.

That 1977 season was the only year I kicked for Coach Majors, and his blood was so orange, you could feel it. He was such a whip-cracker on the field and just as cordial after practice. The great part was everybody was treated the same. Majors, when he came in, brought in this group of coaches who were just so intense about the game of football. For me, it made me realize what football was all about and what you needed to do to win. Majors was on the field with us, getting grass stains—he was involved. He was into every segment of the game.

We needed to be as intense as we could with the program because everybody wanted to beat Tennessee in football. They see the large crowds and the tradition and all the orange. People just want to beat us, and I tell them they are just jealous.

After the opportunity the University of Tennessee afforded my family, I just felt like the Colquitts owed the program. So we set up a scholarship for a player who would walk on and try to make the team on the kicking team. Dustin, my son, came up with the name, The First Family of Fourth Down, and we have been financially blessed to make this happen.

I was a walk-on and Dustin was a walk-on. I might still be working in a warehouse at a department store if I had not been given a chance. It was a tremendous opportunity for me.

Craig Colquitt is founder and stockholder of a national janitorial company, which is a $446 million company based in Cleveland, Ohio. He was All-SEC in 1976 and 1977 and is fourth all-time in career average behind his nephew, Jimmy Colquitt, and his sons Britton and Dustin. Craig Colquitt played in two Super Bowls for the Pittsburgh Steelers. The Colquitts set up a scholarship fund for a walk-on player at Tennessee in 2007 called the First Family of Fourth Down.

ROLAND JAMES
DEFENSIVE BACK
1976–1979

MY CAREER STARTED as another player's career was ending. It was pretty sudden, and I was scared. I mean absolutely scared.

I was on the second-string going into our first game my freshman season, and on the second or third play of the game, our starter, Mike Mauck, got hurt, and his career was over. So there I was, a young, snotty-nosed freshman, and I was the starting free safety for Tennessee. This was a lot different than playing high school football in Jamestown, Ohio, where we had a graduating class of 78 kids.

I got on the field, looked up, and I had never seen that many people before watching one of my games. All I could think to do was run around and try and make plays. I survived. That's exactly what I did that day and for a few games after that—I survived.

That first season, when I finally settled down, I couldn't help but think there was not a better place to be playing football. You could smell it in the air at Neyland Stadium. After a while, you don't hear the people, but you could feel the excitement. It is a town that loves football. The fans were just tremendous, and I haven't found anything comparable to that anywhere.

We didn't have the talent level they have now, so you could get some playing time. The recruiting classes gradually got better and better, but when I was there, we struggled to keep up with the best teams. We were sort of a

Roland James became a starter as a freshman and grew into an All-American in 1979.

mediocre program because it was still a transition to Johnny Majors from the Bill Battle era.

I guess the best thing about me as a player early on was that I didn't know any better. I chased the ball from sideline to sideline. One of the good things about coming from a small school in Jamestown, Ohio, was I played every sport and ran and ran, and I learned to be athletic—and that's the thing I took onto the field at Tennessee. I just played and tried to get my hands on the ball and make something happen.

The early influence came from George Cafego, who coached the kickers. I hung around them some because I was a return man. I learned from Coach Cafego, but also from JC, which is what we called Craig Colquitt. I had never, ever seen anybody punt the ball like that before. When he kicked it, it sounded like the ball exploded. He was special back then, and he got us out of a lot of jams with his punting ability. He could kick deep, and he could have a 4.8-second hang time.

I was around the special teams a lot, and when Johnny Majors came in, man, we went to work on special teams. Johnny came in, and we really worked on punt-blocking drills in teaching us how to block kicks without running into the kicker. We worked on counting steps and taking the right angles. It was a learning process under him. They took me off punt-blocking teams after I fractured my shoulder, laying out trying to block a punt. After that, they started putting the pads down for you to land on so people would not get hurt.

What I liked about Coach Majors was that, after my sophomore year, he let me go run track after a week and a half of spring football practice. He turned me loose, and I was grateful. I ran hurdles, indoors and outdoors, and had a 13.5-second time in the hurdles outdoors. Johnny let the guys who could run track get out there. It was the same for Willie Gault and Anthony Hancock.

When Majors first came in, in 1977, there were a handful of guys running track, but they were on football scholarships. He lined them up and told them, boys, you are on a football scholarship, I expect you to be out there for the start of spring practice. He was okay, though, with us going back over to the track and running. He was the guy that really started using the track guys more.

The one game that stands out for me was against Ole Miss when they beat up on us pretty good in 1977, 43–14. They broke my nose in that one. So it was quite easy to get up for them next season, and I returned a punt for a touchdown and we beat them in Knoxville, 41–17.

I didn't have a style running back punts, I just ran. My freshman year, Stanley Morgan was the punt returner, but in practice one day Bill Battle told Stanley to let me run back a kick. The rule was no fair catches. That's what Battle said.

So I got under one, which had a nice hang time, and I glanced down at the punt team running down at me and figured, *I'm fine, plenty of time.* I caught that ball and got crushed. I didn't go anywhere, except right to the ground.

I wobbled over to the sideline to recuperate. Stanley came over and called me a stupid freshman. He said I should have signaled for a fair catch, but I told him the coaches wanted to see me return one. He yelled at me again, "Don't listen to those coaches, you're going to get hurt."

I had my hands full on defense but did not want to play offense. It was a lot different than high school, where you never came off the field. In college, though, you need to get a break and rest. We had enough on offense with Stanley Morgan, who was not only fast but could run over people at 170. I remember when they finally put Stanley at wide receiver with Larry Seivers, they made a great duo at receiver.

It bothered me that we could not beat Alabama. Don McNeal and Dwight Stephenson give me grief about that. McNeal played on a couple of national championship teams at Alabama and called me this season [2007] to give me heck about Alabama beating Tennessee, which hasn't happened much lately.

I remember Stephenson, who was the best center to play in the NFL. He was on the Dolphins and I was on the Patriots, and we would have these blitzes up the middle through the A gap. He told my wife not to worry in those games where they played us, he would look out for me.

So I would be blitzing, and he would reach out and grab me and say, "Roland, just stay here with me so you don't get hurt." I'd be trying to squirm away, and he would hold on to me. I would yell at the ref to call holding, and Dwight would be laughing and remind me to be still and not get hurt.

It was surprising to me whenever an SEC team got in the national championship race, because we beat the crap out of each other. We also beat up our own guys in practice. Majors would have us out there doing tackling drills on Sunday night. You would have to make five perfect tackles. He wouldn't let the defensive backs tackle a running back, he would make us tackle a tight end or a guard. People were getting hurt left and right, and he was trying to toughen us up.

Mike Mauck taught me about reading your keys, reading your guard, your tackle, and your uncovered lineman, getting your run/pass keys down, and closing the distance as quickly as you could and then breaking down and working on your angles.

There was so much space for error. One of the things I did at Tennessee was stay in the film room with coaches going over all the defenses and learning the playbook. I remember drinking Coca-Cola, a group of five of us, and we were drilled and drilled about different defenses.

Who was good back then? Wes Chandler of Florida was really good. He would run a 4.2-second 40 while the other guys they had could run 4.3 or 4.4, which was plenty fast. We got into it with them in Gainesville in my sophomore year, in 1977, and there were people fighting all over the field. It was a real melee. I'm not even sure how it started, but the worst part was they beat us 27–17.

You always fought hard for Tennessee because you knew the guys who came before you fought for the school just as hard. I remember Lester McClain, who was the first black player at Tennessee, got a lot of the young guys together and told us to keep our noses clean and go to class. He gave us a history lesson and warned us to behave so it would set the table for black players who came after us.

We played cards, and I remember Jimmy Noonan, this tough middle guard, would cheat at 21. Everybody knew it and he knew it, and it was all in fun how he would not turn his cards over and say he had 21. Nobody wanted to mess with Jimmy.

For a young black kid from Ohio in a graduating class of 78 kids, Tennessee was quite an experience. I had an opportunity to go to Ohio State, and I visited Michigan, but when I visited Tennessee, I made up my mind. We had a great recruiter, and my grandmother told me not to come back from Tennessee talking like that recruiting man with that accent. Going to school in Knoxville was the best part of my life growing up.

Roland James was a consensus All-American in 1979. He was a four-year starter and had 288 career tackles. James was an All-SEC defensive back in 1978. He has worked for 11 years for the city of Sommerville, Massachusetts, as a youth director.

The
EIGHTIES

TIM IRWIN

TACKLE

1977–1980

I WAS GROOMED TO BE A Tennessee football player from an early age with my brothers. I grew up here in Knoxville; I didn't come from somewhere else to play football. That was it for me. My father was probably surprised the way it turned out. He thought my second brother, King Irwin, who played full-back at Georgia Tech, was going to be the only college athlete in the family.

We were three brothers, and we all sold drinks at Neyland Stadium growing up. We were hawking around, scrambling for a ticket. Big Orange football has always been in my family's blood. My wife went to the University of Tennessee, and my daughter just graduated from the University of Tennessee. It meant a great deal to me to run through the T for the first time in Knoxville, and in front of people who knew me.

That is one of those "I have made it" moments when you run through the T for the first time. The second "I have made it" moment is when you run out there and get on the field for the first time. That's what it means to be a Vol, those memories of a lifetime.

My main concern when I arrived as a freshman to play football for the University of Tennessee was to prove I belonged. My neighborhood around where I lived had hills that rivaled anything you could find in San Francisco, and I spent the summer before coming in as a freshman running up and down those hills, training and making myself as good as I could be. I remember we

Tim Irwin overcame a serious injury to become a starter for the Vols and go on to have a successful NFL career.

had certain physical tests we had to do when we came on campus, and I remember blowing those tests away compared to the other freshmen.

We had a great, successful group of guys in our freshman class. Roland James, who played several years in the NFL for the Patriots; Greg Gaines, who played a long time in the league; and Brad White, who played for the Bucs. Of the 30 guys we had who started out, nine went on to play pro ball.

I remember telling myself, *If I am not good enough to be here, we're going to find out fast.* The one thing I knew, though, was that I could try and outwork everybody else that was here. I had that mentality, at least starting out. I got into a lot of fights early on trying to prove myself. I started out on defense, so I got into a lot of fights with offensive lineman.

Actually, I got in fights with everybody. I just felt like I wasn't over there to take anybody else's stuff. It was the upperclassmen trying to assert themselves. Let's just say I wasn't going to get picked on. The older guys sometimes can get away with doing stuff to the younger guys. I just wasn't going to let it happen. I got in a lot of fights that first season in Minnesota, too, trying to fit in. I don't know if fighting is part of football anymore.

Pro football never entered my mind when I stepped on the field for Tennessee. Now, pro football is all over the place. I think that's why colleges close a lot of practices; they don't want pro scouts looking at the underclassmen and evaluating them for the next draft. The colleges are also worried about the agents having people get into practice to talk to players and evaluate them.

The NFL never entered my mind, though. It was some remote thing off in the distance. I never thought that playing football at Tennessee was a way to get into pro football and make a living. I wanted to get a good education, and I wanted to be a good Tennessee football player. That was it.

I was redshirted my sophomore year when Coach Majors got there. I was ready to play every week but never got in. I didn't play my freshman year, so you can see I had to wait a while to play. My "second" sophomore year, a game at Notre Dame, that was the first start of my college career.

Back then, when freshman did not play, you wanted to be a starter by your junior year. I sort of picked out that Notre Dame game as the game where I wanted to get in the lineup.

I didn't like Notre Dame very much. I was a Catholic kid growing up and went to Catholic school through the sixth grade before going to public school. When it came time to pick colleges, I wanted a film sent up to Notre

Dame, you know, being a good Catholic kid and all. Dan Devine sent me a letter saying I didn't have major-college potential. I saved that letter and used it as motivation.

We played a great Joe Montana team my sophomore year, and they beat us up there. The next year, 1979, they came down here, and we beat the hell out of them, 40–18. That would've been one of the best games I ever played. It was the first game where I got some notoriety because one of the Notre Dame linemen said, "That No. 78 for Tennessee is as good as anybody I will see all year long." That quote made the papers. At the end of the year, I was Honorable Mention All-SEC, and I think I made that team off the strength of that comment.

When Coach Majors came in before the 1977 season, it was that era when new coaches had the mentality of cleaning house. There were not many guys who came in with me who finished out their eligibility. Of the 30, there were just nine in our class, and we all played pro ball.

You saw the movie *Junction Boys*? Well, we had our own "Junction Boys" when Coach Majors came in for practice in 1977. It was inside the practice bubble, a big tennis bubble, where the football building is now, and those coaches used to take us in there and do things to us that you wouldn't want out in the light of day. It was pretty tough. That was 1977, and it didn't get any better for a couple of years.

It wasn't one of Coach Majors's highlights, and he will tell me in private that he lies awake at night thinking about some of the things he did to guys back then when he first came in. It wasn't just him; it was some of the guys who worked on his staff. Their perception of Tennessee football was not good, and they were pretty much trying to eliminate who was there and trying to bring their own guys in.

As a matter of fact, Jim Dyer, who was a coach here and became a pretty good friend of mine before he died, told me that my name came up at a staff meeting one day, and they asked Dyer if I could play defense for him. He said, "Not only can he not play defense, but he can't play offense, either."

I had had a bad shoulder surgery and got out of the hospital on my birthday. Things were not good that year because the staff was all over players. It was hang-on time right then. They redshirted me but kept me out there practicing against the varsity because I was better than anything else they had, and I would work the guys.

They put some kind of shoulder harness on me. Dyer was being honest; he didn't think I could play. I was 6'7", 265 pounds, and my body had not quite caught up with itself. I don't know that I was the best college football player, so it was all kind of a surprise when I ended up with this long NFL career.

The spring before my senior year, our offensive coordinator, Lynn Amadee, said he had been talking to some NFL scouts who said if I worked hard, I had a chance to make a living at football. That was the first time anyone ever mentioned playing pro football to me, and I was surprised.

After my senior season, I had a chance to go to the East-West Shrine Game. I opted to go to Japan, rather than go to the Senior Bowl. I went over there with Mark May and Russ Grimm, who went on to play for the Red-skins and get in some Super Bowls, and we became good friends. That is when it dawned on me I could play in the NFL.

I had already been accepted to law school, and as I said, the NFL had not been in the plans. I was born big and strong and was able to move a little bit, and I made a living at it for a while.

144

The game that really got me on the radar with the NFL was that Notre Dame game my junior season. Hubert Simpson had four touchdowns rush-ing, and most of them were right behind me. We kicked the hell out of a Dan Devine team that wasn't very good, but it was Notre Dame, nonetheless. Hubert was a great football player; I just blocked the guy on my nose, and we ran a slant play all day. We ran a semi-veer offense back then and ran right over Notre Dame, which felt very good.

My senior year, we had it kind of rough. We were ahead of Georgia 15–0, and then we had a fumble, a muffed punt, and Herschel Walker ran over Bill Bates. We lost 16–15. They went on to win the national championship, but we weren't very far from beating them.

We lost a close game to Southern Cal and then got slaughtered by Alabama and Pitt. That Pitt team was full of all the players Coach Majors had recruited before he came to Tennessee. That was the legacy he left there, and they should have won the national title.

We lost to Virginia and then Ole Miss for a four-game losing streak, and I thought if we came back up here and lost to Vanderbilt and Kentucky, well, people were going to jump off the Gay Street Bridge. But we came back and won both of those games.

What does it mean to be a Vol? Well, I remember my first year in the NFL with the Vikings, looking around in the old stadium and wondering, "Where is everybody?" It was much different playing in the NFL with the Vikings than it was in front of all those people in Knoxville. That's one of the things that is special about the Tennessee program, all the fans that show up on Saturday.

I was All-SEC, All-South, and an Academic All-American. I was always a guy they looked at and said had potential. I was big and I could move my feet, so there were always the expectations.

I had a good career at Tennessee, and some of it had to do with a trainer Coach Majors brought in, Tim Kerin. This was a guy who truly cared about the kids. There are a lot of different types of trainers and coaches, but he really cared. After Bill Yeoman operated on my shoulder, they told my parents I only had a 20 percent chance of playing again.

Tim Kerin stayed with me. He tried to keep the coaches off my back. He never gave up on me. Tim started to stick me out there in the spring for practice after the surgery, but I told him I didn't think I was ready to take a hit yet. He said, "If you're not ready, you're not ready," and he kept me out of spring ball. I scrambled to come back and get playing time that second sophomore year and then started my junior season at right tackle.

Could a career playing football for Tennessee mean a lot to a guy from West Virginia? Sure, but I think it was more special to me, a kid from Knoxville. My dad was a policeman, and I remember walking down the alleys to get to the UT basketball games he would be working. Every year, they would point out the football recruits who were attending a game, and he would tell me, "You're going to be out there some day." It meant a lot for me to accomplish that.

Tim Irwin was an All-SEC tackle in 1980. He also won an NCAA Post-Scholarship Award in 1980 for academic work in pre-law and was on the SEC Academic Honor Roll 1979 and 1980. Irwin was a third-round draft pick in 1981 and played in the NFL from 1981 to 1994, which included a 13-year career with the Minnesota Vikings. Irwin was the Vikings' union representative and later an NFL player agent. He is the presiding judge of juvenile court in Knox County, elected in 2006.

WILLIE GAULT
WIDE RECEIVER
1979–1982

I COULD RUN THE 100-YARD DASH in 9.3 seconds. I had speed, that was my deal. I threatened people with world-class speed. I made the Olympic team my first year. I was fast, I knew I was fast, and it's something you don't teach. You either have it or you don't have it.

Our quarterback, Jimmy Streater, knew to get back fast and set up. In fact, my first catch in college was a 69-yard touchdown pass from Streater in 1979. To hear 90,000 people cheering and getting a standing ovation was great. That's one of the reasons to go to the University of Tennessee. And then when I ran my first kickoff back, it was the same thing. It was very rewarding.

It was more exciting than I thought it was going to be because I came from a small-town where we were lucky to get a couple of thousand people to the game in Griffin.

The post pattern was my favorite route. The thing about the post pattern was the guy did not know if you were going deep or going nine or 10 yards. You could make him think you were going straight up, then cut it inside, and there was nothing he could do because he couldn't run with you. A lot of times, guys were eight to 10 yards deep on defense, and then we went to a lot of short patterns to take advantage of that.

The proof is in the pudding. They know you are fast, but until you do it, until you catch the ball, they are not sure you can do it.

Teams had their strategies for dealing with speed. I saw a lot of cover-2, with a defensive back and a safety over the top, and I had the ball kicked away from me on kickoffs a lot of times. You had to get used to those kinds of things.

If they made a mistake with the kick, I had to be ready to return it. If the wind caught it, or they didn't kick it out of the back of the end zone or out of bounds, I had to be prepared to run it back.

My strategy for returning kicks was first to make sure I caught the ball and then run as fast as I could the first 20 yards—I wanted to be at the point of attack when our blockers first touched the defenders. I didn't want to be there too soon, or too late, I wanted to be there in that split second of contact. That is when the defenders have to think about the block and me at the same time. If you slow down and try to move before you get to the contact, or the hole, everybody catches up, and you get tackled. You need to get there at the same time they are occupied, and then you have a chance to break it. It doesn't have to be a great block, if they are just touching them, it is enough to occupy the tackler.

I was one of the top recruits in the state of Georgia, but Vince Dooley at Georgia did not throw the ball enough for me, being a receiver. Tennessee would throw the ball.

The reason I chose the University of Tennessee over every college in the nation—and I got recruited by USC and UCLA, Georgia, Florida, and many others—is that it was far enough away from home, but still close enough for driving, and it had a major track-and-field program. They had 16 SEC championships in track and were always in the top two or three in the nation in track and field.

They had a football stadium that, at the time, held 92,000 people, and they were on national TV. So it was a big-time program in sports, and I participated in two sports. It was an opportunity to be seen on both the football field and the track. I was recruited by a guy named Bobby Jackson and the head coach, Johnny Majors, for whom I had a lot of respect.

I wouldn't take anything back at all about going to Tennessee instead of Georgia. Tennessee gave me instant credibility. If you can play there—and I think I was successful—people respect you. People knew that if I could play at the University of Tennessee, which was big-time football, then I could play anywhere. I had teammates there, like my roommate, Lee Jenkins, and Reggie White, Jimmy Streater, and Bill Bates, who were all instrumental in my career and becoming the player I was. I learned a lot from them.

Defensive backs gave Willie Gault plenty of cushion when he started into his route because he could run right by them.

148

There are some games I remember more than others, such as running a kickoff back 100 yards against Pittsburgh in 1980, even though we lost the game. I remember it because it was my first kickoff return for a touchdown in college.

There was also a kickoff return of 96 yards against LSU in Baton Rouge my senior year where we were an underdog, and that helped us tie them 24–24. That was exciting because of the big crowd they bring to the games. They were ranked in the top 20, and we were not supposed to be able to play with them.

I remember meeting with Johnny Majors when Tennessee was recruiting me, and I said, "Coach, you have to know that I want to run track in the spring." He said okay, and he was a man of his word. When spring came, he remembered he had said it, and he wasn't one of these guys who was going to go back on his word about my running track, so that was great.

I was able to go the 1980 Olympics, or what was actually an alternate Olympics because of the boycott of the Moscow Olympics. We actually had more countries in our Olympics, so I considered it very competitive. We won the gold medal in the relay in the 4 x 100. I had some good moments in track, in the Olympics, and in one track meet in particular at Tennessee where I ran a 9.95 [100-meter dash], which tied the world record at the time.

When I was a senior, I ran a 13.26 in the 110-meter hurdles, and that was the year I was ranked number two in the world in the hurdles and number two or three in the 100.

I think by the time I finished playing football at Tennessee, people understood I was not just a speed guy. I ran back five kickoffs for touchdowns and two punts for touchdowns against good competition and played well at wide receiver, so that convinced the NFL I could play on Sunday. I was picked in the first round by the Chicago Bears in 1983, and I think playing at a school like Tennessee against some of the best competition in college football showed the NFL I was a football player, not just a track guy.

149

Running through the T was a special thing for me. You can't forget that. The thing that really stands out is playing against the big-time programs, the ones that are on TV all the time, like Southern Cal, Notre Dame, and Alabama. Tennessee was a great university, and aside from the football, I learned a lot and got a great education. That's why you go to a place like Tennessee. You get so many advantages all in one. It speaks for itself.

Willie Gault was an All-American wide receiver in 1982 and All-SEC in 1982. He is the all-time leader at Tennessee in kick returns and kick-return yards. He lives in Los Angeles and handles mergers and acquisitions of companies and also does some acting. Gault was part of a world-record 4 x 100-meter relay team at the alternate Olympics in 1980. (The U.S. did not compete in the 1980 Moscow Olympics because of the boycott.) He was also a bobsledder. He was timed at 9.2 seconds in the 100-yard dash at UT. An All-American in track and field, Gault went on to have a successful career in the NFL with the Chicago Bears and the Los Angeles Raiders.

IN MEMORIAM

REGGIE WHITE
DEFENSIVE TACKLE
1980–1983

EDITOR'S NOTE: This chapter was written by Jimmy Sexton, White's agent and close friend since their time together at the University of Tennessee. Sexton was a manager for the Tennessee football team when White was an All-American defensive tackle and is a professional sports agent with numerous NFL clients.

★   ★   ★

Reggie was an innocent, likeable Tennessee kid. I remember the story about him going out to UCLA on a recruiting visit and committing to UCLA when he was out there. He got spun around by the weather and just told them he was coming. He was from Chattanooga, and, well, when he came home and told his mother he had committed, she told him he was not going to California to play football that far away. And that was that.

I remember another story that Bill Oliver, the famous defensive coach at Alabama, told me about Reggie's recruiting visit to Tuscaloosa. When they flew him down there, they called his mother from the plane. Reggie thought there was a long phone cord connected to the plane from down on the ground. Like I said, just an innocent Tennessee kid.

Reggie White (No. 92) bursts through the line. The former All-American still holds the school record for sacks with 32.

He got recruited by everybody. He loved Steve Sloan and got recruited hard by him, but his mother wouldn't let him go to school in Mississippi because she thought there was a lot of racism still there. He ended up going to Tennessee because it was close to home.

When he got to Tennessee, he had a great freshman year, but his sophomore and junior years were plagued by injuries. That's why he had a better career as a pro than he did in college. He really blossomed after he was healed.

I'll never forget that summer camp before his junior year, watching him practice in the stadium when he made an inside move on Bill Mayo, who was a really good player. Bill grabbed his jersey, and Reggie sprained his ankle very severely. It was a high ankle sprain, and it never got any better for six or seven weeks because he kept playing.

That happened in his junior year, so when he came back his senior year, he was ready, and I don't know if a player has had a more dominant season from that position in college football. He was unstoppable in 1983. He was never blocked all year. So you would probably have to say the injuries those two years kept him from having a greater impact for the program.

He was a nice guy, and he did have to learn to play more with an edge, but I think it is a little overblown that he wasn't mean enough out on the field. Reggie in college was not an overly intense person. He was the nicest guy you could meet and would give anybody the shirt off his back.

He really was an unassuming superstar. Reggie had the charisma, and when he walked into a room, he could light it up. He did not have a lot of that arrogance or the boastfulness of a superstar athlete.

Yes, there was some work by the coaching staff to get him to play with a little more intensity. He had a real keen sense of humility, so the coaching staff worked on that, as far as on the field.

Reggie had a lot of great games as a senior, but the one game that stands out was against LSU in Knoxville. LSU had Lance Smith, who was a very good offensive lineman, and Reggie dominated the game. He hit Dalton Hilliard several times behind the line of scrimmage and was just unstoppable [Tennessee won 20–6]. There was one play where he beat a double team and hit the running back two yards deep in the end zone.

Reggie could do things with his body that other people who were 6'5", 300 pounds just couldn't do. His agility was amazing. He was over-the-top gifted, and that included natural strength. Added to that physical ability, his charisma allowed him to talk to people, his teammates, and get them to follow him.

His hump move is still used in the NFL today, and all the defensive line coaches use film to show it and teach it. He would take one arm and put it under the guy's shoulder and basically throw him out of the way. That was his signature move.

Now think about that. You are taking another 300-pound man and throwing him over to the side in the air like a baseball. Think about that strength. And he could run. They would pitch it to run away from Reggie, but he chased plays and made tackles, anyway. He was probably 295 pounds in college and could run a 4.7-second 40. Reggie could have been a heck of a tight end.

You have to remember that this guy was a high school All-American basketball player, too. He was offered dual scholarships at several SEC schools to play football and basketball.

It was either Haywood Harris or Mark Dyer, who worked for the Vol Network, who coined the nickname for Reggie, which was "Minister of Defense."

I think, at times, he would be frustrated by all the holding, but he would never lose his temper for a long period of time. If he did get upset, it didn't last very long. I think he got more upset if the team wasn't playing well or playing hard enough.

I met him when we lived in the football dorm, Gibbs Hall. We got out of college together in 1983, and he was my first client. I owe everything I have to Reggie White. Had he not believed in us that first year, I don't know where we would be.

Reggie did not look at people for their status and how important they were; he was not a respecter of a person's standing. In some ways, he went out of his way to show respect and be the friend of the person who was down and out. So as for me, as a manager of the football program, he didn't care if I was one of the stars of the team or not. His heart was genuinely in the right place. Reggie was the real deal, and never looked at people in terms of how they could help him.

Reggie would lead with his heart, which is why sometimes in the NFL he would say things that would be taken the wrong way, and I would have to chuckle. It was Reggie being Reggie, and if people didn't know him, what he said probably came off the wrong way.

He wanted to be looked at as one of the best, but he would never push that as his agenda. In other words, he would not boast about how great he was, or that he was this All–American you had to look up to. He was too humble for that.

Reggie White is considered one of the greatest players in the history of the Tennessee program and is a member of both the Pro Football Hall of Fame and the College Football Hall of Fame. He was a four-year starter at defensive tackle, as well as an ordained minister. White was the 1983 SEC Player of the Year and a consensus All-American when he was named to nine All-America teams. He is the all-time sack leader at Tennessee with 32. White died on December 26, 2004, in Cornelius, North Carolina, from a cardiac arrhythmia.

JIMMY COLQUITT

PUNTER

1981–1984

WHAT I REMEMBER VIVIDLY about the start of the punting thing for us Colquitts was when we were walking up to the house one day after caving, and Craig said, "Guess what, I am going to walk on and be a punter at UT."

And I laughed and laughed. I fell on the ground; I laughed so hard my sides hurt. I said to him that Tennessee was the big time, and there is no way one of us was ever going to kick for a big-time program like that. How could you ever play for the University of Tennessee? It's way too out there for us, way too high-scale for us. He said, "Well, I'm going to try, and I'm going to do it."

I remember his asking me to be his center. He was just a walk-on, and they didn't give him a center to practice with. I told him I didn't know how to center a football, I would just throw it to him like we always did, and he could just kick it, and I'd go get it. He was about 19 or 20 years old, and I was 10 years old. Well, I learned how to center it to him in the backyard, sort of. I would just really turn and throw him the ball.

He was bragging, you know how kids brag, and he was telling me how he could kick it over this big tree. I thought, *There is no way*. Well, one day he kicked it over that big tree. That tree was a mile high. I said, "If you can do it, I can do it." I didn't hit it anywhere near high enough to go over that tree.

On my own, I went out there, and I tried and I tried to kick it over that tree. It took a while. Eventually, one day down the road, the ball went over that tree. It was fun. The day he put it over that tree is the day I decided I wanted to be a punter, just like him, for the University of Tennessee.

It all came as a surprise to me, making those All-America teams. I was just kicking the ball and having fun. I just picked up punting from Craig, who always kicked the ball in high school. I remember him more as a tailback and fullback when he played high school football, but I also remember him as a terrific kicker.

He was my uncle, but Craig was like my big brother growing up here. Every Sunday, Craig would pick me up, and we would go up to the mountains, go swimming, go hiking, go caving, and we would shoot arrows from one hill to the next. We just had a lot of fun and were always looking for things to do.

Craig went on and got a scholarship to Tennessee, and a few years later, I started kicking for Doyle High School in Knoxville. I remember as a freshman at Doyle, watching this varsity punter try and kick the ball onto the roof of this building. He tried, and he couldn't do it, and I remembered that tree. I thought, *Shoot, I kicked it over that tree, I can kick it onto the roof of that building in one try*. I picked that ball up and kicked it onto the roof the first time. I grinned and walked away. They still didn't let me play varsity; I had to play the junior varsity as a freshman, but it still felt good to kick it onto the roof.

155

What was a lot of fun at my high school was that, in the games, I could kick it right or left over the head of the other team's return man. I was also a straight-on field-goal kicker. I didn't want to play anything else. I just wanted to kick.

When Craig was done kicking at Tennessee and I was a sophomore at Doyle, he brought one of the coaches over to practice to watch me. I had been going over to UT to watch practice, and I knew Coach Cafego—he was a legend. So they had a coach come watch me and make a report. Cafego was going to retire, but Craig said he wanted Coach Cafego to come over and watch me punt. I was lucky that Coach Cafego stayed around for my career at UT. I graduated from high school in the spring of 1981 and kicked four years for him at UT.

I wanted to go to UT long before they offered me a scholarship. I still remember Coach Majors coming to my house and offering me a scholarship my senior year, and I knew that's where I was going. Coach Cafego had told me, if I went to UT, he was going to stay and not retire.

Jimmy Colquitt is Tennessee's all-time leader in career punting average.

I had offers from Auburn, Vanderbilt, and Alabama and Bear Bryant. They wanted me pretty bad down there in Tuscaloosa. Now, Bear Bryant had a real good way of recruiting. He would have the prettiest girls on campus be your escorts on your recruiting visits. When I visited Tennessee on my official visit, it was the players who took you out. Bear had two good-looking girls escort me to dinner. I think Bear bent the rules a little.

But there was no way I was going to go to Alabama. I would have been in for it up here, and besides my blood was Orange all the way through. There was no way I could be a traitor.

My career didn't get off to such a good start in 1981. In my first game as a punter for UT, Georgia beat us pretty badly. The next week, Marcus Allen and Southern Cal killed us 43–7.

The third game was my first game in Neyland Stadium. I don't care how experienced you are, you are still going to have butterflies. I still remember walking off the field after my very first kick at Neyland Stadium, and I told Coach Cafego, "Coach, I don't remember a thing." He said, "Son, you just barely got it over the line." He added, "It's a wonder you didn't get it blocked." I think it went about 20 yards.

Gradually, from there, my confidence went up. Coach Cafego was a great mentor, and he was always encouraging me, even after that first bad kick.

The game that really stands out for me was when we beat Alabama and Bear Bryant in 1982, and we had practiced the quick kick. We were backed up in our own territory, and we had practiced a play where I would sneak in there as a tailback to kick it on third down and change field position.

So we were facing a third-and-15 against Alabama, and there was not much of a chance for a first down. The plan called for me to run out onto the field and line up exactly where the ball was going to be snapped, so I would not have to move to give myself away. I put my hands on my knees and just acted like I was part of the huddle and everybody lined up around me. I ran out with Jeff Smith, the tight end, who was No. 81, and I was No. 21.

Alan Cockrell was the quarterback, and he said, "Quick kick, on move." He took the snap and tossed that ball back to me like I used to toss it to Craig in the backyard, and I line-drived that ball out of there. We downed that ball inside the Alabama 10-yard line. We held them, three downs and out. They punted, we got the ball, and then Johnnie Jones scored for us, and we won the game in the fourth quarter, 35–28.

The goal posts came down, and I was the MVP of the game. It was great to beat Alabama. I think Knoxville was shut down for a week, people were celebrating that long. To beat the Bear was something else.

It was incredible to be part of all that. I felt I was on top of the world to be a Vol. A lot of people looked up to us—we were heroes—it was a very warm experience.

My punting average went down my junior and senior years. I just didn't have the consistency, and I don't know why. There was a lot of pressure from Coach Majors, and from others. I felt it. I ended up not getting drafted. I had to try to make it as a free agent and went in with the Seattle Seahawks. I played four games with them and that was it. I had gotten inconsistent and couldn't pull myself out of it. In the pros, that is when they ask you to leave. It was tough on me.

I am still the career punting leader at UT, but if the record has to be broken, I hope it is by a Colquitt—my nephew, Britton. He is a good one. He still has another year up there.

I don't know where the ability came from, it is just a technique, hand-eye coordination. You don't necessarily have to hit the ball hard, it is sort of like hitting a golf ball, a lot of it is the follow-through. I truly believe it is a technique. I have parents bringing their kids to me to work with them, and I generally just show them the technique. I show them the sweet spot and tell them to aim for that. People don't remember your good punts, just bad punts, and I tell them to hit the sweet spot and you will get the good punts.

The Big Orange is the circle of love for the First Family of Fourth Down, which is what the Colquitts are. I told Coach Cafego one time that I loved fourth down, and Coach Majors got mad at me, but I told him he had to understand my point of view. We would get a first down, and I couldn't go out there and kick. Coach Cafego told Coach Majors that was understandable. You had to want to kick the ball.

Jimmy Colquitt is the all-time leader at Tennessee in career punting with a 43.9-yard average. He was a four-year starter for the Vols and was named to All-America teams in 1982 and 1983. He holds the record at Tennessee for highest season punting average of 46.9 yards, set in 1982, as well as the highest single-game average (53.0), set in 1982 against LSU and tied in 1983 against Auburn. He works in natural stone sales in Knoxville, selling stone to builders, landscapers, and homeowners, and is the uncle of current UT punter Britton Colquitt.

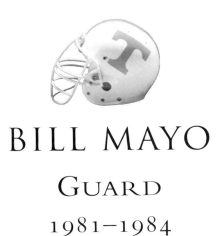

BILL MAYO

GUARD

1981–1984

THE SEASON JOHNNIE JONES became the first Tennessee running back to rush for 1,000 yards, I was the right guard. What made it special was that Johnnie made us feel like a huge part of it. He was such a humble guy, and he kept telling people—the newspapers, the television folks, whoever—that the guys on the offensive line had a hand in it. You wanted to block for him because he was such a good guy. That's what it means to be a Vol, to have the stars make room in the spotlight for guys on the offensive line.

I still have the painted football that Coach Fulmer gave each of us on the offensive line. It says, "Tennessee's First 1,000 Rusher, 1983, Johnnie Jones." I still have that in my office. On the bottom, it says, "Right Guard, Bill Mayo." He gave one of those to all five of us. Johnnie could still play today, the way he looks. He was so quiet back then, nobody knew he was there sometimes.

I was never a great athlete, as far as some as the other guys who played with me and through the program just before or just after me. I could never overpower somebody, I did not have great strength, but I took great pride in being a good blocker with what I had to work with.

Coach Fulmer was a stickler for technique. You would get a grade sheet after every game. You could go out and mash the guy in front of you, but if you stepped with the wrong foot, you would get a minus and a plus. The plus would be for making the block, the minus for poor technique.

Bill Mayo was an All-SEC guard in 1983 and 1984.

160

I took a lot of pride in using the proper technique, and it helped me. I won a lot of battles with good technique. There were more physically gifted defensive lineman, but I tried to read what they were going to do, used proper technique, and won a lot of battles.

My last two years at Tennessee, I played at 6'4", 280 and 290 pounds. I was one of the biggest guards in the country, but I tried to do as much as I could with fundamentals and technique.

When I got to Tennessee, we were really hurting for offensive linemen. The class that was supposed to be seniors had a lot of problems with keeping the class together, so the program was really thin in terms of upperclassmen. A lot of them either left school or something happened, and I ended up having to start the first game of my freshman season, which was against Georgia, the defending national champion.

I had to play against a guy whose name was Eddie "Meat Cleaver" Weaver. They beat us 44–0. It was brutal. Starting my freshman season meant that I was there for 48 games—11 regular-season games and one bowl game each year for four years. I missed just four starts, one for an ankle my freshman year, and three my sophomore year. For a while, I had the record for most games started at Tennessee, but it has since been broken.

I would say the biggest game of my career was in 1982 when we beat Alabama 35–28 in Knoxville. That win ended an 11-game losing streak to them. It was a huge deal for Coach Majors.

It was Coach Bryant's last game against Tennessee. The most vivid memory I have came right after an interception to seal the win for our offense. We were going to snap the ball and take a knee to end it. Well, we snapped it, I turned around to celebrate and jump up and down with the other guys, and people were just pouring out of the north end zone. The fence came down and then the goal posts came down. All of a sudden, it seemed like there were 30,000 people on the field.

The last time I saw those goal posts, they were being marched up and down Cumberland Avenue, along that strip of bars, by the students. It was wild and a lot of fun. Some guy cut up the goal posts and was selling pieces of them.

That game with Alabama was back and forth, and we never quit. They were No. 2 in the country and had been so dominant over Tennessee for years. There were a couple of guys, former players, on the sideline, and you could tell that they were thinking something was going to happen and we were going to lose to Alabama again. You could just see how pessimistic they were, and they were getting ready for the disappointment, because it seemed like we would never get that monkey off our back.

And then we won. We finished it. It wasn't one of those Alabama games where the Tennessee team played well, only to lose at the end. The streak had gone back all the way to 1970, and we ended it.

That was a big win for the whole program, and not just players, but for all the fans. Tennessee went on a streak where we beat them four years in a row.

I guess the most disappointing game was against Ole Miss in 1983 in Knoxville under the lights. The game was on TBS, nationally televised, and we scored on our first possession of the game but never scored another touchdown. If we had won that game, we would have been in position to win the Southeastern Conference championship. We just could not get anything done.

I paid a lot of attention to Coach Fulmer and to David Cutcliffe, who joined the staff in 1982. He had been in Alabama, a high school coach, and he sold everything so he could come to Knoxville and be a graduate assistant. He did such a great job, then in 1983, Coach Majors put him on the staff full-time.

Fulmer and Cutcliffe were our position coaches. They used to give us these massive tests where they would list every play we had against every defensive front known to man, and we had to draw it up.

It started out with having to know your position and ended up where you had to draw all five positions. The linemen had to know more than one position. My very last year we were playing Maryland in the Sun Bowl, and a day before the game our left tackle sprained his ankle pretty badly. Phillip came up to me and said, "You know left tackle, right?" I said, "Yes," and he said, "You are now the starting left tackle."

Phillip had been so insistent on our knowing each position, I had no problem playing left tackle. That is how they prepared us every week.

My son, Cam, was first offered a scholarship by Ole Miss when David Cutcliffe was the head coach there. Cam went over for a visit and considered it just because David was there and I thought highly of him as a coach. That was exciting that David was the first coach to offer Cam a major-college scholarship. I'm glad Cam didn't go there, though, because of what happened the next year. Ole Miss made a terrible mistake by firing David, and they are paying for it right now.

I still remember the time when Tony Robinson was our quarterback. He was a great talent. But there was a day in practice when Walt Harris, who was our offensive coordinator, ran us through our check period. Well, we came up to the offensive line and were all in our stance. They threw up another defense, and Tony was supposed to check into the correct play. He checked into a play, and Walt yelled, "No!" Tony called another play, and Walt yelled, "No!" This went on for six plays, and we were still down in our stance and starting to get tired. Our thighs were burning.

Finally, I turned my head a little and whispered, "Tony, check to 48," and Walt went ballistic. He started yelling at me, he started yelling at Tony. I said, "Coach, he's killing us."

Now, you talk about somebody who could run and throw the football. Tony Robinson is what Texas's Vince Young looked like 20 years ago. It is terrible what happened to Tony with some of the trouble with the law.

It was sort of disappointing not to get drafted. I played in the Senior Bowl, the Hula Bowl, and I went to the NFL Combine. It just goes back to what I said earlier, that I was not the best athlete. I did not have the measurables that they like to see, such as the 40 time, and the bench-press number. I made All-American, and I made All-SEC, so not to get drafted was disappointing.

Playing at Tennessee was like having another big family when I was there, and it still means that for me. I'm sure other schools think they have great fans, but I can't imagine any like ours. I still meet people today who say, "Oh yeah, I remember you. No. 67 from Dalton, Georgia," and, "You did (this) in 1982," or, "You did (that) in 1983," and, "How is Cam doing?" and on and on. They wrap their arms around you and they don't forget you. They love Tennessee football so much and they are so passionate about it, that's what makes it fun to be around. It was so motivating to see all those people up there excited about Tennessee football.

We had a lettermen's reunion two or three years ago, and we all got a jersey with a number on it and we did the Vol Walk behind the current team. That was incredible. We didn't have the Vol Walk when I played. I can see why those kids get so fired up and excited about that. We used to come to the stadium in the bus, and it was nothing like the Vol Walk is today.

I think what I was really proud of was being part of that class of 1981 that came in. Alan Cockrell was in that class, along with Johnnie Jones. We helped, I think, pave the way to that 1985 season when Tennessee won the Southeastern Conference championship.

Up until 1981, the year we came in, the program was trying to get going under Coach Majors. There were some losing seasons, and Tennessee was not accustomed to losing seasons. Coach Majors thought our class was the start of turning things around. He said they were recruiting better players and better people, and things started going well consistently. Coach Majors was always very nice to say that our class was the start of getting things turned around.

It was like Johnnie Jones when he ran for more than 1,000 yards. People were always giving credit to others in the program when I played there.

Bill Mayo was chosen to the United Press International, CAMP, Football News, and NCAA All-America teams in 1984. He was a two-time All-SEC guard (1983, 1984). Mayo started at guard as a freshman and was a four-year starter for the Vols. When he graduated, he held the record for number of starts all-time (44). His son, Cam, was an all-state lineman who was recruited and signed by Tennessee before injuries ended his career. Mayo lives in Dalton, Georgia, and works for Lifegas as an area manager.

JOHNNIE JONES
RUNNING BACK
1982–1984

ONE THING I THINK ABOUT from playing at Tennessee was the fax I received my junior year from Curt Watson. I had just broken his single-season rushing record—this man's record!—and he sent me a fax congratulating me. It was so nice. He is a big-time pilot with the Blue Angels and a famous player in the history of the school, and he took time to do that.

When I finally met Curt, he was just as nice to me. It made setting the record much better—that someone like that would stop and send a note and then treat me so well. I think that's what it means to have played football at Tennessee. Having players like that.

I gained 1,116 yards, and that was the first 1,000-yard rushing season for a Tennessee running back. I never thought I would be the first back to get 1,000 yards in a season, not just because I didn't play very much my first two years and wasn't a starter that season, but because of all the great backs that had come through the University of Tennessee.

I didn't start playing, really, until the third game of my junior season. All those running backs in front of me on the depth chart started to get hurt, and they finally let me play. I was almost about to leave Tennessee. I was doing well in practice, running against the first-team defense, but I wasn't playing in the games. I don't know why they wouldn't give me a chance. I didn't understand at the time.

Johnnie Jones was the first Vol to rush for 1,000 yards in a season.

I talked to my dad about it, and he said I couldn't quit. That wasn't what I was supposed to do. He just told me to practice hard and, when they called my number, make sure I was ready and let them know I could play. You have to use it to your advantage and not get mad and pout about it. It was discouraging because I remember a long run against Georgia Tech my sophomore year, but they made me sit even after that. I didn't play much that season.

My sophomore season, they were going to redshirt me, which would have been really disappointing, but then everybody got hurt, and I got to play some games. I had my mind set to be redshirted, played some, then was out again sitting on the bench.

I finally got my chance in Memphis against The Citadel my junior season [1983]. That was the first game I started because of injuries to two backs in front of me. We won 45–6, and I gained 148 yards. The next week, we played LSU, but I didn't play much then because the backs who were hurt were back in the lineup. I don't understand how I made somebody mad, going to the bench like that after a good game.

The week after that LSU game, we played Alabama, and the starters were out again. I got a chance and made the winning run against them. After that, I guess, they thought I was okay and let me play.

The Alabama game stands out for me because we beat them 41–34. I had the winning run, and it was in Birmingham on their field. It was a 66-yard run, and it was in the fourth quarter, so I remember it well. It was an option play, 49 option. It was going left-handed, and I got some great blocks from the receivers, Tim McGee and Leonard Taylor. They made tremendous blocks downfield, and I cut off each block.

I was pretty much wide open because the defensive end took Alan Cockrell, the quarterback. It was on a blitz play by their defense. When I got past the line and had a clear field because of the downfield blocks, my first thought was, *Don't get caught.* Before I knew it, I was looking for the official to hand him the ball. I was in the end zone.

I didn't know how important that game was until I made that run and we won. We beat Alabama, which we didn't do much back then. People were very happy with that win.

That was a big game for me and so were the 200-yard games. I had three of them. When you get that many yards in a game, the offensive line is really blocking well. Coach Fulmer was the offensive line coach, and I remember how we practiced so much running those plays. We could option, we could run off-tackle, we could pitch and sweep.

I was 5′11″, 195 pounds, and I was pretty strong back then. I was squatting around 500 pounds, which set records for my weight. I could run inside and still run outside. I had some speed and power, which is good for a tailback. I could also catch some of those swing passes, which allowed me to get outside. I ran low, behind the pads, and that was a key for me. You had to make yourself hard to tackle and couldn't be making all those dodging moves. It was one move and into the hole. I think with all the weights it made me stronger as the game went along.

The Vanderbilt game in 1983 stands out for me when I got 248 yards. It was one of those days you just enjoy being out there running. They always played us tough, and they wanted to beat us, so you had to run hard.

I just had a point to prove with some of the big games I had. I ended up being the MVP of our Citrus Bowl win over Maryland [30–23] and had 154 yards in that game.

I'm still glad I went to Tennessee. I could have gone to Memphis State or Ole Miss, but once I went inside that Neyland Stadium—whew, it was loud, it was big. That's where I wanted to go. I also didn't want to go too far from home in Munford. But the big thing was playing inside that Neyland Stadium in Knoxville. It wins you over. I was used to playing in front of 300 people— and that was for the big games. I had a big senior year—2,100 yards—and could have gone some other places, but I wanted to try Tennessee.

If I had to do it all over again, I would do the same thing. Sometimes, life doesn't treat you fair, but you have to keep your head up and wait for your chance.

Johnnie Jones is third all-time in rushing at Tennessee behind Travis Henry and James Stewart. Jones gained 2,852 yards and averaged 5.5 yards per carry. He set a single-season rushing record in 1983 with 1,116 yards, starting just seven games. He broke his own rushing record in 1984 with 1,290 yards. He was first-team All-SEC in 1983 and 1984. Jones is a resource officer with the Alternative and Court School in Covington, Tennessee. He is a youth league football coach in his hometown, Munford.

TIM McGEE
RECEIVER
1982–1985

I F YOU WERE A WIDE RECEIVER in high school, you immediately thought
about the University of Tennessee. It was Wide Receiver U because of
people like Clyde Duncan, Willie Gault, Anthony Hancock, and Mike
Miller. They gave it that tradition. It was the same reason you went to Miami
if you were a linebacker. You go to schools where they are known for certain positions, and Tennessee was definitely known for wide receivers when
I was making my decision where to go. My choices came down to Ohio
State, Purdue, and Tennessee.

The special part of it was that, once Willie and Clyde and Hancock came
along, we started getting every high school All-American wide receiver, and
the competition to be a starter was very intense. If you separated yourself
from the other guys, you had a good idea what the end result would be: a
chance to play in the NFL.

When I went down on my recruiting trip, I saw African Americans and
more African Americans. The coaches took me around, and the guys they
paired me up with were African American. I went to some parties, and there
were more African Americans, and I was thinking, *This is like Tennessee State*,
which is one of the historically black colleges and universities. I mean, I was
a young kid from the inner city, just a puppy.

When I went down for the summer camp before the start of my freshman season, school was not in session, so no one was around. Then we got

All-American Tim McGee, who had a successful career in the NFL, helped Tennessee become known as Wide Receiver U.

to the first game, and I looked up in the stands and I thought, *Where are all the African American people?* That was hilarious to me just because of how naïve I was.

Then you went on to appreciate how much you appreciated the fan support. If you had a tough game, they loved you; if you dropped a pass, they loved you; if you had a great game, they really loved you.

Now, when I came in, we had Johnnie Jones, who was a great runner, so we used him a lot, and I played the wingback. We played three receivers, and the wingback moved around to create matchup situations. We used to run this wheel route in this two-receiver set, and the Z would clear out for you, and I would come underneath. We also had the go route, but you didn't get the go route very often at Tennessee, because people played off of you so much. People respected our speed.

Alabama was not a big deal to me because I was from Cleveland, Ohio, and I didn't have the sense of that great Southern rivalry like a lot of guys had. I heard about it, but it is totally different than being a part of it.

The special games for me were when we were on national TV against Auburn and against Florida. Those games were big for me because it was a chance for Tennessee to get some notoriety.

Back in the early '80s, Tennessee had not yet become a national power again. People knew about the wide receivers, and that's what they would talk about on TV: "Oh, by the way, Tennessee has good wide receivers, but they're going to lose today." We were going to light up the air with the football, they said, and then blow it.

So, when we got on national TV against No. 1 Auburn in 1985 and beat them, that was a turning point for our program. That was my senior year, and we won 38–20. They had Bo Jackson, and he was being heralded as the Heisman frontrunner, and sure enough, he went on to win the Heisman. People thought they were going to blow us out. That was the first of two games where we were on national TV and people thought we were going to get blown out and we ended up stealing the spotlight.

It was supposed to be Auburn's running game against our passing game. We bombed away on them; we absolutely drilled them. I think Bo got hurt in the first quarter and wasn't himself, and we shut him down. He left the game.

Myself, Joey Clinkscales, and Eric Swanson were the receivers, and I tell you, by the end of the third quarter, I felt bad for their cornerbacks. We were in attack mode. I remember Kippy Brown, the receivers coach, telling me before the game, "Be ready, we're not holding anything back."

Tony Robinson was the quarterback, and he was absolutely the best quarterback I have ever witnessed, and I have played with some Hall of Fame–type quarterbacks. He had the arm, the speed, the mind, and was the most athletic quarterback I have ever seen.

I think we lost the chance to play for the national championship when Tony Robinson got hurt against Alabama. We tied Georgia Tech the next week, and there's no way Georgia Tech should've tied us. We would have had one loss, one tie, and had a chance to be considered for the national championship game.

Tony had it all; he was a Randall Cunningham type. Peyton Manning is Peyton Manning, taking nothing from Peyton, but Tony could have been the greatest quarterback at the school. He was the bomb. Then he got hurt against Alabama, and the bottom fell out. He took a nose dive. He got in trouble a few weeks later and got picked up by the police, and that was it.

We still got into one of the major bowl games, the Sugar Bowl, and routed Miami 35–7. That was a classic example of over-confidence by Miami.

That game was won prior to the kickoff. The behavior exhibited by the Miami team throughout the week lost the game for them and won it for us. In all my years in sports, I have never seen anything like it, at any level, where an opponent totally disrespected another opponent. We would go to press conferences, and it was like we weren't there. It was as if the game had already been played and we were having postgame press conferences.

Jimmy Johnson was the head coach, Vinny Testaverde was the quarterback. Bennie Blades was a star defensive back. They had Alonzo Highsmith and Jerome Brown. I mean, they were loaded.

They weren't saying anything negative about us, but what they were saying was that they should be No. 1 in the country after beating us. It was them and Oklahoma who were in contention for the national title. The question from the national media was, who should be No. 1 in the event of a tie and both teams finishing undefeated?

This was back in the day when point spreads had a lot to do with national rankings, and the Miami guys were talking about how much they had to win by against us to be considered for the national title.

They felt they couldn't beat us 10–9 and win the national championship. It was pretty amazing to hear it at the press conference.

It was kind of laughable for me because I had spent so much time on the All-America team tours and banquets with several Miami players, notably Willie Smith, the two-time All-American tight end. On one of the trips, he was my roommate. He wasn't just talking about how they were going to hammer us, he was talking about how Miami had set a standard for winning national championships, and this was their birthright to play for the national championship. They looked right past us, and the Tennessee players took it very personally all week.

When we came out to warm up in the Superdome for the game, 80 percent of the fans were Tennessee fans. That was great to see. The other 20 percent were Miami, and they had on orange because of their school colors, so there was this sea of orange out there. It was amazing to me. You couldn't tell the other 20 percent belonged to Miami.

Miami marched the ball right down the field and scored with their first possession of the game. I looked at other people on the sideline, and there was this look of, *Uh-oh, we are about to get drilled.* If people don't admit it, they are lying. That wasn't in the back of their heads, it was in front of their heads. We had gone three-and-out, and they went right down and scored. It was like, *Oh, shoot.*

And then we got back in the game. It wasn't a big play. It was just a steady thing. Our defense stopped them, and we started to play our game. Our defense's confidence got going. We were conservative at first, then we opened up with our passing game. We had the most unlikely hero, a walk-on running back, Jeff Powell. He played great; the defense played great. It was a highlight for me.

There was a disconnect for a long time between me and the Tennessee program because I played for so long in the pros. You don't get a chance to go back and see the games and follow them because you are so busy on the weekends with your NFL career. I did go back during my NFL career when I was on injured reserve and get my degree in human services. I follow them and still want them to win for the bragging rights.

I cherished the relationships and the discipline taught by Coach Majors, Bob Harrison, and Kippy Brown. I don't say that in cliché way, I mean that in a true way because it was so valuable to me. What you learn in the first two or three weeks at the University of Tennessee carries through the rest of your life because of what you learn those first two weeks you repeat over four years. You hear some of the proverbs they use and put them to work.

I was able to take the experience at the University of Tennessee and use it to prepare myself for the rest of my life. It wasn't just football for me. It was the most fun I ever had. I wouldn't trade the four years at Tennessee for the 10 years in the NFL.

I am an agent now, and I tell kids to enjoy it because it's a game in college, it is work in the NFL. It's still fun, but it's work. Those four years there were the best. It was the most awesome experience a kid could have. You go back and think about it, and that orange uniform was the ultimate experience.

Tim McGee led Tennessee in receiving in 1984 and 1985 and was a consensus All-American in 1985. He was an All-SEC wide receiver in 1985 and was selected in the first round of the 1986 NFL Draft by the Cincinnati Bengals. McGee played in the NFL for nine seasons with the Bengals and Washington Redskins. He is currently an NFL agent based in Cincinnati.

BRUCE WILKERSON
OFFENSIVE LINEMAN
1983–1986

WHEN YOU LOOK BACK at that 1985 team, the team that surprised everybody by beating Miami in the Sugar Bowl, you have to look at the chemistry. We had all kinds of chemistry on that team.

We only lost one game that season, and one of the big reasons was we trusted each other to do our jobs. You could go out there on the field and really concentrate on your assignment because you knew the guy next to you was going to take care of his business. That was the identity of that team.

We had more than chemistry, though. There were a lot of guys on the offensive line who played in the NFL. We also had wide receivers who played in the pros. Our quarterback, Tony Robinson, would have been an All-Pro in the NFL if he had not gotten hooked up with drugs.

Daryl Dickey came in as quarterback to replace Tony when he ran into trouble and managed that team and all that talent. He was not asked to win the games, necessarily, but just manage the game. That's chemistry; that's doing your part.

The experience I had being on two championship teams in the NFL has made me look back at that Tennessee team and understand why it was a winner and that the win over Miami was no fluke. That particular Tennessee team had what it took to be a great team, which was talent and chemistry.

On that team, you didn't have to worry about somebody else doing the job, which was just like it was in the NFL with championship teams.

On that offensive line, we had John Bruhin, who went to Tampa Bay in the NFL. We had Harry Galbreath, who played in the league a long time. David Douglas played with the Bengals. Daryle Smith played in the NFL and in Canada. And we had myself. Out of the six-man rotation, five of us played in the pros.

Also, if you look back at that offensive line, all of us, except Todd Kirk, were from the state of Tennessee. He was from the coalfields of Virginia, which wasn't far away, and he understood the tradition and pride of Tennessee football as much as the guys who were from the state. David Douglas was from Rhea County and John Bruhin and Daryle Smith from Powell. David Douglas and I grew up in the country listening to Tennessee games on a radio that was sitting on the fender of a tractor.

That's what it means to be a Vol. Having that pride of playing for your state team, the Big Orange. Kirk wasn't from Tennessee, but he had that pride, too.

What we learned to do back then was pay attention to the offensive linemen who had played at Tennessee when they came back in the NFL off-season to work out. They were Tennessee guys and they were still teaching us. I would watch Tim Irwin, who was playing for the Vikings, and he would work with 405 pounds in sets of eight and sets of 10, which I never could do.

175

I would be shocked by what he could do, but I would see the commitment and the work he put in, and I would try and copy it.

What makes a good program is when you have your juniors and seniors setting a strong example for the underclassmen. That was part of playing for Tennessee—you had to set the expectations for the younger guys. They had to know what was expected of them.

I could tell you exactly what is going on inside a weak program. The guys are coming in and doing the bare minimum. Those programs have players who only do what the coaches say and nothing more. Back then, in the '80s, we had a lot of guys doing extra work because that's what it took to be successful on our level. Then, from watching guys like Irwin after my junior year, you also learned what it took to play in the NFL.

Phil Fulmer taught us that technique carries you. If you look at the NFL, your best players are the guys with the best technique. You are going to run

Bruce Wilkerson was an All-SEC guard in 1985 and 1986 and appeared in two
Super Bowls with the Green Bay Packers.

into guys who are just as big as you are, just as strong as you are, so you are going to have to rely on technique to get things done and be successful.

We had always been taught that in the hype of a football game, like that Miami game, the first five minutes were critical. You had to survive the first five minutes and the intimidation factor, because that's what Miami liked to do to opponents. Win the battle of the first five minutes, withstand the initial rush, and then they have to line up and play football just like you.

That Tennessee teaching and mental toughness were big in that Miami game, which was one of the great wins in the '80s for our program. We went three-and-out on our first possession, they went down and scored, then we settled down. We didn't quit, we didn't get discouraged or lose our confidence.

On offense, we had wide splits and created natural running seams for our backs. You can do that if you have confidence in guys to block one-on-one. Miami's defense was a penetrating defense, they liked to get upfield, penetrate, disrupt things, and cause havoc. They lined up on edges on the offensive linemen and wanted to get into the backfield. They had powerful players like Jerome Brown, who was one of the best defensive tackles of all time to play college football.

177

We did some cross-blocking in that game, which was favorable to our angles. We had a veteran enough team that Coach Fulmer allowed the offensive guard, if he had to, to block a defensive tackle, even if that defensive tackle was in a wide-three on him, and hard for him to reach. You make the call that the tackle would block down and pin him, and the guard would pull around and block the linebacker the tackle was supposed to go up on. We communicated all night.

By our having a veteran offensive line, we were able to get some favorable blocking angles on Miami and create some seams and use their aggressiveness against them.

In the first half, you would use a word to make that call on blocking assignments. In the second half, if you knew they were keying on your word, you would change it up and make a call amongst yourselves. It was very satisfying to handle them as we did. They talked a lot of smack all week about how they deserved to be national champions, and they really just overlooked us. We were from the Southeastern Conference, a really good league, but they kept it up all week that we were going to be stepped over.

A key part of that game came when Jeff Powell broke a long run. They assumed their All-American defensive back, Bennie Blades, or maybe it was Brian Blades, was going to run down Jeff and tackle him. They didn't realize Jeff was a track athlete who had world-class speed. He took off. I'm sure they were looking at Jeff like he was a backup who didn't play much and had little experience.

They never caught Jeff. We were up by two touchdowns, and his run of 60 yards put them three touchdowns behind, and we went on to win easily.

That was the great thing about that team, somebody getting hurt, somebody stepping in. Tony Robinson was on crutches and hurt, and Daryl Dickey stepped in. Davis was hurt, and Powell stepped in. That was very key to our season. When somebody got hurt, our depth showed when somebody jumped in and did well.

One of the reasons we were so good on the offensive line that season is that Coach Fulmer, who was the offensive line coach back then, wanted everybody to have that no-mistakes attitude and mental toughness. That's why he was so good as a coach.

When I was there, Coach Fulmer was mean as hell at times, but probably a nice guy. I thought Coach Majors was mean, but they were pushing us to get the best out of us. As a young kid, you don't know how far you can push yourself to get the most out of your ability. They taught me that your body will do a whole lot more if you release your mind enough.

For instance, when I came to UT, I thought I could run a mile and a half; I didn't think I could run two miles, but I did. I kept thinking, *Mile and a half and I'm done.* Then they started pushing me, and I did more than I ever thought I could.

Coach Majors, if you look back at it, taught us about the hidden yardage in the game and how crucial field position was to winning. He would fill up the field-position chart and talk about these intricacies of the game, and we were like, *What's he talking about?* We didn't get it, but he did, and it made us a better team.

That stuff carried over for us from college to the NFL, things like making teams drive 80 yards to score, and the percentage of times they could actually make a long drive without making a mistake. He taught everybody about making sure teams did not have a short field. Coach Majors would come in and say all this stuff about short fields, and when this same stuff came up in the NFL, I was on it. He taught us to be students of the game.

I've been gone 20 years, and that tradition of being part of Tennessee football is with me every day. Being part of the pride that people from this area take in football is special. The whole East Tennessee area rallies around UT football, and I get a lot from it because I actually played there. You don't realize some of these things when you are young, you are just there to play football and have fun in college. You don't care about the tradition and all that as much. But it grows and grows on you, and you come to understand what it means to be a Vol.

Bruce Wilkerson was a three-year starter, played four of the five positions on the offensive line for the Vols, and was a team captain. He was a two-time All-SEC offensive lineman (1986 and 1987) and one of the mainstays on an offensive line that helped Tennessee score 35 points against the vaunted Miami defense in the 1986 Sugar Bowl rout of the No. 2 Hurricanes. Wilkerson was drafted in the second round of the 1987 draft by the Los Angeles Raiders. He played in the 1997 and 1998 Super Bowls with the Green Bay Packers. Wilkerson lives in the Knoxville area and is a machinist for the Alcoa aluminum company.

HARRY GALBREATH

OFFENSIVE LINE

1983–1987

Let me tell you where I was when I came in as a young player. My first spring I had no concept of technique whatsoever. We used to have these things called "Harry Drills" where everybody would do the drill one time, and the rest of the time was dedicated to me. I was not very polished.

It was one of those make-you or break-you type things. I got better. Coach Fulmer pretty much ran us all off at one time or another. I was on the cusp of wanting to leave a few times. He tried to push all of us to the edge, especially me with those Harry Drills. There were a couple of guys who actually left campus, and he had to go get them. They were good players, too; he was just very demanding.

It was confusing, we felt like we were being picked on, but it was nothing personal. He was just trying to get us better. Once Coach Fulmer started working with me, he realized I could be a good player. You have to understand I came from a small program where we didn't have a lot of coaches, so I was not a finished product.

My first year was really challenging because I went to a high school [Clarksville, Tennessee] where we did not have a bunch of coaches, maybe one guy on offense, one guy on defense. We had a "cat" scheme—you block that cat and I'll block that cat. There wasn't a lot of individual coaching going on.

That's why I say I was at the right place at the right time. It was truly a blessing that Tennessee recruited me and I had that coaching from Coach

Harry Galbreath (No. 76) leads a runner into a hole. Galbreath has an award (the 76 Award) named after him because of the punishing blocks he put on defenders.

Fulmer. He helped make me into something. I was not a highly recruited player, and you're right, when other big schools see that you are not highly recruited, they can wonder about you.

Coach Matthews recruited me for Tennessee and would call me every week. I was recruited mostly by OVC [Ohio Valley Conference] schools and took an unofficial visit to Memphis State. I was supposed to take a trip to Kentucky after my Tennessee visit, but I didn't go.

The thing that you have to do is prepare yourself for when the opportunity comes, and I was ready. I wrestled in high school, and I think that gave me some mental toughness. I hung out at an old sweatbox gym, the Cobra Gym, and I'll never forget the guys who helped me. We didn't have any of the fancy weights, but they helped me get stronger so I could play in college.

Tennessee recruited me as a nose guard, and I was the MVP of my district on the defensive line. By the time school started my freshman year at Tennessee, though, I was on the offensive side of the ball. I still weighed 252 pounds, the same as in high school. I had trouble gaining weight.

It was an uphill struggle here that first year because, like I said, I was not what you'd call a polished guy. In the preseason, I remember going to meetings, and then one day they gave me an offensive playbook and told me to go see Coach Fulmer. Just like that, I was on offense.

I was a little bit heartbroken. It was easier to play defense because all you had to do was find the ball. They wanted you running after it, though. We were in practice one day, and there was a long pass down the field, 40 yards or something, and I just stopped. I was on the line and figured I didn't have to chase it. Coach Bill Shaw said to me real calmly, "Hey, Harry, where's the ball?" I pointed down the field, and then he yelled, "Well, get your fat ass down there!" The habits you had in high school came with you—the ball is gone, why follow the ball? You don't have the concept that if you follow the ball, anything can happen.

I was on offense a few days later. I don't think that particular play where Coach Shaw yelled at me had a lot to do with it; I think they just needed some players over there. I was behind the eight ball, though, because there were a lot of guys who were highly recruited, and they were in front of me.

I went to work with Coach Fulmer, who was the offensive line coach then, and he was a stickler for details. You had to have the right step, the right head placement, you had to get off the ball. When he graded us, he was pretty tough. You could put somebody on their back, but if you took the wrong step or you weren't low enough, he gave you a minus.

I was the strongest guy on the team four of the five years I was there. I felt so blessed to be here, playing for Tennessee, that whatever they asked me to do I tried to do 110 percent, and that included lifting weights and getting stronger. I was very competitive, and no matter if it was horseshoes or rolling dice, I wanted to be the best that I could be. Going to the weight room was just a mindset.

I got into the weights at that sweat gym at home. Just going in and working with those guys made a difference. They kept telling me, as big as you are, you should be lifting this and lifting that, and on and on. They pushed me. I'm never going to forget that place, the Cobra Gym. I had some records at Tennessee and made the Strength All-America team. Bruce Wilkerson was pretty strong, too, and we had a quiet competition, and that helped.

I had a little chip on my shoulder, and I wanted to make sure I succeeded in life. I knew there were people that might pat me on my back and then maybe stab me in the back and say they knew I would be back in Clarksville eventually as a failure. So I went to class and I studied, just in case things did not work out in football. I was not the world's greatest student when I first went to Tennessee, but I got better.

Early on in my career at Tennessee, I would run into guys who had had more coaching in high school, and there was some peer pressure, and they would say to me, "You can't do this, you can't do that." When someone tells you that, you get a chip on your shoulder. When the players say something like that, it can carry more weight than what the coach says. Being from a small town, not wanting to let people down, I wanted to put forth my best effort.

The day I took my first rep with the starters, Coach Fulmer told me, "Act like you belong." It was his way of telling me that my level of play had to come up to where the others were. I ran with it. I started three years and lettered four.

183

The guy I played behind one year, Bill Mayo, was a great technician. Raleigh McKenzie was a good technician, too, but he was also a tough guy. Dave Moon was very smart, and he beat most opponents before he got on the field. I sat behind those guys and watched them in the film room and soaked it up.

They would put the play up on the board, and then I just watched them and how they dissected it and understood it. Some guys would go in to watch film and just watch the screen; they weren't really there. These guys—Mayo, McKenzie, Moon—paid attention, and I learned from them. I wanted to add those things to my game, all those things these guys were going over in meetings. Harry the sponge, that was me.

At Tennessee, they have something called the "76 Award" for intimidation blocks, which was named for me because I wore No. 76. It is an honor. I think Coach Cutcliffe started it. He said one day in practice, and this was after I left, that we needed more guys like Harry Galbreath. I think it was because we had the competition when I was there to see who could get the most intimidation blocks. It was when you just mauled a guy. You couldn't cut them, you had to flatten them. They would show a film to freshmen who came in to play offensive line of some of my blocks.

If you stayed the course, paid attention, good things could happen to you. I started three years and never missed a game, and then got the Jacobs Blocking Trophy in the SEC, and I was drafted into the National Football League. It is a tribute to a lot of things, especially to my mom who raised me, and the way she raised me. Then you have to think about the influence of Coach Fulmer. Even though I was an eighth-round pick of the Dolphins, I started 13 games as a rookie, and that is a testament to what I was taught at Tennessee. It was not a tough transition. The terminology, everything, was nothing. Coach Fulmer is the best coach I ever had.

I just started working at Tennessee this year, and even though I don't have a big background in weightlifting, these guys are working with me every day on fundamentals and technique with no problem, no hesitation.

When I get a chance to talk to these young offensive linemen, I tell them that when I was here it was called "Wide Receiver U," but a lot of people don't realize how many offensive linemen we have playing in the NFL. They may not have been taken in the first round, or second round, but we had guys who played a long time. If you play here and go on to the next level, you can have a career. There is a rich, strong tradition of offensive linemen at UT.

Tim Irwin wore No. 76, just like me. I used to see him around, tall, lanky, and working hard. He had a good career in the NFL. I don't know if he will remember this, but he told me one time, "Don't embarrass that number."

I don't think I did. I think I played hard and represented the school well. What is great about this program is that guys will come back and work out after they have left, and you can ask them questions, and they will share their time. I think that is a part of what it means to be a Tennessee Volunteer.

There is an award in the Tennessee football program called the "76 Award," named after Galbreath, who would lay out defensive linemen with his fierce blocks. A three-year starter at guard for the Vols, Galbreath was a first-team All-American (*The Sporting News*) and was All-SEC in 1987. He won the Jacobs Blocking Trophy in 1987, which is given to the top blocker in the Southeastern Conference. Following a successful career in the National Football League, Galbreath returned to Knoxville as the assistant strength and conditioning coach at UT.

ERIC STILL
GUARD/TACKLE
1985–1989

I F YOU HAD TO DESCRIBE MY COLLEGE CAREER, it was like being fixed to a roller coaster. It was an up-and-down career. My freshman year, when I redshirted, we beat Miami in the Sugar Bowl. The next year we had a rough season, 7–5. My sophomore year we were 10–2–1. Then came the infamous 0–6 start to the 1988 season—and that was something to be a part of because then we won the next five.

Finally, my senior year we were 11–1, SEC champions, and finished No. 5 in the country. We went through the highs and lows of it; there was something for everybody during my career at Tennessee.

We ended on a great note my fifth year. We finished in a three-way tie for first place in the SEC, and then beat a good Arkansas team in the Cotton Bowl. We ended up as the highest ranked of the SEC teams.

To get there was some trip. That season got the program on a fast track going into the next decade. Tennessee, I think, has been a powerhouse since that 1989 team.

That 1989 team was very good on offense. We had a good offensive line with Antone Davis, who was an All-American, and Charles McRae, who would be an All-SEC tackle and get drafted in the first round of the NFL. Charles was 6′7″, 290 pounds, a big old country boy.

We ran the ball very well with two good running backs, Reggie Cobb and Chuck Webb. Chuck still holds the record for yards rushing in one game, 294

Eric Still was an All-SEC guard in 1988 and 1989 and an All-American in 1989. He helped plow holes for one of the most overpowering running games in college football in 1989.

against Ole Miss. I think he had 250 in the Cotton bowl against Arkansas. If he had not wrecked his knee, he would have won a Heisman Trophy. That's how good that guy was.

We were definitely a run-first offense with Cobb and Webb. The offensive line was a strength of our team, in fact. From the mid-'80s to early '90s, Tennessee had some really good offensive lines under Coach Fulmer, who was the position coach, and we had a reputation.

There were guys who came through the program when I was an underclassmen who did not get a lot of recognition in college, but played seven, eight, nine years in the NFL. Bruce Wilkerson, the McKenzies, David Douglas, and John Bruhin come to mind. That was one of the reasons I got better as I progressed; I had a chance to be around guys like that and emulate them.

What struck me about Tennessee was the East Tennessee and Knoxville area had a blue-collar-type environment, which kind of fits for an offensive lineman. I think that had something to do with my going there in the first place.

Bill Mayo, an offensive lineman, took me out on my recruiting trip, and I noticed how tight-knit that group of linemen was, and I think that also had a lot to do with my going there. Bill was a storyteller and could probably write a book about Tennessee football.

The system that Tennessee ran fit my abilities. We ran the I formation the whole time I was there. The feature back was obviously the tailback, and he just kind of read the holes and did what he did best. That allowed me to be as effective as I was because you did not necessarily have to make the right block, you just had to stay on the block long enough for the tailback to hit the hole.

I wasn't very strong, and I didn't think I was very big, but the system just allowed me to succeed. Coach Fulmer could take an average lineman and make him good. I was not gifted athletically and probably in the lower half as far as strength among offensive linemen. Again, Coach Fulmer had a knack for getting every ounce of ability out of somebody like me.

Coach Fulmer was a technician. We would be at the hotel Friday nights before games, and we would take these tests that would last until 2:00 or 3:00 in the morning. You better finish it because you did not want to be the guy who did not turn it in the next morning.

It would be 100 plays, 100 sheets, against 12 different defenses. So what that meant was you were drawing plays against 1,200 defenses. It sounded complicated, but all the plays fit together—you just had to figure out all the looks of the defense.

In all the time I played, there was not a game in which I was not prepared for something I saw on the field. That is a result of those tests, among other things. The strength of Coach Fulmer's coaching was that he had you ready for what you were going to see from the defense on Saturday. There was never a moment like, "Wow, what was that?" It allowed an average guy like me to do well.

We would get together at 3:00 o'clock on Sunday afternoons, the day after the game, and it would take him four or five hours to get through the game film. We were always the last ones to the training table on Sunday night. That was in the days before they had limitations on how much time you can spend practicing. Coach Fulmer would start at left tackle and go straight across every position. He never left anything unturned, he covered it all. He was pretty attentive to detail.

I feel a little bad for him for what he has gone through this season [2007]. He has been getting a lot of criticism. I know his intensity and I know he prepares, but sometimes you just don't have the talent. I can appreciate what he has been through; it is very tough to be a college football coach. They work 18-hour days, and I don't think people realize how much goes into the preparation during the week. That is just during the regular season and does not include recruiting, when you're gone from your family for five days at a time.

I think that good season we had in 1989 really started in 1988 when we won those last five games of the season after starting 0–6. We also changed a lot of stuff up going into the 1989 season after what happened at the start of the '88 season. We revamped a lot of the training and weightlifting and nutrition. It was nothing drastic, just a different approach. We had been embarrassed as a team with that 5–6 season, and I think Coach Majors wanted to get it fixed.

What I remember about the 1988 0–6 start is that the only people talking to us were our girlfriends and our coaches. Nobody knew what to say to us. You have to give the coaches a lot of credit, because when we started 0–6, we could have easily finished 1–10 or 2–9. They got things fixed and got the wheels back on and did not let the season become a total disaster.

We came out in 1989 with a sense of direction to right the ship and get back to Tennessee football. None of the games really came easily because we would grind it out on the ground and play physical football. We kept winning and winning with that style.

188

I remember we beat UCLA 24–6 early in the season when they were ranked No. 6. They really weren't that good, but it gave us some confidence to beat a team ranked in the top 10. The fact that we beat them in the Rose Bowl really set the tone.

We beat Duke, and then we had a big game against Auburn when they were ranked No. 4, and we beat them 21–14 in Knoxville. We beat Georgia in a close game, and then stubbed our toe against Alabama. That was the only loss all year. We then won our last six to finish 11–1. Tennessee football was back.

That 1989 season was a nice little year tucked in there between the big Sugar Bowl win in 1985 and the Peyton Manning years in the '90s. I really think that '89 season was big for the program because it got Tennessee back on track as one of the elite programs in the country. You don't hear a lot about that season; it was a blue-collar-type team that was not flashy. If you look back at it, there has not been a team in the last 18 years or so that has rushed for as many yards in a season as we did in 1989 [2,701]. We averaged something like 245 yards per game, even though Reggie was dismissed halfway through the year.

Reggie Cobb and Chuck Webb were two of the best backs I ever played with. They complemented each other very well. After Reggie got dismissed following the Georgia game, we went down to Alabama trying to find our identity again and got beat.

Then Chuck came on and was great down the stretch of the season. Like I said, if he had stayed healthy, he would've won the Heisman Trophy.

In 1990, after I left, he had those two great offensive linemen in Antone Davis and Charles McRae, and he would have been great, but he got hurt. Nineteen ninety was the year Tony Thompson had a great year rushing for more than 1,200 yards.

Reggie Cobb was one of the nicest guys I've ever played with. He got along with everybody. He was a super person, a super football player, he just got hooked up in some wrong things. It was disappointing that that happened to him. He is a fine individual.

Reggie was a local hero in Knoxville in high school football. He was extremely talented and ran for 225 yards against Auburn in 1989. It was the first time Auburn had given up 100 yards rushing in a game in a long time. They were loaded on defense under Pat Dye, and Reggie went to work on them.

The fans rushed the field before the game was even over when we beat Auburn. They tore down the goal posts, and it was a wild time. We had to get off the field, it was so wild. The fans were hungry for success because we had been down the season before, and a win against Auburn was special. Pay Dye's defenses were very good, the best in the country, and we took the fight to them. They were scary with all the talent they had and were as good as anyone. But we ran on them all day.

It was a workmanlike year for us because we took it one game at a time. After what we had been through the year before, we knew we just had to do it one game at a time. I remember after that Arkansas game in the Cotton Bowl, when we were 11–1, there was not that tremendous excitement. I think we had worked so hard that season, we were exhausted.

That was a year that got Coach Majors going in the right direction. He had had his ups and downs, but he was at his best when his back was against the wall. I liked Coach Majors, he was old-fashioned, old school, ruffy scruffy, and I was glad I played for him. He was the bridge from the old-time Vols of the '50s to us. I hated to see what happened to him in 1993 when they took his job. I still don't know what happened.

What I remember about Coach Majors is he could remember situations and scores. I think he had a photographic memory. He had a different personality, and a lot of guys like to imitate him. He would have his pet phrases, and guys would try to imitate him. I'm not sure anyone did it perfectly. We got a lot of kicks and laughs out of that in the locker room.

The thing I liked about Coach Majors is if you went to school, went to class, and stayed out of trouble, he was right there with you. If you didn't do those things and you got in his doghouse, it was very hard to get out.

Everybody from different schools can make their case for their program, but I think I can honestly say Tennessee is a unique program in college football. It's more than the school colors, it is the 100,000 people in the stands, and it's the support and year-round enthusiasm of the fans.

The thing that stands out to me was in 1988: we were 0–5 and came back to Knoxville to play Alabama, and the place was packed. Some other schools with an 0–5 team might have a stadium two-thirds full or empty seats here and there. I looked into that crowd, and there wasn't an empty seat. Once a person falls in love with Tennessee, they are there forever.

One of the reasons there has been so much criticism of the program is that no one wants to win more than a Tennessee fan. They want to continue to see that success and hang onto it. I didn't grow up a Tennessee fan because I lived in Baton Rouge and Missouri. But even though I didn't live in Tennessee, the school had a reputation outside the state lines.

I still remember when I was a sophomore playing high school football in Baton Rouge, a dad of one of our players said, if I ever had the chance to play college football, I should go to Tennessee and play for Johnny Majors.

You can just look back and see that Tennessee has had two head coaches in 30 years, both of them ex-players, and that shows you the history and the tradition. Two coaches in 30 years shows you just how solid the program has been.

Eric Still was a consensus All-American in 1989. He was All-SEC in 1988 and 1989. He was a senior in 1989, when Tennessee rushed for 2,701 yards, the second-highest total for a UT team. Still was on the SEC Academic Honor Roll for four seasons. He is a commodity trader in the Memphis area with Crow Trading. He earned a degree in business administration with a concentration in transportation.

The
NINETIES

ANTONE DAVIS

TACKLE

1987–1990

COACH FULMER AND COACH DONAHUE flipped a coin with me to see if I would play offense or defense. I kid you not. I came in as a nose guard, so Coach Donahue wanted me for defense. Coach Fulmer recruited me and thought I would make a good offensive lineman for him.

So there I am, as a freshman, and they have this tug-of-war and say, "Okay, we're flipping a coin." Coach Donahue won. Coach Fulmer then grabbed me off on the side and said, "Look, if you make one damn tackle for them, I will run you from now on."

Coach Fulmer recruited me at TMI [Tennessee Military Institute], where I was a nose guard. He saw something in me that said I could be an offensive lineman. He was not going to let Coach Donahue have me. I was going to be an offensive lineman. I had played the whole year at TMI as a nose guard, and Coach Fulmer couldn't just say, "He is playing offense." I had to have that one audition with Coach Donahue. I personally didn't like defense.

My playing defense lasted one practice. I was on offense with Coach Fulmer after that. True story.

Playing football at Tennessee taught me how to be a man. It was the biggest thing I took away from that program and that experience in Knoxville. I say that because, growing up in Fort Valley, Georgia, it was all about survival. That was the most important thing. School was important, but it was not at the top of my list when I was worried about what I was going to eat the next day. Manners were not at the top of my list; football was not at the top of my list. Survival was at the top of my list.

I didn't understand a lot of things about life until I got to Tennessee. I started wearing suits because on travel days Coach Majors demanded it. I learned how to address people properly. Instead of saying "Yeah" and "Nah," I learned how to say "Yes" and "Yes, sir" or "No" and "No, sir." I learned how to carry myself and how to interact with other people.

I learned at Tennessee how to carry on a conversation with adults. And it was a rounded conversation. I wasn't a horrible kid growing up, but I was in a different mix, and those kinds of social skills were not the most important things when I was trying to just survive and worry about what I was going to eat. Those kinds of things were around me, but they weren't important. I had six brothers and one sister growing up, so we had some challenges.

Fort Valley, Georgia, hasn't changed. I tell people it is cryogenically frozen. I can drive around with my eyes closed because I know where everything is. What's important is that I have changed, I have grown. Playing football at Tennessee and going to school in Knoxville helped me grow immensely.

193

I was one of the better run-blockers who came through Tennessee, at least that's what people tell me. That's what felt more comfortable to me. Pass-blocking didn't feel natural to me. I did it well enough to make a living in the NFL, but it didn't feel as natural as run blocking.

In 1989 and 1990, when we were a run-first team and really getting some yards on the ground, the best play was "6 and 7 gap" all day long. I remember it like it was yesterday. It was basically a cross-block between guard and tackle, kick out, and then lead-block on linebacker. Reggie Cobb and Chuck Webb just had to make one defender miss, and we're out of the gate.

When I played with Philadelphia and we went to play the 49ers, we beat them 40–8, and the play we ran was "6 and 7 gap." It was the exact same play we used at Tennessee. The running back that day for us? Charlie Garner of Tennessee. We ran the same freaking play we did at Tennessee. It was great.

Coach Fulmer had a lot to do with the success of the run game when he was offensive line coach. He always made sure we were more than ready. Always.

For instance, there would be a conditioning test players would have to take before training camp started. Coach Fulmer would always make sure that a

Antone Davis was an All-American and won the Jacobs Blocking Trophy in 1990.

week prior to Coach Majors giving the running test to the rest of the team, the offensive linemen did the running test and passed it with him.

People dreaded doing that test once. We did it twice, under time. We always passed. When we ran the test with Coach Majors, we actually did better, and it was Coach Fulmer who made us look good in the eyes of the head coach.

When I got to Tennessee, I honest-to-goodness didn't know how to play football. I was 6'5" and tried to play around 305. I always struggled with my weight.

When I was at TMI, I pretty much got whatever I wanted to eat. Then, when I was being recruited, I got whatever I wanted to eat. They weren't going to hassle me with food on recruiting trips.

I took some recruiting visits, committed to Tennessee, then decided I needed to take a real recruiting visit, and wound up taking a recruiting visit to South Carolina. I ate everything I could eat under the sun. I came back to Tennessee, got on the scale, and weighed 349.

So, a few months later, I showed up in the summertime to get in shape for camp, and up until now, Coach Fulmer and I were pals. We were buddies. He recruited me, and it was like, "Where have you been all my life?"

One day, I saw Coach Fulmer walking up to me on the sidewalk, and he said, "Antone, how much do you weigh?" I said, "Three forty-nine, Coach." And I stuck my chest out because I was real proud. He said to me, "Three hundred," and walked away.

195

I thought, *Holy cow, who was that guy? Not my best friend, surely not my pal.* I had two months to do it. My best friend was no more. The day I had to report, I was 299. I had to get down quick. He was the coach, and I was his player.

The game that stands out for me at Tennessee? Easy. Auburn.

It wasn't a blowout, but I had my best game against Auburn's David Rocker. He was one of the best in the country, and I ate his lunch. He was a great player, and they had great players all over the place. It was the 1990 game where we tied them 26–26 at Auburn. That was the best game I had. He was lined up as defensive tackle, defensive end, right over me.

Rocker was well known, and I wasn't. The year before, in 1989, it was all Eric Still. He was our marquee player, so people didn't pay any attention to me.

In 1990, I was still a sleeper, so to speak. I wasn't on the cover of everything. David Rocker, on the other hand, was up for this award or that award, he was all over the news. People knew who he was. So I had the toughest matchup on the field that day.

I'll never forget that game because their fans blocked our buses. Tom Myslinski got up and mooned them all, and Coach Majors got all over him. My goal that day was not to make any mental mistakes and have the game of my life, and I did. We went right at Rocker. I have a highlight film here at the store that some of the workers watch, and there are four or five plays where I just crush him. I hate saying that—maybe I should not say that because I never brag—but I had a good day. He had a lot of good days, except for that one. For so many years, I was afraid to say how well I did, but my wife says that now that we have kids, I have to talk about it.

Coach Fulmer was of the attitude that, if he saw one of us having a real good game, he would call plays to take advantage of our matchup. We wouldn't run the draw play, or this or that. He would call plays where I would go one-on-one with a guy. He was not calling plays where we were pitching the ball and running away from this guy. He was calling our base plays. After a while, Rocker basically gave up. The plays were 34 and 35, and all five linemen were up against the five guys in front of them. It is the essence of football: line up and get the guy in front of you.

The 1989 Auburn game at Neyland Stadium in the rain with Reggie Cobb and Chuck Webb, when we beat them, stands out. Again, "6 and 7 gap" all day long. It was unstoppable. We won 21–14. Eric Still and I were on the right side of the line and blocked people, and Reggie and Chuck ran it.

The other thing I am proud of is that we helped turn things around after that 0–6 start in 1988. That was my sophomore year, and it was the year somebody made the comment that Tennessee's weakness is that Tennessee is weak. Bruno Pauletto, the strength coach, took it personally.

In January, we went around to all the players and said, "Who is coming back?" I will never forget that Sterling Henton was one of the biggest catalysts. Bruno had shirts made up that said, "Body Under Construction," and we went to work for the 1989 season.

Sterling and Tony Thompson, a running back, made it fun. They started giving us shirts for the weight club. That brought us together like you wouldn't believe. I remember that better than some games. Everybody was there in those workouts.

The next season, in 1989, we broke out and were 11–1. We got up at 5:00 in the morning to run, and everybody was excited, people did not gripe all the time.

That was also the time Coach Fulmer told the offensive line it had to be the leaders of the team, not the quarterback, not the running backs, no one. It was us. He said we had to be the best group on the field. He said if one of us got in a fight in practice, he wanted to see every one of us backing him up. When he gave us that freedom, we started to jell as an offensive line.

So that offseason was the change in Tennessee, and by the time we got around to playing football in the fall of 1989, we were ready. Look at where Tennessee has been since that 1989 season. We've been a national powerhouse most of the time.

In that offseason, we also started to pick up the zone blocking on offense, because Washington State had come in 1988 and just beat us up with it. We started to learn it, understand it, and perfect it. That turned our running game around. They had scored 52 points against us, so we started studying that film and other film of them.

The most frustrating part of my career was in 1990. Charles McRae had played on defense but was moved over to offensive line and got a lot of pre-season hype. It was like I just showed up and was nothing. I never missed a meeting, never missed a practice unless I was hurt. I never got in trouble. I never did anything wrong, I was by-the-book, but my teammate got all the hype.

I can tell you that I was bitter for a while when I left Tennessee because of it. When I first got there, I saw Harry Galbreath and Bruce Wilkerson get recognized for all their hard work. By the time I was a senior, I thought it was my turn, but then I didn't get my turn. I still made money and went to the NFL, but there was some resentment.

I'm not bitter now because I have had time to grow up. I am over it and thankful for that university and for everybody who touched me. I am forever grateful to Coach Fulmer. He made me the person I am today. Coach Majors had an impact on that, too. I wish I was more mature back then, but I can honestly say I wish I had gotten more spotlight.

Then again, Tennessee got me prepared to make plenty of money in the NFL, and I had a good time and I'm thankful for what they did.

We have a little bit of a sports bar here in the restaurant, so I have some Tennessee stuff up. Actually, I have two booths with Tennessee stuff and one with everyone else from the SEC. There is a small dirty booth in the corner with Florida Gator stuff.

I appreciate Tennessee football a lot more now than when I was there. Before I went to TMI, I had played one year of high school football. That's it. I didn't know how to play. Coach Fulmer taught me from scratch. I am so grateful.

I never understood the impact the team has on the public. We have all done the Vol Walk and run through the T; we have all looked up and seen 90,000-plus and now 100,000-plus.

But you do not understand what that team means to the fans until you go back and share in the pregame atmosphere. It was totally different than I imagined it. You have to go out there and live it. These people feel it in their bones.

To the players, it is: go out there, don't make any mistakes, and win. To the fans, it is a way of life. I never saw it that way. If I had to run through the T now with what I know is going on around that stadium, I would pee down my leg. How can anyone play in this environment?

Now, when I watch a Tennessee game, I am proud to say I played for the Vols. I am thankful that I played. It is unbelievable that I played.

Antone Davis was a consensus All-American in 1990 when he was named to nine separate All-America teams. He was also named All-SEC in 1989 and 1990 and won the Jacobs Blocking Trophy in 1990, which is voted on by Southeastern Conference coaches and given to the best blocker. Just two Vols, Davis and Arron Sears (2006), have won the Jacobs Blocking Trophy in the last 17 seasons. Davis was named Outstanding Lineman by the Birmingham Monday Morning Quarterback Club in 1990. Davis was drafted in the first round of the 1991 NFL Draft and played in the NFL from 1991 to 1997. He and his wife, Carrie, own a Buffalo's Southwest Café in Clermont, Florida, near Orlando.

HEATH SHULER

QUARTERBACK

1991–1993

WHAT DOES IT MEAN to be a Vol? It can be best described by the feeling you get when you run through the T for the very first time. It is an incredible sensation, even when I am just watching from the stands at games I attend or see it on TV. Words cannot describe what it means to run through the T. I think it is special for the players and it is special for the fans to watch it at home games. I won't forget my first time running through the T. It was in 1991 in our first game against UCLA. It was 105 degrees on the turf that day.

When I came to Tennessee, Andy Kelly was the fifth-year starter and I was a backup. He was a great leader and made terrific decisions on the field. I owe him a debt of gratitude for what I was able to accomplish, and of course, he went on to set all kinds of records in Arena League Football.

It wasn't my job until 1992 when we played Southwestern Louisiana in the opener in Knoxville. I completed all my passes, which, you should know, includes an interception. So, when one of my guys caught it, I was 7-of-8 passing. We played very well, and the fact that we had some incredible tailbacks to hand the ball to helped me get settled. We didn't have to throw the ball, but we played at a high level with the running game, the special teams, and defense, and won comfortably, 38–3.

The next week, we played Georgia, and that started my career, really, at Tennessee. It turned things around for us because they were the higher-ranked team [No. 14]. We were in the top 25, but not as highly ranked [No. 20].

It was an exciting game—a big game for me—because we went Between the Hedges in Athens, Georgia, and had an 80-yard drive at the end to win the game. We punched the ball in to win the football game 34–31, and it was huge for our program because it was an SEC game and it was on the road.

You can't help but think about the fourth-down play we converted on the drive. It was fourth-and-16 or -18, and they had called the play from the bench, which was "62 Mirer." I remember our working on that play in practice, and we weren't that successful with it, actually, during the week.

But Coach Cutcliffe, as usual, had their defense figured out, and that's the play they wanted. In the huddle, I told Craig Faulkner, one of the wideouts, to run off the safety deep, and I told Ronald Davis to get in the middle. Sure enough, they jumped Craig, and Ronald Davis came underneath and caught the ball. We got the first down and sustained the drive.

When we got close to the end zone, I ran the option play and we scored. That particular season, when we got inside the 20-yard line and were moving in for the score, we used the option, and I think I scored 11 touchdowns on the ground that season by the option.

It was very, very difficult for teams that had not seen the option to suddenly defend us because we would go from the five-wide receiver set to the option on the very next play. Teams had a difficult time with our offense because we were so balanced. We would go from five-wide to two tight ends, and I would run the option. They could not substitute quick enough. We had the type of wide receivers, like Cory Fleming, who was very big and could come in tight and block a bigger defensive player or split out wide. We were 50-50 run-to-pass, and it helped us perform at a high level inside the red zone.

We were setting school records for scoring in the red zone. I had run the veer offense, which is an option scheme, in high school, so I was familiar with it. We had the kind of versatile personnel at Tennessee that allowed us to do a lot of things, either spread it out or go to a traditional formation. I had some great running backs behind me with Charlie Garner, who had a good pro career, and Little Man Stewart, who also played in the NFL, and Aaron Hayden, who was another good back.

You could not ask for a better group of tailbacks than we had. Charlie and Little Man were able to split out and play as wide receivers. Just look at the

Heath Shuler, the Southeastern Conference Player of the Year in 1993, said the hardest decision he had to make was to skip the 1994 season and enter the NFL Draft. He was a first-round pick.

statistics from that season and you can just see the balance in our attack. Craig caught 31 passes, and Cory Fleming caught 40 passes. We had other receivers who were competing at a high level.

Then Florida came to Knoxville, and we beat them quite handily in the rain. It was another big win for us, 31–14. They were ranked No. 4, and we had climbed in the polls to No. 14, so that win really got some recognition for us.

The next year, I had a good game against Florida with five touchdown passes, but we lost down there. We didn't run what you would see a lot of today, the no-huddle offenses, but we ran at a high pace, and that's what gave Florida some trouble. You can't say enough about the front line, because I didn't get sacked much. Our guys were in great shape and kept things secure up front. They did not allow defenders in our backfield.

You can't forget your offensive line. Bubba Miller, Jeff Smith, Jason Layman, Leslie Ratliffe, and Kevin Mays. That was my offensive line. Kevin would have gone down as one of the best offensive linemen in the history of Tennessee football. In fact, Coach Fulmer said he was one of the best pure talents he had ever coached. He blew his knee out right before the NFL Combine, which is the only reason he did not have sensational pro career.

One of the things that was so great about David Cutcliffe, who was the quarterbacks coach and then offensive coordinator, was that he could take the personnel and craft something to their talents. Far too often, you will see offensive coordinators try and fit their personnel to a particular offense. Coach Cutcliffe saw that I made much better decisions in a faster-paced game. You didn't have that time to think, you just reacted.

There were plays that we made that David Cutcliffe actually set up during the week. There was one particular call against Alabama where, in practice the week before the game, he said if you see this defense, call this audible. I did that against Alabama, and Charlie Garner went 60 yards on a play called at the line.

David Cutcliffe's coaching went beyond the Xs and Os. He taught you so much about getting prepared and studying opponents. If you look at the players he has coached, like Peyton Manning, you can see how well-prepared his quarterbacks were at Tennessee.

Charlie Garner could go as fast right and left as straight ahead. He made moves in college that I only saw from a couple of players in the NFL. He was an amazing talent. Emmitt Smith of the Cowboys made those plays, but so did Charlie. He was as good a talent as I ever saw.

The Georgia game when I started for the first time was memorable, and so was the Boston College game in the Hall of Fame Bowl in Tampa when I threw three touchdown passes and ran for two. BC was ranked No. 16, and we were ranked No. 17, and we were peaking at the end of the season. We scored 38 points and just had a high-performing offense that day.

I think one of the most uncertain and uneasy times for me as a player was when they made the transition from Johnny Majors to Coach Fulmer. We all felt like we were caught in the middle. Johnny Majors was the coach who recruited us, and Phillip Fulmer was the offensive coordinator. We didn't want to do anything to hurt either of those coaches.

Maybe things could have been handled differently on campus with regard to that situation. I had a lot of respect for Coach Majors and know it was very hard on him. Phillip Fulmer was more of a players' coach, while Johnny Majors was a practice coach who preached fundamentals. What really impressed me with Coach Majors was that he was very adamant about special teams and how we performed in the kicking game.

One of the things that made it special to be a Tennessee Volunteer was the kind of help we got from players who were in the program ahead of us. Jerry Colquitt and I competed for the job, but we were roommates, too, and he helped me with the offense and with the reads. He was doing what he felt was right for the team. What was unfortunate was that Jerry waited and waited for his turn and then blew his knee out. Here he was, a fifth-year senior who finally got to start, and his season ended. We were in California playing against UCLA, and he blew his knee out. It was just the first or second series of the game. That was in 1994, the year after I left early, and I'm sure some people said, "Well, we could have used old Heath."

But I had my time there, and it was Todd Helton's turn. He got his opportunity to go in and play. We know what kind of athlete he is because he has gone out and played like a Hall of Famer in baseball.

Jerry was the starter, then it was Todd Helton, Branndon Stewart, and then Peyton Manning. It didn't take Peyton long to assert himself and become the starter in 1994, and the rest is history with that guy.

I turned pro after my junior year, but my mom did not want me to go. She wanted me to stay in school. I went back and I have my diploma up in the office here. Mom didn't care what happened on the gridiron; she wanted that sheepskin, and I had to promise her I would go back. Leaving Tennessee was the most difficult decision I ever had to make. There was unfinished business because we didn't win a national title, and I was leaving my friends behind.

In the back of my mind, though, was a childhood dream, since the time I could hold a football, to play in the NFL. To be able to capture that dream, well, I couldn't wait. I had to seize the moment. I was rated the top quarterback in college, and it was likely I would go in the first three picks. I ended up going with the third pick overall to the Redskins.

Two weeks ago [November 2007], I took my son, Navy, down on the field. That was an incredible feeling to take him down and see the team run out on the field. The memories came back at me, and I realized how special and unique a feeling it was to play for the Big Orange and wear that jersey. When you go back, you feel what it's like all over again, and you think about what it means to be a Vol.

Heath Shuler was the SEC Player of the Year in 1993 when he completed 65 percent of his passes and threw for 25 touchdowns with just eight interceptions. His 2,353 yards passing was the second-highest total in school history. Shuler was the runner-up in the Heisman Trophy voting and first-team All-SEC. He is seventh overall in school passing yards with 4,088 yards, and his career completion percentage of 61.6 percent ranks in the top five all-time. Shuler played in the NFL for the Washington Redskins and New Orleans Saints from 1994 to 1998. He is currently a member of U.S. Congress as the representative from the 11th district of North Carolina.

JOEY KENT
WIDE RECEIVER
1993–1996

I DIDN'T COME INTO THE PROGRAM thinking I could be the all-time leading receiver. No way. Even now, with the most receptions in the history of the program, I do not consider myself the best receiver in the history of the program. There are so many great receivers who had more talent. At least I can be in the argument, and that's enough. It's just an overwhelming honor to be in the record book at a place like Tennessee.

There were a couple of years there in the early '90s, maybe 1991 and 1992, where Tennessee had lost a little bit of its notoriety as Wide Receiver U. Carl Pickens had left and he was a great one, and there was a lag in there. Then, in my junior year, 1995, we put up some amazing numbers, it wasn't just me, it was Peerless Price and Marcus Nash. The numbers we put up with Peyton Manning had not been achieved in the history of the program, and we were back to being Wide Receiver U.

I remember the summer before my junior year, the receivers coach, Pat Watson, called me in and wanted to know what my goals were for the season. I looked over the media guide and what some of the records were and the reception record was in the fifties. I figured if I caught six or seven balls a game, I could have an 80-catch season. I told my receivers coach that at the time, and he told me these numbers have never been put up before. It was also going to be hard to do because Peerless and Marcus were also very good receivers.

Joey Kent, Peyton Manning's favorite receiver at Tennessee, led the Vols in receiving in 1994, 1995, and 1996, was named All-SEC in 1995 and 1996, and is UT's all-time leading receiver.

I didn't catch 80 balls that year, but I think I was at 68 or 69. I think going in and telling the coach that I could get to 80 balls a year was showing him that I was willing to push myself to another level. We had the best quarterback in the country, so why couldn't I have a big year? As a group, we put up some really good numbers.

I think Peyton liked my leadership capabilities. I was actually two years older than him, but I redshirted one year, so when I was a senior, he was a junior. I was considered a leader of the receiving corps. He knew I was going to be at the right place at the right time and that I would work with the younger receivers in the passing game. That helped build our relationship.

We played together in 1994, 1995, and 1996, and over those three years our favorite route was going over the middle. We had a route called "Meir." I don't know why they called it that. That was our bread and butter. It was a 14-to-15-yard crossing route where I would run across the middle and the guy opposite me ran a post pattern to clear out the middle of the field. It was a great route for us and a favorite call of Coach Cutcliffe, especially on third down. A lot of teams knew what was coming but still could not stop it.

We had alternate versions of the route, too, where we could change it up if defenses tried to cheat on us. We could run an option route off it, or Peyton could dump it off to the running back. That was our favorite route in the 1995 and 1996 seasons.

The game I remember most was the Alabama game in 1995, which we won 41–14. I am from Huntsville, Alabama, so it was especially big for me because Alabama had beaten Tennessee seven or eight straight times. The Florida-Tennessee game has taken over as the big game in a lot of people's eyes, but that Alabama-Tennessee game is still the biggest to me.

As a senior in high school, Alabama and Auburn did not recruit me very much, so I had extra incentive. My senior season in high school, our starting quarterback got hurt, so I had to play six games as the quarterback and did not get much attention as a wide receiver, which was my primary position. My receiver stats were very low, so Alabama recruited me as a safety; they did not see me as a receiver. Auburn started to recruit me only after Alabama started to recruit me.

So you can see how the Alabama game was such a big deal to me. I had a lot of family and friends there, and then I scored on the first play of the game, an 80-yard touchdown pass from Peyton.

People still come up to me and say, "Joey, we remember that game and that catch, because we finally beat Alabama. It was like it happened last week." I have listened to so many stories from people telling me they were just sitting down to watch the game, or where they watching the game, or people who were still trying to get into the game when I made that catch. I never get tired of hearing about it because of what it meant to the program and what it meant to me.

The best part is being able to go back home to Alabama with that little memory right there. We turned things around in the rivalry with that win, and Tennessee started to get the best of them after that. They did not beat Tennessee again until 2002.

That's what it means to be a Vol, because you never know when there is going to be one of the big plays that it's going to be remembered through the years. You never know when that one play will make somebody known in Tennessee football history for the rest of his life, like it did for me. The emotion is so strong around the program, these big plays are not easily forgotten.

I went into that game hoping it was going to be a game to be remembered. Peyton and I talked about it and how much it would mean for Tennessee to beat Alabama again. I told him I wanted to get involved in the game early.

In some previous games that season, I was involved in the second half, but this was too big a game for the university and for me, and I wanted to be involved right away. We talked about what kind of coverage they were going to be in at the first snap, and when we came to the line for the snap, we sort of looked at each other and said, we have a shot at something here.

It was a perfect play. We knew from running that play over and over during the summer and practicing what was going to happen. It was a cover-3 defense, and I was the slot guy. I don't think they were looking for me in the slot because Marcus Nash was usually in the slot.

When it was cover-3, I tried to cut the distance between the corner on the outside and the safety playing in the middle. Peyton just had to get the ball over the linebacker. It is not a deep route, but when I caught it, the safety overran it, and I took off. It was the biggest play of my Tennessee career. I didn't think about it like that at the time because I was just a 19-year-old kid, but when I look back at it, it was huge for me. This was a seven-year deal where we had lost to those guys. As time passes, I understand how big that was for the program. If I think about it, it was huge then. I was a little naïve in knowing the scope and scale of the program at the time. The tradition is huge, and the people who have come before me are amazing. It is a tremendous honor to have played there, and there are so many friendships I made there that I still have today. I root for Peyton every Sunday and am a Colts fan just because of him. He had some amazing ability and helped me make a lot of plays. It wasn't just his passing ability but his leadership and being a good guy that I also appreciated.

It is a special feeling to hold those receiving records, knowing all the receivers who came before me and after me. It is an honor when I think about guys like Tim McGee and Willie Gault and Alvin Harper and the rest. Being in the company of great players, that's what it means to be a Vol.

Joey Kent is Tennessee's all-time leading receiver with 183 catches from 1993 to 1996. Kent also holds the record with the most touchdown catches in a career with 25 and the most 100-yard receiving games with 15. He was All-SEC in 1995 and 1996. Kent lives in Nashville and is a pharmaceutical rep.

PEYTON MANNING

QUARTERBACK

1994–1997

Playing football at Tennessee was one of the best things that ever happened to me, and I'm always proud to say I played there. I feel I had a chance to play at one of the great places ever in college football, and I'll never forget it.

One of the things I will remember most is all the pageantry in Knoxville for the home games all four years I played. To start that many games in front of that crowd, I will always consider it an honor and a privilege.

It just wasn't the athletic side of it. It was also the social and academic side. That had a lot to do with my staying all four years. I could have left early following my junior season, but as I said, it was a privilege to play there, and that's why I wanted to stay for my entire career.

Just start with all the people who came from every corner of the state—Middle Tennessee, East Tennessee, and West Tennessee—to watch games. How could you not want to be part of that if you had one more season?

They came by boat. They came by car. It wasn't even an option for so many people about what to do on Saturday. You watched Tennessee football. To have that many people come watch you play football and invest so much in the program is truly a special experience.

The Tennessee fans were extremely consistent in supporting the team, and that had a lot to do with the great experience I had there. I think a lot of

Peyton Manning's legacy at Tennessee is of a player who produced points and victories, but also put in the extra time on the practice field.

players who played for Tennessee will tell you that they appreciated the support and backing of the fans during their careers.

I felt lucky to have Coach Fulmer and Coach Cutcliffe to be my coaches while I was there. I'm proud of the fact I still have a close relationship with my college football coach, and we have stayed close these years since I left. Coach Fulmer and I try and visit with each other when we can.

What makes it special between Coach Fulmer and me is that he and I were pretty much starting off together at Tennessee. I was the quarterback in just his second season as head coach. He was in the early part of his head coaching career, and I was just starting my college football career, and it was kind of fun to grow with him.

It was great to get Tennessee football established again as one of the dominant college football programs in the country. He worked very hard, and he was the guy who would go in the trenches with us to get things done and win games.

Coach Cutcliffe had a big influence on my career because he always stayed on top of my fundamentals and made me pay attention to details. I feel fortunate that I had both of them coaching me in college because they had a lot to do with my development as a football player.

I think the thing I was most proud of accomplishing during my career was the amount of games I was able to play for Tennessee. I never missed a start, never missed a game, and never missed a play because of an injury. If I ever came out of the game, it was because we were ahead and they wanted to give the backup a chance.

The one thing that was big in my book was being accountable to my teammates, because I knew they were going to be out there on the field for me and the team. It was a big deal to me to stay out on the field and play because I knew there were others out there playing hurt and being accountable.

I think Joey Kent, who was one of my wide receivers, had a lot to do with my being successful. At every level I have played, there was always that receiver I connected with, and it didn't take long to get things down pat, as far as running routes and completing passes. There is a chemistry. In high school, it was my older brother, Cooper. In the NFL, it is Marvin Harrison. In college, it was Joey Kent.

Joey was one of the older receivers when I got there. He was a year ahead of me and the guy I leaned on heavily. Joey and I just had the timing down, and I knew when he was coming out of breaks and when I had to throw it. There are some guys you play with where you cannot get the timing down, and it just does not click. With Joey and me, we got the timing down; it didn't take long at all when we started working together.

I was there the summer before my freshman season in 1994, and even though I was not the starter, Joey and I got a lot of repetitions in before actual practices started. He was a great route runner and had dependable hands. I always felt like I knew where he was going to be. That's one of the things you want in a receiver; that consistency in running routes and catching the ball.

When I think back about memorable moments in Tennessee, I always think about the firsts, the first time something happens, the first time I started, things like that.

I remember the first time I went in the huddle for Tennessee. It was against UCLA, and I went in, handed the ball off three times, and then came out. The starter, Jerry Colquitt, had been hurt, and the backup, Todd Helton, was injured, so I got to go in. I wasn't in very long, and I didn't throw a pass, but I still remember the first time going in as the quarterback for the University of Tennessee. That was a special moment.

The other game I remember was against Mississippi State when Todd Helton was hurt and I went in the game, handed off twice, and on the third snap threw a 76-yard touchdown pass to Kendrick Jones. That's something you keep with you. That is when I became a starter for Tennessee.

213

I think the other big game was beating Auburn for the conference championship in Atlanta, 30–29, my senior season in 1997. That was a big win for our program and my last SEC game. To win the SEC championship was special for the program.

I think one of the more memorable games was beating Alabama my sophomore season in 1995. That was big because a lot of juniors and seniors, who had never beaten Alabama, just had a big thrill in their eyes. We won in Birmingham, and the older guys in the program who had lost to them the year before and tied them the season before that were extremely excited to get that win.

The first play of the game set the whole tone because it was an 80-yard touchdown pass to Joey Kent. We were not necessarily trying to score on that play; he just caught the ball in the right seam of that defense, made a move, and it was off to the races.

We were picking a side of the field to go to on the pre-snap, saw the defense line up a certain way, and thought we had a shot at something, maybe not a touchdown, but a play for a big gain. We scored and went on to a big win. Being an Alabama guy, it was a great day for Joey.

The other game I remember was when we played my dad's school, Ole Miss. There was a lot of media hoopla, and part of it was just trying to break it down so I could play the game and not get caught up in that. We played down in Memphis in one game, and I just tried to take the emotional side out of it and concentrate on its being Tennessee versus Ole Miss, as opposed to Peyton Manning versus his dad's alma mater.

Eli and I both benefited and learned a lot from David Cutcliffe [who went on to coach Eli Manning at Ole Miss] because he had such a great way of communicating with players. He was a very detail-oriented guy who went over things time and time again. One of the things I really liked about him is that he is a high-energy guy who is very excited about life, and it rubs off on you.

College pride with some NFL guys is very important. When Tennessee is playing a rival like Georgia, you can see that pride in guys from those respective schools. I'm always proud to represent the university, and it's fun to run into guys who also played for Tennessee. Those are usually the guys you talk with after games. You certainly have that bond.

I try and get back to Knoxville as much as I can in the offseason. I enjoy watching the basketball there, and also working out with the team. Every off-season since I've been in the NFL, I have tried to go back for a week and work with the quarterbacks and receivers. I stay a week and see Coach Fulmer, visit with old friends, and try to help the players who have followed me in the program. I try and do that every June.

The decision to come back for my fourth year was extremely difficult and one of the toughest decisions in my life. I had my degree, and I could've been a high draft pick, and there were a lot of things to weigh. It was a nerve-racking decision, but I woke up one morning and knew what I wanted to do, which was to stay in school one more year and finish my career. Coach Fulmer, I remember, was very excited when I shared that with him.

A lot of that decision to come back had to do with the way people treated me while I was at Tennessee. That was a big part of my decision. I was treated so well there, and people were so supportive of the program, it helped me decide to come back. There were some lifelong memories.

College football is special, it is one of the great institutions we have. When you go through the recruiting process and stay in school four years, you go from a boy to a man. You have dinner with your offensive linemen, which was always special, and live with these guys and share a lot with them. In the pros, guys go home to their families, and it is not anything like being in college. It is four years I will always cherish.

If there was one thing I wanted to pass on to Tee Martin, who led Tennessee to a national championship the year after I left, it was work ethic in practice. He was always working hard in practice and had a sense of urgency. That's what I was so impressed with about him; he really worked hard in practice to get better so he was ready when it was his turn to start. I think you have an obligation as an older player to help the younger players, and the best thing to do is to lead by example.

I like to stay involved in the school with the Peyton Manning Scholarship Award, which has had nine winners. It's given to a high school student who excels in sports and academics, and who also gives back to the community with service. There are students who have won, and I keep up with all of them to see how they are doing. They write me letters, and I try and stay in touch.

215

I tell people who have a checklist of things they want to do in life that one of the things they have to do is see a Tennessee home game in Knoxville. Some of them want to see the Yankees and Red Sox in Fenway Park, or something like that. But right up there is the pageantry and the excitement around a game at Neyland Stadium. When they finally go to a game at Tennessee, they always come back to me and say it was one of the best experiences they have ever had.

Peyton Manning is the all-time career leader in passing yards at Tennessee with 11,201. He is the all-time leader in touchdown passes (89) and completions (863). Manning was an All-American and All-SEC in 1997, as well as being named 1997 SEC Player of the Year. The Birmingham Touchdown Club named him the Outstanding Senior in the SEC in 1997. He was awarded an NCAA Post-Graduate Scholarship Award in 1997. In his 10-year NFL career with the Indianapolis Colts, he has made All-Pro six times. In 2007, Manning led the Colts to victory over the Chicago Bears in Super Bowl XLI.

JEFF HALL

KICKER

1995–1998

ONE OF THE KEY THINGS FOR ME and my success at Tennessee was that Coach Fulmer truly made special teams one-third of the game. It was offense, defense, special teams. I had a full-time snapper and a full-time holder. What did that mean? In four years, we had one mishandled ball. That's all.

Isn't that amazing? I mean this is in the Peyton Manning era and the national championship season when we had all kinds of scoring chances, and we had only one breakdown.

My approach to kicking was, once Monday rolled around, that is when the preparation began. The physical preparation was taken care of, and it was a pretty level playing field in that regard. It was the mental preparation where there was separation between kickers in the SEC.

So I started preparing myself mentally on Monday. The first thing is, you know what to expect, that the crowd is going to be loud, and wherever you play is going to be a packed stadium with 80,000 to 100,000 people. So when you go out for a kick, you block everything out; don't think about anything and let muscle memory and instinct take control.

Every night, Monday through Friday night, I thought about the game. I had a very good mental-preparation coach, Craig Wrisberg. Coach Fulmer told me to go see him, and he taught me how to prepare myself mentally for the game. He would have me visualize what it would look like standing on the

Jeff Hall is Tennessee's all-time leading scorer.

side, what it felt like after we just scored a touchdown, and what it would look like or what I would hear when Coach Fulmer would call for the extra point.

Craig had me thinking about what I would see as I ran out onto the field. He had me visualizing everything, from taking my steps back, to kicking the ball, to running off the field after I made the kick and getting ready for the kickoff. I tried to play through all kinds of different scenarios every night, as I lay in bed trying to fall asleep. By the time I got to Saturday, I had already visualized all these different scenarios.

Mentally, I was as prepared as anyone, and it helped me start for four years. The big thing was knowing how to prepare myself mentally, and it made a big difference in my career. Once again, it also made the difference that Coach Fulmer made special teams one-third of the game and placed an emphasis on it.

My snapper my freshman and sophomore years was Mark Ingram, and my holder was Jason Price. My junior and senior years, the long snapper was Kevin Gregory, and the holder was Benson Scott, who is the son of Bobby Scott, the former quarterback. Among the four of them, there was one time we had a problem with a hold. That was the only time we had a mistake, and we're talking about almost 300 place-kicks.

The biggest kick for me personally was the Georgia game in 1995. It was the game-winning field goal in Knoxville.

In the grand scheme of things, for the fans and for the university and my teammates, it was probably the Florida game in 1998 that broke the losing streak against the Gators. We beat them in overtime, 20–17, and went on to win the national title. It was a 41-yard field goal.

I mentioned the one against Georgia being important for me because it was the second game of my college career, and we won 30–27. It really laid a foundation for me personally and showed me what I needed to do to succeed on that level.

I had just one game under my belt going into that game with Georgia, which was also my first SEC game, so that added to the pressure. It was the first time playing on television, and it was against a very good Georgia team that had Robert Edwards. The talent on both sides was fairly similar, and the game went back and forth. We had Peyton Manning going up against Mike Bobo and Robert Edwards. You just never know how you are going to react in that kind of situation. Looking back at the tape, it wasn't my best technique, but I made the kick and went from there.

I was nervous on every kick I went out for, whether it was an extra point, field goal, or kickoff. That is just my mentality, my make-up. It probably took a few years off my life because it's just how I am geared. When you get to game-time, there is nothing else, you have to play, and you have to be ready, so you make the most of every opportunity in practice and make sure you are in the weight room.

How did I end up in Tennessee? I committed December of my junior year. I took an official visit to Knoxville and I knew God intended for me to go to Tennessee. I started 50 games there, and that's where I was supposed to go all along.

Maryland really, really, wanted me. The first day you could get phone calls from the recruiters, I got nine or 10. I had some big kicks in my high school career, including one of 62 yards my sophomore year and another my junior year, and that helped me get on the radar with some big programs early on.

Alabama, Notre Dame, and Clemson were very interested, but I never got to the point where I was serious with anyone besides Tennessee. I can still remember telling my dad after I went to see a game in Tuscaloosa that it did not feel like home. Knoxville was where I was supposed to be.

Coach Fulmer and I had a great working relationship. One of the best things he did for me in my career was in the spring of 1995 when we talked about expectations. Coach Fulmer told me, "Jeff, as much as I love your being from Winchester and my going to school with your folks, if you are not the best, you are not going to play."

His reputation was on the line because I was from his hometown, and neither of us wanted people to think that I was only kicking because I was from his hometown and he went to school with my parents. It was one of the best things he could have ever done. Every year going in to the season, I made sure I was the best, and I was the best. No one was going to push me for that job.

After we won the SEC championship in my junior year and then the national championship in my senior year, I remember Coach Fulmer telling us it would not hit us until many years down the road, what we accomplished for the program. I just turned 31, and my business is here in Knoxville, my relationships are here. Looking back now, it is very important to know that I was involved in the Tennessee football tradition and that, while I had a small part, I was on teams that won the SEC championship and the national championship.

I was a captain on a national championship team and a team leader, which is special. Going over there to watch games still gives me chills. I was a legitimate part of the program. That was a blessing and an honor that I will never be able to match.

I got drafted by Washington in the sixth round of the NFL Draft in 1999, went to camp, and could not have kicked the ball into the ocean if I was standing on the beach. It was one of the hardest experiences I have ever had. I was doing everything I had done before, but nothing was falling for me. It was hard.

The fact I am the all-time leading scorer at Tennessee is testimony to the guys I played for. We had great receivers and running backs, and maybe the greatest quarterback to ever play the game, Peyton Manning. No one was more committed, and no one worked harder; we all saw it, and now so many other people are starting to see it because he won a Super Bowl. We scored a lot of touchdowns or got in position to kick field goals, so I was able to score and score. Now, when you factor in the defenses we had that took away the ball and gave the offense field position or more possessions, you understand how I was able to be the all-time leading scorer.

Of all the football players I played with—past, present, future, whatever—Al Wilson was my all-time favorite. You could take Al and put him in any group of people, from any background, and he would be able to lead any group of guys with his intensity and his passion and his work ethic. He just had that look. He was a hard worker, and he was that warrior who everybody respected. His motor never stopped.

Peyton left a legacy at UT that stayed around a while. When he was here—we were in the same recruiting class—he would organize these optional workouts, and the whole team was out there. He would trash-talk with defensive backs and the linebackers and tell them to bring it on, and the receivers and backs were going to be out there running routes and seeing if anybody could stop his guys.

Peyton left that legacy for Tee Martin and other quarterbacks to follow. What he started stuck around for a few years; it did not just leave with him when he went to the NFL. I think he was a huge part in our winning the national championship in 1998, even though his last year was 1997. His mentality and his work ethic were so good, and that attitude just stuck around the program.

What is special about Tennessee is that there have been players like Peyton Manning, who have come through the program over these many years and contributed to the legacy of Tennessee football and left their stamp. He was special, but this program has had some other special players who hand down something from era to era.

Jeff Hall is Tennessee's all-time leading scorer with 371 points. He is one of just four Vols ever to be named All-SEC in three seasons (1995, 1996, 1998). Hall was on the All-SEC Academic Honor Roll for four seasons at Tennessee. He is a money manager in Knoxville.

TEE MARTIN

QUARTERBACK

1996–1999

WE WON A LOT OF CLOSE GAMES in 1998 and had a chance to play for and win the national championship. Here's why.

Phillip Fulmer, the head coach, made sure he put us in game situations during practice. There were times when practice was harder than the games, and the staff was committed to that philosophy.

Once Peyton Manning and some of those seniors from 1997 left, Phillip thought it was even more important to make practices harder to get us ready for big games. We challenged each other more and made it a tough time. A lot of us were young—I was a first-year starter—and we needed to get ready. I left the practices sometimes feeling worse than I did after a game.

I remember the practices where Phillip would put in a blitz of the team we were going to play that Saturday and not tell me it was coming. Everybody had to know their role against that blitz and be prepared. It made practice like a game. They threw stuff at us all the time, and if we got it done, we got it done. If we didn't, we worked at it again in a game-type environment.

If you ask me, we made plays on offense because of the O-line. That was a close-knit group that protected well and knew their assignments. I spent a lot of time in the summer throwing with the wide receivers, but when the season started, there was a lot of communication between the quarterback and the offensive line, and we built a trust in each other.

Tee Martin led the Vols to a perfect season in 1998. He was also All-SEC in 1999 and is sixth all-time at Tennessee in passing yards.

We went through a 13-game season, and they gave up just eight sacks—
two of which were me running out of bounds. That is just amazing that they
would allow the other team to sack me just six times. I was really close to
those guys, Chad Clifton, Mercedes Hamilton, Spencer Riley, Cosey Coleman, Jarvis Reado. They were spectacular that season.

They did not panic a whole lot. I would see some blitzes, and they
wouldn't worry, they would pick it up. It got so I could drop back and not
panic and make plays. They were awesome people in the trenches. They
stayed healthy for the most part, but even if they were injured, they played.

The fact the offensive line held things together was big for us because early
in the season we lost Jamal Lewis to an injury, and Coach was trying to figure out who was going to be the next leader, the next big-time running back.
Well, we had some leaders, it was the offensive line. We didn't want to have
it on one person, like me, because I was young and trying to figure things
out. We had it on a group of guys, that offensive line.

That first game of the season against Syracuse, we had to play against
Donovan McNabb. It was a close game, but it wouldn't have been that close
if I had not missed two open receivers, which cost us two touchdowns. That
was my first game as a starter, and it took me two quarters to get settled
down and play better. Donovan would make a play, and I would just try to
keep us in the game and not make mistakes. That's what drove me, not making mistakes and ruining things for our team.

By the time the Arkansas game came around later in that 1998 season, I
was ready for a lot of situations. That game almost cost us the national championship, but we held it together and pulled it out. We looked up in the first
quarter, and we were down 14–0, and we had just touched the ball once. We
needed to stay on the field, but they had done a good job of holding on to
the ball and finishing drives.

We got a touchdown just before halftime on a deep ball to Peerless Price.
We felt like we could beat them all day throwing the ball deep because they
had focused on stopping our running game, which at the time was the best
way to stop us. We went into halftime and decided to be as aggressive as we
could with the run game and try to take shots with the passing game.

I remember late in the game, we were down and went for it on fourth and
10. The pass to Peerless was batted down, and it looked like it was over for us.
Sometimes in those situations, you untie your shoes and take your shoulder

pads off, but for some reason, I thought we would get the ball back and get one more chance at it.

I had a pretty good idea that, if we could get the ball back, I knew Arkansas's coverages, and we could make some plays. Then they fumbled on the 42-yard line, and we drove the rest of the way. That was the first week we were No. 1. We didn't want to give it up, so we just used that second chance. I don't think we threw a pass at all that winning drive. We just handed it to Travis Henry, and he went with it.

That game scared us, shocked us, and woke us up. We had been very confident, but after that game we took the rest of the teams a lot more seriously. We beat Arkansas 28–24 and then went after the next three teams on the schedule, beat them, and got into the national championship game.

My favorite play that season was when "Cut" [David Cutcliffe] would let me choose the play. I never wanted to tell him what to run, because you don't want to come off as arrogant, but I think they gave me the kiddie package at the start of the season. I would get bored during games because, being around Peyton, you wanted more of a mental challenge.

Eventually, Coach Cut would let me choose some plays, and I felt like I was part of the game and not there just to manage.

I think it was after Jamal got hurt that Cut told me he wanted to see what I had, that he wanted to see me play my best and put everything to use. It was the South Carolina game when everything came together for me. I was able to be a little more wide open with the offense, and the offensive line protected me. My confidence went through the roof.

Coach Cutcliffe and I started to think a lot alike. The whole idea was not to be a play behind. I had an option to keep the ball on the ground or pass it. I even had the option of what pass to throw in some situations. He gave the formation and the play, and I could change it if I had to.

Coach Cutcliffe knew what I understood about the offense; he knew what I knew and what my capabilities were at that point in the season. He gave us a test every week, and he was a phenomenal teacher. He was great at preparation. When game day was there, he knew he did not have to worry about his quarterback on the field in terms of decision-making. Once he could trust me with making good decisions, he opened up the offense to me.

We finished off a great season with the win over Florida State in the national championship game, 23–16. I don't even remember the two days before the game. I just had tunnel vision, focusing on how to beat Florida State. It was a special game for me in a way because I grew up a Florida State fan. I am from Mobile, which is in that area where a lot of FSU people live. Florida State, though, wanted me to be a wide receiver, and I wanted to be a quarterback.

A big play in the national championship game was the deep ball to Peerless Price in the fourth quarter for 78 yards. They had us backed up, and what Florida State likes to do when they have you backed up is to blitz and use single-coverage on the outside. Coach Randy Sanders said we were going to take a shot at them if that happened, and we scored. We thought that, if Peerless was one-on-one with anyone in the country, we would score. I didn't see the completion; I took a big hit on their blitz. As soon as I threw it, I was hit and down, but I heard the crowd and knew we got them.

That game was the epitome of having to forget the last play and move on to the next. If you didn't, you were in trouble. The teams were so evenly matched, you couldn't get down when you made mistakes—both sides made mistakes. I made mistakes.

Normally, I could tell you play by play about a game, but not the game with Florida State. We had to think about the play we were in and not look back or look forward, because any emotional drop could hurt us.

225

We had two chances where a touchdown pass was dropped and I threw an interception. If I had wanted to chew somebody out, or they wanted to chew me out, that would have been a waste of time in a game like that.

It meant a whole lot to win a national title. I did not grow up on Tennessee football. I am from Alabama. My decision to go to Tennessee was based on that old decision of going to the place that best fits you. Tennessee was going to let me be a quarterback; Florida State wanted me to be receiver.

I'm glad I came back to Tennessee and experienced games like Syracuse and then helped Tennessee win a national championship. When Peyton announced he was coming back for his senior season in 1997, I contemplated transferring. I didn't know if I could sit on the bench again because I was just so hungry to play.

There was a period then when I had decided to transfer. It was nothing against Tennessee, nothing against anybody, I just wanted to play badly. It was best for Tennessee and the program for Peyton to come back. He was a great quarterback; I didn't hold it against him.

My first plan was to redshirt and then try to have three seasons remaining, but I think the team needed me to be the backup in case Peyton got hurt. I took that second year with Peyton pretty much to learn and set the stage for being a starter. I knew there were some very good recruiting classes that had come in, and I knew there were going to be some very good players left in the program when he left, so I didn't want to mess up that chemistry.

I guess people can say he would have wanted to trade places with me—the stats for my national championship ring—but I think that Super Bowl ring he has looks pretty good, too.

Peyton taught me a lot of little things that I needed to know to be a quarterback. I tried not to bother him too much my freshman year, just ask questions when I could. My second year, he had grown to respect me. We were roommates on the road, so we talked about football a lot. My respect for him grew as player and a person. I got to see a side of him a lot of people did not see.

It was a great decision because I came to appreciate the program and all the people connected to the Orange who helped me. We had crowds there to support us, and I grew to love wearing the orange and white and the players who had built the program to where it was before I got there.

There are a lot of awesome places to play—Ohio State, Penn State, Michigan—but I don't think any of those places compare to having the Vol Walk, the checkerboard end zone, the Vol Navy, 109,000 people in the stands. It was great to be part of history and not just being on a team that came and went, but a team that went down in the history book.

Tee Martin was named All-SEC quarterback in 1999. He is sixth all-time in passing yards with 4,592. Martin coached briefly at Morehouse in Atlanta and was the passing game coordinator. He is currently a director of Playmakers Sports in Atlanta, which tutors high school athletes and aids in their transition to college.

DEON GRANT

SAFETY

1997–1999

WHEN YOU LOOK AT THAT national championship team in 1998, we had weapons all over the field, from running back, to quarterback, to linebackers, to secondary. We also had a mentality that we were not going to stop until the last second of the game. So, if another team eased up or made a mistake, we took advantage of it and won the game.

That was my sophomore year at Tennessee, and you saw all the excitement building around town as we kept winning close games. The Orange was especially big that year, and you could sense it was one of the top programs in the country. There was a lot of attention on us because we were winning, and winning exciting games.

The first game of the season helped set the tone for winning that title. We played Syracuse, and they had Donovan McNabb and a very good offense. Donovan brought his A-game that day and put up a lot of points. Both teams made mistakes, so it ended up being a high-scoring game.

They were the team that slipped up in the fourth quarter and allowed us to come down and kick the winning field goal. It was a great feeling to beat a team like Syracuse and Donovan in the first game of the season. That gave us a lot of confidence.

The next week we played Florida, and that was an even bigger game because we beat them in overtime in Knoxville. They were considered one of the best teams in the SEC and ranked No. 2 in the nation. That gave us even more confidence.

That was a hard-hitting game, and one of the reasons I came to Tennessee was to beat the Gators. We had it in our mind that we were going to stop this Florida-Tennessee thing—this idea that Florida had our number and was the better program.

Jamal Lewis was a big-time running back out of Douglass in Atlanta, and he and I got together one day during the recruiting process and decided we wanted to go to Tennessee to beat Florida. We could have done the same thing with our home state team, Georgia, but we liked Tennessee, and the Orange were having trouble with the Gators, too, so we picked UT.

I was the number-one-rated safety in the country coming out of high school in Augusta, and we had beaten Florida in the Georgia-Florida High School Football All-Star Game. Jamal and I got together and said, "Let's start something up there in Tennessee against these Gators. Let's take care of Florida once and for all."

People in Georgia were mad at me, Jamal, and Cosey Coleman because we were all from Georgia and were very highly rated players. Tennessee had a very good recruiter, Coach Rodney Garner, and another coach, Kevin Ramsey, and they got me up there to Knoxville. They said the right things that my mother and I needed to hear, and I signed. They had a good engineering program, which is what I wanted to go to school for, plus they have a tradition of getting one defensive back into the NFL every year.

A big thing, though, was getting a chance to beat the Gators. They beat us in Gainesville my freshman year when I played special teams and some nickel back. That was Peyton Manning's last year at Tennessee, and it was a hard game for us to lose because we thought we had a good team.

That next season, 1998, we got them. We stopped them in overtime, and came down and kicked the winning field goal.

The Florida game was my coming-out game. I didn't start my freshman year, so people really didn't know me on the college level. So the Florida game was my second game as a starter, as a player Tennessee was really counting on, and that was the game where I made a one-handed interception in the middle of the field.

If I hadn't made that play, it would have been a touchdown for Florida, and they would have beaten us. The receiver was wide open, and I just read the quarterback and came across the field to make the play.

Defensive back
Deon Grant had 14
interceptions in
three seasons
(1997–1999).

After the win over Florida, we beat Houston pretty good and then beat Auburn. We went down to Georgia, my home state, and beat the Bulldogs. They were the home team, but it wasn't very close, 22–3.

We had some close games that season, but we also showed how much talent we had by dominating some teams. We beat Alabama by 17 points, and we beat South Carolina by 35 points.

We had another great game in Knoxville against Arkansas, where we had to make one big play after another. They were winning the game late, and it didn't look good for us because they had the ball. It was raining, and they looked like they had control of us. If they had kept control of the ball, that would have been the game, our title shot probably would have been over.

I remember being up near the line of scrimmage, ready to blitz to try and make something happen. Billy Ratliff, one of our defensive tackles, then made the play of the game. He pushed the Arkansas center so hard on the snap, the center fell back into the quarterback, and the quarterback tripped over the center. He fell to the ground and fumbled [with 1 minute, 43 seconds left to play].

We recovered the football and scored the winning points. That Tennessee team was like that. We made plays when we had to make plays, all season long. We won the close games because we didn't quit. If we got the ball in our offense's hands, they did what they had to do that season to score points and seal the deal.

I remember how hard that Arkansas game was for us. That was the game where I blocked a field goal to keep us close.

We were a great team. All you had to do was look at the roster and see all the NFL players we had—Peerless Price, Chad Clifton, Jamal Lewis, Travis Henry, Travis Stephens, Al Wilson, Raynoch Thompson, Darwin Walker, Dwayne Goodrich, and me. That's a lot of good players.

We won the SEC championship, were undefeated, and were set to play Florida State for the national championship. Once again, it was us against Florida guys in a big game, but this time it was FSU, not the Gators. Those Florida boys are real cocky, and they talk a lot.

Peter Warrick was a wide receiver for Florida State, one of the best in the country, and he and I went at it pretty good that week, talking back and forth through the media. We had competitions going on at this sports place, games and things like that—we went at it there, too. We went at back and forth on TV all week.

Peter was saying all kinds of stuff, like nobody could stop him but his momma. I went back at them, saying we're not the type that does a lot of talk in the media, so we'll prove it on the field. We did a lot jaw-chappin' that week. I can say all this now because Peter Warrick and I have become good friends.

We did what we had to do and won the game 23–16. I remember a lot of plays from that Florida State game, especially one: I told Dwayne Goodrich before one play that they were going to run a curl to Peter Warrick, and to sit on it, and I would cover over the top. Dwayne picked it off and took it right to the end zone. It was a 54-yard touchdown return, and we led 14–0.

Peerless Price was big on offense for us in that game. He caught a long pass [78 yards] from Tee Martin for a touchdown and had a strong game overall.

Once we had the lead, we used our running game and shut down their running game. I couldn't even tell you if it was hot or cold in Arizona that night. We were so amped up, we didn't notice.

The next season, 1999, I thought I had a great year. I intercepted something like nine passes, which led the country. They told me "D, you have to be the leader back there." That was because Al Wilson was gone to the NFL, and they left it in my hands. I was able to do a lot of freelancing, making plays all over the field. They trusted me to try and make plays, and not be caught out of position.

I had a two-pick game, a three-pick game. I returned an interception for a touchdown. I played receiver also. We beat Georgia badly that year, too. We lost some close games that year, though, the kind of games we won the year before. All three games we lost were very close.

I haven't had a lot of chances to go back up there because of my NFL career. My first year out of college, after I broke my hip, I was up there, but not much lately.

One of the reasons I went to Tennessee was that I thought I could have a big career in the NFL, and I am having a big career. I still bleed that orange, too. Once you bleed that orange, it stays with you no matter how good the team is, no matter how sorry the team is. That goes for the basketball teams, the baseball teams, the tennis teams, soccer, whatever the case may be. I root for them all.

The thing you remember most is running through that T before the games. That was really big. We won an NFC championship when I was at Carolina, but there was something special about winning a national title wearing the orange.

We run into SEC guys all the time in the NFL, and I will make friendly little bets on the side about games. Sometimes I'll get my car washed by a guy who played at another SEC school after Tennessee has beaten his team. I am quick to stand up and say, "I went to UT," and feel good about that.

Deon Grant was an All-American safety for Tennessee in 1998 and 1999. He was drafted in the second round of the 2000 draft by the Carolina Panthers. He signed a six-year contract with the Seattle Seahawks in 2007.

DARWIN WALKER
DEFENSIVE TACKLE
1997–1999

WHEN THE 1998 SEASON STARTED, Coach Fulmer brought out a staff—a big long stick like that one Moses had in the movie. He called it a "synergy stick." We had lost Peyton Manning, and everybody thought we were going to be terrible. He brought out the stick and said, "This is going to be the center of all our focus." He kept that stick around all year and even had it the week of the national championship game.

I don't know that he pulled it out every week, but he pulled it out that week of practice for the Fiesta Bowl, and it seemed almost eerie, because there was a synergy around that team. We won close games and we made plays.

Now, we all knew already that we were going to have a great team. We knew what Tee Martin was all about as a quarterback, and we knew the talent we had on top of that. We were never concerned about taking it all the way because of the level of our talent.

Everybody thought we were done in 1998 and that were going to fall off because Peyton Manning left for the NFL. The whole world thought we were through, but we were so talented in 1998, and nobody knew about it.

We went out there and started killing people. Look back now at some of the guys who were on defense in 1998, and eight or nine, maybe more, went on to play in the NFL. Also look at two of the backups, who were freshmen,

Darwin Walker, an All-SEC defensive tackle in 1998 and 1999, closes in for the sack.

Albert Haynesworth and John Henderson. They ended up as very good players who went to the NFL, and we had them as backups.

Look back at 1997, and you will see our defense was made up of a bunch of nobodies, with the exception of Leonard Little, who went on to the NFL. Al Wilson was not that well known yet, and some of us were just getting into our careers. The 1997 season was all about a bunch of guys on defense trying to climb to the top.

Then 1998 rolled around, and we were still on a serious grind and trying to get better. We matched effort with talent and won the national title.

Playing with Donovan McNabb in the NFL, we have had many, many discussions and arguments over that first game of the 1998 season, the game that started our path to the national championship. We played Syracuse, and Donovan was their quarterback. He still believes the key pass interference call against them was a bad call. And I say, "What about that sack and caused fumble I got on you?"

That game was a wake-up call for us because we felt we were Tennessee, from the mighty SEC, and these guys, Syracuse, should not be able to play with us. We're supposed to win. That was an unconscious thing in the background that we all thought, including myself. We all thought we were going to go up there and beat up on them. They came out and played their best game, and we played our worst game, and we barely got out of there with a win.

What do I remember specifically about the 1998 season? I made my biggest play of my career at Tennessee that season, which was a sack in the national championship game against Florida State. It was in the third quarter, and it took them out of field-goal range in what was a close game. Bobby Bowden, the Florida State coach, came out and said that was the key play of the game, that my sack changed the game.

I was in such a zone throughout that game, and I still don't exactly remember the play or how it happened. I do remember the roar of the crowd and the reaction, because that stadium was filled with orange.

That 1998 team was all about getting to the next level individually and as a team, and then that dynamic changed in 1999, the season after we won the national championship.

Guys started to think about getting to the next level individually and forgot about the team, and that led to our demise. I think we had better talent in 1999 than in 1998, but we did not have that grind-it-out mentality. Everybody knew about all of the talent we had because we had so many preseason

All-Americans. But guys got more concerned about the next level—the NFL—when the 1999 season began.

I will take some responsibility for that. I was a captain and maybe I should've done more. We underachieved, no question about it. We lost three close games and finished 9–3. We could have been a great team that year, too. We had so many top-tier players, but it was a season where it was hard to develop a chemistry.

I was hurt a lot my senior year with a shoulder injury against Kentucky and an MCL sprain. I didn't have as good a year my senior year as my junior year in 1998. I might have been better off, from the standpoint of the NFL, leaving school after my junior year. I think it hurt me in the draft to wait, but I was determined to come back in the fall of 1999 and finish school.

The engineering curriculum is so dynamic, and the technology changes so fast, I needed to graduate and get that degree in 1999–2000. It would have been hard once my NFL career was over to come back to school.

One of the greatest honors I have ever had was speaking at the commencement in the engineering school last spring [2007]. The core of the speech was what I called Darwin's Keys to Success, which is utilizing the things that you have.

The NFL—and I talked about this in the speech—can get you in some doors you otherwise might not have open to you. What I stressed is not just getting in the door, but what you do once you are inside. You have to prove you are competent.

Most businesspeople and entrepreneurs find getting in the door is the hardest part. Just getting the right door open is the biggest hurdle, and that's what I talked about with the students. I told them there was something special about them that they needed to uncover and highlight that could get them in the door.

What helped me in business was the determination that I learned in football. I had an obsession to get to the quarterback and punish the guy who was in front of me on Sundays. You need the same type of drive in business. And that is what I tried to stress to the students; have that focus and have that determination. The same tactics that work in football can work in business.

I think the coach who had the biggest impact on me was Dan Brooks, the defensive line coach at Tennessee. He was a players' coach and a good man. He understood a lot of what players were going through when we were trying to handle academics and playing major-college football. You can just see what kind of coach he is by the number of defensive linemen who came through the program and went into the NFL. You had me, Albert Haynesworth, John Henderson, Turk McBride, and others.

Dan Brooks helped me learn how to relate to other people on the team and share what I knew. I did not consider myself anything special, but he helped me understand that I should share what I had learned in the program with other players and to consider myself as a valuable asset to the team.

The problem was I did not want to act like I was this great player and start telling people what to do. But Dan Brooks said that is exactly what I needed to do. It wasn't just football he was talking about, it was also about my success in the classroom and that I needed to have a serious talk with some of these guys so they could accomplish those things.

I was an overachiever in the classroom. The engineering curriculum was very hard, and I had to overachieve to get my degree. Don't get me wrong, I got my share of partying in, but there are times when the guys would come by to get me to go out, and I would say, "Not tonight, go on without me, I've got to deal with this engineering lab," or something like that.

Being part of the Tennessee program is huge, because everywhere you go, you run into alumni—not necessarily players—who remember that 1998 team. It was the team after Peyton Manning, and we won the national title. People have not forgotten it and they never will.

Darwin Walker was an All-SEC tackle in 1998 and 1999 and was a captain in 1999. Walker was selected in the third round of the 2000 NFL Draft. He played for the Arizona Cardinals, Philadelphia Eagles, and Chicago Bears. Walker earned his civil engineering degree at the University of Tennessee (2000) and cofounded Progressive Engineering in Knoxville with fellow Tennessee grad Paul Tucker.

The
NEW
MILLENNIUM

TRAVIS STEPHENS

TAILBACK

1997–2001

WHEN THE 2001 SEASON STARTED, people were questioning my durability. I was just 5′8″, 190 pounds, and there were media who stayed on me and on me. People thought I could tote the ball maybe 15 times a game and that was it. They were questioning the "little" guy.

Then, in the second game of the season, I carried the ball 41 times against Arkansas. It tied a school record. People couldn't question my durability after that.

I trained hard for that season. The team would have its own workouts early in the morning, but I got up even earlier, 5:00 A.M., with a track guy, Vince Martin. It was an underground workout, and it was an intense hour—so intense it felt like we were working out for three hours.

That's how I was able to build the strength, power, and endurance for that 2001 season. I set a school record for carries for a running back that season, and those workouts were a big reason why. I carried the ball almost 300 times, and it was made much easier because of those workouts.

I knew I was going to be all right, but it didn't hurt to have people saying I was too small. It made me work harder, and I made sure I was ready for the SEC games. It all started with the workouts—I took all that negative stuff with me into the workouts.

I still remember this big lineman from Arkansas falling on my stomach in a game, and I just got right back up. My abs were tight, all muscle. That's how

Travis Stephens
waited his turn
to start at UT
and rushed for
2,336 yards
(1997–2001).

239

hard I worked out for that season. That was my one season to be the feature
guy, the man, and I didn't want to miss out on my chance. I averaged 30 carries a game for the first five games in 2001.

What I was proud of was that most of my big games came against big
schools, the SEC games. That second game of the season against Arkansas, I
had 206 yards rushing. I got 226 yards against Florida when we beat them in
the Swamp. There was a 176-yard game against Georgia. You really get

pumped up for those big games. I played hard every game, but those SEC games I really got up for.

I remember going to Florida in 1997, my freshman year, which was Peyton Manning's last year at Tennessee. I just watched from the sideline, and I remember how loud it was. That's what I wanted to experience. For a young player, that's why you are there.

On the sideline that day, I kept telling myself I wanted to experience the pressure of all those Gator fans screaming at me. I was blessed to get that experience my senior year, and it was my best game because it meant so much for the team.

That Florida game was the game that was postponed because of 9/11. It was a good thing they postponed it out of respect for the people who died, but it also turned out to be a good thing for our team. This doesn't mean much compared to what happened to all the people in New York and Washington, but it was good for our team because Donté Stallworth, one of our best wide receivers, broke his wrist and was out. John Henderson, who was an All-American on the defensive line, was also out with an injury. So if we had played that game when it was scheduled, we would have missed those two. But, like I say, that doesn't mean much compared to what happened on 9/11, it's just something that made a difference in that Tennessee-Florida game.

Whoever won the Tennessee-Florida game back then usually represented our side of the SEC in the conference championship game. So, you can imagine, it was the biggest game of the year for us every year. It was for the East Division championship, a chance to play in the SEC championship game, and a chance to play for the national title...and it was the Gators.

I felt like I was in the zone that whole game. They were No. 2 in the country, and we were No. 4, but we were still 21-point underdogs. It was the perfect setup for me; it was the game I wanted to play and I needed to play in. I think it was Steve Spurrier's last SEC game at Florida, and we won 34–32.

The moment I remember from that game came right after they scored a touchdown. The crowd was going crazy, and I stood back there as we lined up for a play, waving my arms up and down as if to ask the crowd if that was all they had. I was kind of taunting the crowd, asking them to pump it up, pump it up. We snapped the ball, ran one of our zone plays, and I busted them up for 60 yards to set up a touchdown. That was the kind of play I came back to school for.

I think people were surprised I decided to redshirt my junior season in 1999. People couldn't understand it, coming so late in my career, but I knew I was third-string behind Travis Henry and Jamal Lewis. They were great backs and would go on and play in the Pro Bowl. I wasn't going to get many carries that season.

So I asked Coach Fulmer if he would let me redshirt. I think I would have transferred if he had said no, because I really wanted to have one season at Tennessee as the feature back. I wasn't trying to be selfish; I just wanted to play. Each of us got our own year. All I wanted was my opportunity, that's it.

I gained most of my yards off my zone plays, 4 zone or 5 zone. I just made my own reads as far as hitting holes. That was my bread and butter. That's what I was doing against Florida when I had 226 yards.

My fullback, Will Bartholomew, was the best fullback I ever ran behind. We were actually rivals in the same region in Tennessee high school football. Scott Wells was the center; Fred Weary was a guard. Will Ofenheusle was a tackle. Anthony Herrera was on that line with Reggie Coleman. What a line!

My style was to get north-south and run downhill. I idolized Walter Payton, and he was always downhill, and charged the defender. He liked hitting rather than being hit. My line would hold blocks and make it easy for me, where I could get through the line and then make a move on the linebacker before they could get up into the hole.

Coach Fulmer will tell you that Travis Stephens played in the games the same way he practiced during the week. I remember Coach Fulmer saying on a television show, or interview, that watching Travis Stephens was like watching a coaching clinic. That's one thing some of us learned from Peyton Manning that one year he was with us. I wanted to be a perfectionist, just like he was. I wanted to be a player/coach out there on the field.

After we beat Florida in that last regular season game, we played LSU in the SEC championship game. All we had to do was win and we could play Miami for the national title. We lost in an upset, and it was very disappointing.

You don't get too many chances to play for a national title. LSU played us very well during the regular season when we beat them, but we made too many mistakes in the SEC championship game. They had a nice little scheme—this quarterback draw with Matt Mauck—that we could not stop, and they beat us. They lost their quarterback, Rohan Davey, and their running back, LaBrandon Toefield, was hurt, but we still lost.

It was the big game—before the really big game for the national championship—and we weren't ready. We weren't looking ahead, really, we just made some turnovers.

Even though we didn't get a chance to play for the national championship that season, it finished a good career for me at Tennessee. All I wanted to do was go to a big program, and there aren't many programs as big as Tennessee. It was closest to home, too.

I could have gone some other places and played, like Kentucky, but I wanted to compete against the best players. I was never afraid of that. My first two years at Tennessee and my junior year, I had guys in front of me who were playing well, so I had to sit. But I finally got my year. I was the only back to rush for more than 1,000 yards that season in the SEC.

My first recruiting letter was from Tennessee in my junior season of high school. You get five visits, but after I went to Tennessee, I didn't want to take the other four. I ended up visiting Kentucky because my sister ran track there, but I was going to Tennessee. It was the big-time, and I wanted to play against the best. It may not have worked out quite the way I wanted because I didn't play much my first two years, but you have to respect the two guys I was playing behind, they were going to be Pro Bowlers.

When you look back on it, I was able to get some rings there because we won the national championship one season and two SEC championships. Tennessee was a place that made you strong because of the competition, not only the competition on the other side of the field, but the competition on your own team. That's why it is a great program.

Travis Stephens had the greatest single season for a running back in Tennessee history when he rushed for 1,464 yards in 2001. He was a finalist for the Doak Walker Award, given to the top running back in the country, and was a first-team All-American. Stephens is the ninth-leading rusher all-time in Tennessee football history.

JOHN HENDERSON
DEFENSIVE TACKLE
1999–2001

ONE OF THE BIGGEST HONORS for me in my football career was that I won the Al Wilson Leadership Award two years in a row at Tennessee. I was also a captain. Instead of doing a lot of talking, I worked hard to try and lead by example. I trained hard and tried to be a good teammate, and I can't describe the feeling I had when I was named captain or when I won the award.

Al Wilson played linebacker on Tennessee's national championship team in 1998, and he set some great examples for me because his play was so real. He played hard every play; I just liked the way he intimidated people. He could come up to the line like a pit bull, which reminded me of some of the stories I have heard from NFL guys about Lawrence Taylor, the All-Pro with the Giants. People would get concerned about where Al was and what he was going to do. I liked that about him.

I learned a lot from Al and from Shaun Ellis and Leonard Little, some great Tennessee players who were upperclassmen when I got there. I tried to feed off them and the whole thing about what it meant to be a Tennessee Vol. Once they were gone, I wanted to have the same presence they did before the snap of the ball and try and bring some confidence to the rest of the defense.

My identity was to try and play fundamentally sound and have good technique. I have some natural skills, sure, but Coach Dan Brooks would drill

John Henderson was the Outland Trophy winner in 2000 and an All-American in 2000 and 2001.

into my head that it wasn't enough to have skill, you had to play the game correctly. I think that's why I had such a good year in 2000 with the 12 sacks and all the tackles. I'm still trying to do it now with Jacksonville, to play with good technique and stay low.

One of the things Coach [John] Chavis at Tennessee told me was that he wasn't sure I could play defensive tackle because I was so tall. He didn't know if I could stay low. Well, I did it. I stayed low and learned to play. There was some terrific coaching by those guys at Tennessee. Keep your pad level, follow your coaching. It's easy when you have some ability and you listen to what they have to say. That's why I am here today. Taking in the coaching and going with it.

Coach Brooks, who was the D-line coach, teaches the basics. He came out fired up all the time and would not take a day off at practice. He had the number-one saying in the world: "It's a great day to be alive, gentleman." He said that every day, I will never forget it. It has stuck with me.

When I got there, I was supposed to be an end, but they switched me out in camp and made me a tackle. From that point on, I just went from there. That was my freshman year. At the time, I said, "If they need me there, that's where I'm going." I didn't complain about it because I knew Tennessee's staff had a reputation for finding the right position for guys.

Jason Witten came in as a defensive end, and they made him a tight end, and look at the career he is having in the NFL. He's gone to the Pro Bowl and is one of the top tight ends in the league. The coaches on Coach Fulmer's staff know how to evaluate talent and can make the call about where a guy should line up.

Look at Fred Weary. He started as a defensive tackle and got moved to offense. Now he is having a career in the NFL and starting with Houston. The coaches see you, they understand your personality, your body type, your feet, then they make the move. They don't do it with everyone, of course, but the ones they switch seem to get better and better.

I know I came in as a tight end, and they moved me. They've just got this knack. I think it helps that they have this belief in you and it gives you confidence that you can master another position. It's been working for them for a long time. We should count up the number of players in the league who came into college playing a different position, got switched to another position, and are now playing in the NFL.

I had all kinds of offers coming out of high school, but I committed early so I didn't have the pressure. I was close to Mom by going to Tennessee, and I knew I could relax and enjoy my senior year.

I was Prop 48 when I got there in 1998. I had some academic issues. I couldn't play in the games and didn't have to practice—just go to school and get my grades up. But I wanted to practice, so they let me practice. So I got my Bs and As and got into the books, which was part of the deal. I worked out and got myself ready to play by my sophomore season. I didn't have to be there at practice, but I wanted to be there. They let me stay as long as my grades were kept up.

In 1999, I played tackle with Darwin Walker and Billy Ratliff and then started after Billy got hurt. I kept thinking early in that season that we had so much talent that we were going back to the national championship game. We lost one game early to Florida when we were ranked No. 2, but then we won a bunch of games going into the Arkansas game. That's when it got away from us, on the road at Arkansas.

We had gotten back to No. 3 in the country and then lost to Arkansas 28–24. Then we ended on a bad note losing to Nebraska in the bowl game, but we were still 9–3, which was a good year.

I started when Billy Ratliff had that bad injury. I had to take the coaching and step up and stop being a rookie. I think he got hurt midway through the season, maybe the South Carolina game, and that's when it hit me that was I going to be counted on and needed to play like a starter, like someone they could trust.

We were really good. There were a lot of players back from the national championship team, which brought a lot of experience to the 1999 team. We felt like we could be just as good, but we weren't.

Going into the 2000 season, what really got me ready was my offseason conditioning. That was the year I won the Outland Trophy and had 12 sacks. I dedicated myself in that offseason and went to work. It was all about getting my body ready and working hard.

Then, in 2001, I thought we would finally get back and play for the national title. All we had to do was beat LSU in the SEC championship game, and we were going to play Miami for the championship. We did not play well, and they used this quarterback draw. I remember the key play of the game was their draw when we were in our 30-package and I blitzed the 1 gap.

Somebody else got blocked, and Matt Mauck ran it on in. They caught us in the blitz. We had some pass interference calls, too, and we turned the ball over and lost our chance to play for the national title, which was disappointing because we were certainly talented enough.

That was my last year at Tennessee, and I was ready for the NFL. I was ready for the NFL because of the coaching I got at Tennessee. They would ask me to do things in Jacksonville when I got to training camp, and I already knew what they were talking about. They asked me if I could do this stance, and I could do it with both hands. My pad level stayed low in drills, and I could move my feet.

The only thing that changed was the money and the uniform color. Everything else I was ready for. I think that's what you get from being a Vol. They didn't have a drill I couldn't do when I got to the pros.

I'm from Nashville, so you grow up hearing about the tradition and running through the T. You only have to run through the T one time to bleed orange the rest of your life. That's pride, that's what that is.

It's real like that, all the time. The Vol Walk was one of the greatest things, too. You never get that back. I still remember before the last game I played in Neyland Stadium, we were getting ready to run through the T, and I just paused. I put my hands on my hips and didn't move. It was emotional; it was Senior Day. I just looked around and took it all in. We beat Vanderbilt 38–0. That was a good sendoff. I had been part of the Tennessee tradition, and I was very proud.

John Henderson is only one of two players in the history of the Tennessee football program to win the Outland Trophy. He won it in 2000 and was a finalist in 2001. Henderson was an All-American in 2000 as a junior and then made seven more All-America teams his senior season before entering the NFL Draft, where he was a first-round pick of the Jacksonville Jaguars. Henderson was All-SEC in 2000 and 2001.

DUSTIN COLQUITT

Punter

2001–2004

Y BROTHER AND I TRIED real hard to break the chain of Colquitts going on to punt for Tennessee, just because we played a lot more soccer than football when we were kids. We were not being groomed, as you would say, from the time we were little kids to be punters for the Vols.

I just got into it by accident. The way it happened was the field-goal kicker for our high school team at Bearden went down with an injury before the start of the season during the summer two-a-days. My club soccer team had started all of our tournaments, and I was in Texas—this was in the summer before school had actually started—and the high school coach called and said they needed a kicker. He was desperate.

I went out there two weeks before the high school season and started kicking in practice for them. There was a linebacker doing the punting in practice, and he actually hit a ball that went over the back of his head. I said, "You know, my dad did some punting, maybe I should try that, too." It went from there.

Now, this was right before my senior season in high school. I had never played football, even with all the relationships to Tennessee football. My dad had wanted us to be quarterbacks, but we ended up in soccer.

So while I was out there, my younger brother, Britton, said if Dustin was going to be out there, he wanted to be out there to play freshman football.

The first game we played was against West, and I will remember this punt forever. I never had another punt like this my entire senior year. We were winning 16–14, and there were two minutes and 15 seconds remaining in the game. I was backed up eight yards deep in my end zone and had to punt.

You have to remember. I had never played football before. On top of that, I'd had two terrible punts prior to that that had helped West get good field position—they scored both times.

So what happened? I hit a 74-yard punt out of the back of the end zone. That next day, somebody must've called the Tennessee coaches and said that Craig Colquitt's son just had a 74-yard punt. I got my first recruiting letter on Monday from Tennessee.

I think I made the first five field goals I tried at the beginning of the season and then went 0-for-8. The punting was the same, not very good. My dad was working full-time, so he couldn't come help me, and I struggled.

Before that letter came, I figured I would just go play soccer at Brown in the Ivy League and get a great education up there. After that letter, I decided I was going to walk on at Tennessee, and that's the way it was going to be.

249

David Leaverton was the punter when I enrolled my freshman season, and there was no way I was going to out-punt him; I could barely punt in high school. But my dad's office was closer to the campus, so he started coming over to practice to work with me. He took his lunch off and came every day to practice for a year and a half until I got it figured out and got a little more confident.

All of a sudden, we had a third Colquitt—me—as a Tennessee punter. Jimmy, my first cousin, my dad, and then me. My brother Britton is the punter now.

It was very disappointing to our club soccer coach, who poured his soul into our program, to watch me take off before my senior season to play football. It really hurt him, and only recently have we been able to talk. He bought a bus, he carted us all over the place, and he was very upset that I skipped the national tournament to play football. He called me six months ago and said he was proud of what I accomplished by getting into the NFL.

My dad was always about not pressuring us to be football players as he was. I think that helped me out a lot, not feeling that pressure.

I remember a practice one day the spring before my second season, after Leaverton left. I kicked the ball so well that I thought, *If I can do that, I could*

Dustin Colquitt's left-footed punts caused opponents trouble because of the ball's odd rotation on descent.

250

eventually be the starting punter. Phillip Fulmer came over after one of my kicks and said, "That's what I'm looking for, right there." He sat me down, and he said, "Dustin, I want you to think about one thing, and that's that people come to practice for one thing, and that is to watch you punt."

That helped me feel more confident. Would people really come just to watch me punt? Phillip became almost a second father to me. I found my consistency with his pushing me like that and started taking things a lot more seriously.

Phillip was the ultimate player's coach. He was not just involved in preparing us for games, he made sure he got involved preparing us for life. It wasn't just football, it was going to class, it was being respectful to women. I remember the times I got frustrated, and he would say the right things to keep me from getting too frustrated. He loves winning football games, but he also tried hard to develop character and manners and make us respectful people.

There are a lot of memorable games, but the most memorable was beating Miami down there my junior year because they had a 26-game winning streak in the Orange Bowl. You could feel our energy and that something special was going to happen in the plane ride down and in the locker room before the game.

Kevin Burnett and Kevin Simon gave huge speeches before the game and pumped us up. Our defense kept their offense in a funk the whole game.

Late in the game, we had to punt the ball. Their guy dropped it, and Derrick Tinsley jumped on it. We took a knee three straight times to run out the clock and won the game. Miami's return guy was Sean Taylor, and we ended up going to some All-American banquets together, and he wouldn't talk to me. My punts had that weird left-footed draw that could make it difficult to catch the first time.

Miami had a deal where they would put two return guys back, and for any punter, that is intimidating. Roscoe Parrish was the other one, and he was very fast. I couldn't have run faster than them if I had a motorcycle.

On the one kick Taylor dropped, I kicked it to the sideline, and I could tell he was getting nervous because of the rotation. He looked down a couple of times, he looked up, and he bobbled it, then dropped it. The ball cuts really hard right, and it can be tough to catch. Most people don't face left-footed punters.

The other big game I can remember was playing in the Swamp in 2001 against Florida. We were ranked No. 5, and they were ranked No. 2. If we could win that game, we would get to play for the SEC title and have the chance to face Miami in the national championship game. That was an awesome game against Florida, and we won 34–32.

We could have played for the national title if we had just beat LSU in the SEC championship game in Atlanta a week later. We knocked Rohan Davey, their quarterback, out of the game, but Matt Mauck, their backup, just ran all over us. He had two rushing touchdowns. All of our fans came with roses in their mouths because they thought we were going to beat LSU and go play in the Rose Bowl for the national title. It didn't happen. They beat us 31–20.

This will be my third season gone from Tennessee, and as I look back, what I valued most was the camaraderie and knowing guys from all sorts of places. Tennessee has a national recruiting base, and we have players from all over the country.

Some of the college rivalries, for instance, with the Alabama guys, can linger. Brodie Croyle is on the Chiefs roster with me, and we looked at each other the first time and sort of said to ourselves, *I will never talk to this guy.* We were not going to hang out or let anyone see us hang out.

So now we hang out together all the time. I hate where he went to school, but he is a super nice guy. On the Saturdays we play Alabama, I don't talk to him; we won't hang out that day.

The Alabama-Tennessee fans do not understand it. I was at a banker's convention with my father-in-law in Florida, and I had a guy walk up to me in Florida, who was a Tennessee fan, and he had heard Brodie mention on the XM radio that he was a friend of mine. The Tennessee fan had a hard time understanding that I could be a friend of an Alabama player, but that's what makes the rivalry between the schools special.

When you are in the NFL, it is a job. On the college level, however, the whole environment is special, and it is not a job. It's tough to go back and watch sometimes because it can choke you up. It's a special feeling that you were part of that program. I've gone back four times since I left, and it's great to take it all in again.

Dustin Colquitt led Tennessee in punting for four seasons. He was an All-American and first-team All-SEC in 2003. He is third on the all-time list for career punting average (42.6) behind his cousin Jimmy Colquitt, who kicked for Tennessee from 1981 to 1984, and his brother Britton Colquitt. Dustin Colquitt kicks for the Kansas City Chiefs in the NFL. The Colquitts have set up a scholarship fund for walk-on players at Tennessee.

JAMES WILHOIT

KICKER

2002–2006

I CAUGHT THE TENNESSEE EXPERIENCE on both ends. I grew up as a huge fan in Hendersonville and then got to play and experience it that way, too. I remember the day Tennessee called and told my coach they were going to offer me a scholarship while I was on the recruiting trip to Knoxville for Junior Day. When he told me, it was an unbelievable feeling. I was sitting in Spanish class, trying to concentrate, and all I could think of was, *Wow, Tennessee just offered me a scholarship.* I am from middle Tennessee. This was the team I'd watched my whole life, and I was going to get a chance to play for them.

But, of course, I was a stubborn kid. Michigan had been recruiting me all along, too, and had offered me a scholarship before Tennessee. Michigan saw a film of me a month after my junior season ended and offered me a scholarship on the spot. They wanted me to come in and kick off, punt, and handle place-kicking right away as a freshman.

So I thought, *If Tennessee is not going to recruit me as hard as Michigan even though I'm right in Tennessee's backyard, well, I'm going to have to give it some thought.* When we got up to Neyland Stadium, Coach Fulmer asked me if I was ready to be a Vol, and I said, "I'm going to have to think about it."

My parents looked at me, and they were white as ghosts. So was Coach Fulmer. I looked at them, saw their reaction, and said, "Oh, I'm just kidding."

James Wilhoit is number two in scoring all-time at Tennessee.

I guess I was kidding, but maybe not. I guess I wanted my home state school to be first. I knew if I had gone to Michigan, I would have been on Tennessee's website checking to see how the Vols were doing every week.

I talked to Coach Fulmer about it later, and he said they did not expect anyone to offer me that early. They were going to offer me after camp going into my junior season in high school, but that was my first year starting for the high school and they wanted me to get a season in. They always said the ball sounded different when I hit it than others in the camps they had and that I was going to be a kicker for them.

I remember the first game I went to when I was younger. Tennessee's Jay Graham ran 80 yards for a touchdown. We scalped tickets, and my parents let my friend and I sit on the 50-yard line while they went up in the nosebleed section. I was hooked. We got to see a game-winning touchdown against Alabama.

Jeff Hall was the guy I idolized growing up. I remember I was at a party the night he had a game-winning kick against Florida. A couple of girls had asked me to dance with them, and I said, "I don't think so, the Tennessee-Florida game is on."

Everybody else was outside. Eventually, people came into the house and wanted to watch a movie. I ended up in the back corner of the house watching the game on this little TV. Tennessee won, and at the end of the game, I was running around screaming, and these people thought there was a fire— I was doing victory laps.

I played more soccer than football when I was younger, and I remember when I was in the seventh grade, I could kick 40-yard field goals. I kicked the ball into the end zone in the eighth grade. One day, I was out there as a seventh-grader kicking as far as some of the backups on the high school team.

The kick that I will always remember, and one fans remember, is the game-winning kick against Florida in 2004. I had missed a game-tying extra-point kick but came back about two minutes later and kicked that 50-yarder to beat the Gators 30–28. I remember it most because it showed my character. Some people at that point would not have recovered from missing the extra point; I never missed extra points, but I was just complacent.

I was not upset I missed it; I was just mad. I told myself I was not going to be the guy who cost us a win over Florida.

Coach Fulmer asked me where I would be good from when we got the ball back. I told him just to get me across midfield, and I would kick it. There were six seconds left, and as soon as I kicked it, I knew it was good. I was jumping around before everybody else, celebrating the win. It was an incredible moment. There was such a celebration on the field that I lost my breath from all the pats on the back. We still had to kickoff, so they assessed a penalty for delaying the game.

The other game I remember was my redshirt freshman year [2003] against Alabama, when we won in five overtimes [51–43]. I kicked three field goals, but I remember having to make a tackle in that game to keep them from winning. There were 30 seconds left in regulation, and I did a bloop kick because

255

we did not want a return. Tyrone Prothro caught the ball—he was a speed-ster, and he just took off running. We ran down the field like there was not going to be a kickoff and got surprised by him coming through us.

I took an angle backwards to try and get him on the sideline. I reached out, grabbed his face mask, and was able to tackle him. That was the fastest I ran in my life. They missed the field goal to win, and we played five overtimes.

I hit a field goal in the fourth overtime to send it to the fifth overtime, and we won. That was the first game I had been under that kind of pressure. It was nerve-racking. It was definitely a growing experience for me.

Some of the out-of-state guys embraced the tradition, and then there were those of us from Tennessee who were in awe of it. That's the way it is at Ten-nessee with some guys. They try and embrace it, but I think it hits the guys from the state more.

On my recruiting visit, they brought guys into the locker room and talked about all the great players who had come through that locker room. I was in heaven. Some guys were saying, "Okay, let's get this over with." The recruits from Tennessee ate it up; they loved hearing it because that had been their dream, to play with the Vols. You had some out-of-state guys who got drawn into it like us. Omar Gaither, who is from North Carolina and plays with the Philadelphia Eagles, said he makes bets with guys from other schools that Tennessee will win a game against his teammates' team. You see that pride in Tennessee after you leave.

The hardest game for me was losing to Vanderbilt in 2005. Being a kid who grew up near Nashville, that was pretty tough. We finished that season 5–6. It was a very difficult season to take because we were used to being in the mix for the SEC championship and the national title.

That season, you had to really focus on getting ready for games. A lot of guys had a tough time with losing, and it affected us on the field. I think if we'd been any other program than Tennessee we would not have been so despondent and won more games. But a lot of people were just so down, and it cost us.

So when we came back for the 2006 season, we felt like we needed to make a statement in the opening game against Cal. They didn't have a chance because we worked so hard to win that game and make a statement. The peo-ple in Knoxville were not very happy about that 2005 season, and neither were we, so we took out a lot of frustration on Cal, which was ranked in the top 10. We won 35–18.

Through the spring and then in summer camp, all we could think about was getting back on the field for the 2006 season. That Cal team came into Neyland Stadium as the favored team, so we were even more motivated. For a non-conference team to come into Neyland Stadium as a favorite, well, that wasn't good for Cal. I have never seen us play that well.

We ran into some trouble later in the season. We were one play away from beating Florida but lost to them. Then Erik Ainge, our quarterback, got hurt, and that was a setback. Then there was a fumble in the LSU game by JaMarcus Russell that would have ended the drive they had in the fourth quarter to beat us. The officials said it wasn't a fumble, they kept the ball, and then won. Aside from the Arkansas game, there was not a game that we couldn't have won.

We had some good seasons when I was there, but if you had told me that after the 2001 season, when we almost played for the national championship, that we would not have another SEC title before I left, I would have been very surprised. I think that's what it means to be a Vol, the expectations. You go to a place like Tennessee, which is filled with tradition and winning teams, and you expect to be near the top in college football.

James Wilhoit is the second-leading career scorer in Tennessee history with 325 points. He led the Vols in scoring for four seasons (2003–2006) and was named All-SEC in 2006. He was selected Academic All-American in 2006 by the College Sports Information Directors of America.

ARRON SEARS
OFFENSIVE LINE
2003–2006

WE WENT 5–6 MY JUNIOR YEAR in 2005, and it was one of the worst seasons for Tennessee football in a long time. Coach Fulmer had never been through it as head coach, and none of us were expecting it. It was very disappointing to all of us.

I put in my waivers for the NFL draft right after that season, and the NFL came back and said I had a third-round grade. I thought about it a long time, whether to jump or stay for another season at Tennessee. I thought about that losing season and the guys who were going to be left behind to try and get Tennessee back to where it was supposed to be.

I couldn't leave them, not after what happened, not after 5–6. We didn't make a bowl game, and I didn't feel like leaving on a bad foot. You only have a chance to go through it for four years and you want to say you stuck it out together with your guys.

So I stayed for another season and we went 9–4. I am here in the real world now, the NFL, but there is nothing like college and playing for Tennessee, and I'm glad I stayed for that extra year.

It's funny, when I was growing up, I was an Alabama fan first because I am from Alabama. Then I had a first cousin go to Auburn, so I had to change over from the Crimson Tide to the Tigers. After my junior year in high

Arron Sears grew up an Auburn fan, but became a Tennessee All-American.

school, my brother also went to Auburn, so I became really tight with the Auburn football family.

It stayed that way right up until the day I decided where I was going to go to school. It came down to Tennessee and Auburn, but Coach Fulmer can sell water to a well, so I ended up at Tennessee.

I think Coach Fulmer's work throughout the years speaks for itself. You can just look at the names of the offensive linemen who have come from Tennessee and see what a major impact Coach Fulmer and the program can have on your career. You have a chance to get drafted into the NFL, which I was, and a lot of it had to do with the coaching I received there.

Coach Fulmer is a former offensive lineman, and he had a major influence on me. It's good to have a coach who has been through it, who has played the offensive line, and who can teach you the ins and outs.

Just look at the guys who came right before me and went on to the NFL. Chad Clifton, Fred Weary, Cosey Coleman. The list goes on and on. It makes a difference in your decision. Coming out of high school, I took four visits— Ohio State, Miami, Auburn, and Tennessee. I picked Tennessee because the work there speaks for itself. There is talent all over the field, and it is productive at every position, but the offensive line was one group that was never going to be overlooked by the coaching staff.

My sophomore year, we played in a big game down at the University of Georgia where I had to block their All-American defensive end David Pollack, who was the best defensive end at the time in the Southeastern Conference. Michael Munoz got hurt early in that game, so I had to step in at left tackle. I didn't practice that whole week because I was injured and was sitting out after rolling my ankle against Auburn.

I was starting at right tackle, and when Michael got hurt, I was able to come in and play left tackle and block a great defensive lineman, which contributed to our win. It was a great opportunity, because David Pollack got a lot of sacks for Georgia and was an NFL-type player. So to be able to block him and keep him from getting sacks really helped the team, and we beat them 19–14.

I didn't practice at all that week, but I stayed in the film room and studied Georgia and its defensive line and schemes. It's what you do at Tennessee. You find a way to get ready, even if you are not 100 percent and can't practice. You don't lay down, you find a way to be productive.

My junior year we played another game I won't forget. It was down at LSU, and we fell behind 21–0. I had moved from right guard to left tackle, then to left guard, and then right tackle because of injuries. I played every position but center in that game. I remember having to step in at halftime and try to rally our guys because we were playing terribly.

I came into the locker room, and guys had their heads down. They looked like they had already lost the game. I can't repeat all the things I said to people in there, it was pretty strong.

I get really excited about the game of football. I thought I was one of the leaders of that team, and I needed to say something. We came out and turned it on in the second half and won in overtime, 30–27. Everybody responded to what the coaches had to say. We didn't really change our scheme; we just started playing better.

A lot of people turned that game off and walked away from their televisions because we couldn't get anything going in the first half. But as soon as our guys stopped feeling sorry for themselves and started doing their jobs and executing, we started to play well.

I've moved around to a lot of different positions on the offensive line, but I didn't care as long as I was getting a chance to play football. Some guys might want to stay at the same spot, but it was okay that I moved around.

There was a Monday before a game with Alabama when Coach Fulmer came to me and said he needed me to move to the inside, to play guard to try and keep the line stable, instead of playing on the outside at tackle. It was fine with me. Coach thought it was the best matchup against the defensive linemen we were playing. That Alabama defense was rated as one of the best in the country, and he wanted to be able to move me inside. They had Anthony Bryant at defensive tackle. He was a very good player, and we needed to get some movement on the inside. We won 16–13.

I am in the NFL now, and I look back and see how short college was for those four years. I went to a school that had a great tradition, and I got to play before 110,000 fans. There is nothing like it in college football, especially the 7:00 o'clock kickoffs in the fall. Running through T is great, but the best part is playing out there with that Tennessee helmet on your head.

Saturdays are my Tennessee T-shirt days in the NFL. It is supposed to be our day off, but we come in and have meetings and guys show up in their T-shirts from the schools where they played in college.

The SEC guys really get into it because we think we played in the best college conference. You have to represent your school, and I do it every chance I get. I am a Vol forever, Big Orange, no question about it. Once you are a part of it as a player, you are always a part of it.

Arron Sears was an All-American offensive tackle in 2006 (Camp, Coaches) and won the prestigious Jacobs Blocking Trophy, which is given annually to the top blocker in the SEC in a poll of coaches. Sears was also a two-time All-SEC offensive tackle. When he was named first-team All-SEC in 2006, it was the first time since 2000–2001 that a Vol was named All-SEC first-team in back-to-back seasons. He was drafted in the second round of the 2007 NFL Draft by the Tampa Bay Buccaneers.

HONORABLE MENTION

*These men did not play football
for Tennessee, but through their words
and deeds, they proved that they knew
what it means to be a Volunteer.*

BEN BYRD

THE KNOXVILLE JOURNAL

1948–1991

I CAN GIVE YOU A QUOTE from a player from the great teams of 1938, 1939, 1940. It was Leonard Coffman, a fullback. Somebody interviewed him after a game in Memphis against Ole Miss, and he was all beat up from a tough game. He was dripping wet with sweat, he looked pretty worn out, and he said, "To play football for Tennessee, you have to get wet all over."

From Neyland's time on, you learned that you had to work for it. Nobody was going to give it to you. Tennessee football was about intelligent preparation. You hear about the game maxims; the players and coaches live by them.

You know, Neyland stole those from his Army coach, a guy named Charles Daley. It's a funny thing about those maxims, because Neyland produced more coaches than any other program ever, and those maxims got around the country. There are 20 coaches, I believe, in charge of major programs, and they took the maxims with them.

They were players who became coaches, and they spread them from coast to coast. It was coaches like Frank Broyles at Arkansas and Doug Dickey at Tennessee and Florida.

Tennessee has not turned out a head coach in a while, but those maxims are still circulating in college football. Tennessee's influence is all over college football, whether people know it or not, because of what Neyland passed on.

Ben Byrd's career at *The Knoxville Journal* lasted more than four decades and spanned the career of some of the greatest players in Tennessee history.

Tennessee and Princeton were the last two programs to get rid of the single-wing, which is funny, because Hank Lauricella and Dick Kazmaier fought it out for the Heisman Trophy in 1951, and they were single-wing tailbacks.

The T formation caught on in the 1940s, starting at Stanford. By the time Neyland got back from the war, the T was in over 50 percent of the college football programs, but not at Tennessee.

I talked to Neyland after he had retired, and he was the UT athletic director. He said, "I didn't care about the single-wing, I didn't care about any kind of offense. You win football games with defense and the kicking game. And I kept it because maybe it gave me a little quicker power between the tackles."

It would have taken two years to make the conversion to the T formation, and Neyland didn't want to waste the time on offense. He believed in defense and the kicking game first.

That is who he was as a coach. He wanted to spend his time on field position, defense, and taking advantage of breaks. When he went to two-platoon football, he put his best players on defense. In 1938, 1939, 1940, they shut out people. One year they didn't give up any points in the regular season.

Now, they had some offense with a backfield that was called "Hack, Mac, and Dodd." Buddy Hackman was the wingback, Gene McEver the tailback, and Bobby Dodd the quarterback.

Tennessee did not fill its stadium back then because Neyland played out-and-out breathers early in the season. He did not want to play a tough game until the third week, just to make sure his team was ready. You can't talk about Tennessee football in the same numbers as there are today—I mean in terms of people that come to the game—because the university was not as big, the town was not as big, and the stadium was not as big. But as far as feeling and intensity, it was as big.

They had not gotten to the marketing and advertising that turned it into such a financial success. The only income the athletic department had was from the sale of tickets and concessions. You could get a hot dog and a Coke for a quarter.

Back then, nobody wore all of this orange. People dressed in their Sunday suits and wore hats. It was a different culture then, but they made noise. A lot of people think football started in the late 1950s with Jim Brown and Johnny Unitas, but it started a lot earlier than that.

Red Grange played for Illinois in 1924 during the Golden Era of sports in the 1920s, with Babe Ruth, Jack Dempsey, Bobby Jones, and Big Bill Tilden. That is when Tennessee established itself as a national power in football, in the late '20s.

People were just becoming fascinated with sports, and I think that the Depression added to that. It was tough, it was hard, and baseball and college football provided some relief. It did not cost that much to go to a game, $3 or $4 a ticket, when I was a kid.

I went to my first game when I was seven years old in the middle of the streak where Neyland had five undefeated seasons in his first seven years. I think that was the last time that you'll see a team with that kind of streak. That was in the late '20s and early '30s.

Beattie Feathers was the tailback, probably the greatest player at that time. He was also a heck of a punter, and I remember a game with Ole Miss when one of their guys broke through to try and block the kick. Beattie's punt hit that guy right under the chin. He blocked the punt, but he got up and wobbled around before they could get him off the field. Feathers was magnificent. He was a half-Cherokee Indian. He ran with great grace.

Neyland said McEver was the best he ever coached. He was a broken-field runner and a supremely confident player. He was the one who ran that kickoff back against Alabama 98 yards that many say was the play that got Tennessee on the map. He was barely touched.

All my life, I have heard that kickoff return by McEver was the play that put Tennessee into the big-time. Alabama was the big dog in the South then, even though that particular year they were not that good. The 'Bama fans were giving Tennessee fans 21 points in the stands before the game. That was 1928 in Tuscaloosa, and Tennessee won 15–13. So much for those 21 points.

That was the same year Tennessee beat Vanderbilt, and really, Neyland was hired to beat Vanderbilt. Vanderbilt was a king back then, and a few weeks after beating Alabama, Tennessee beat Vanderbilt. McEver, Dodd, and Hackman were sophomores then, and the program was on its way.

Other towns had football success back then, and then it went away and came back—or never came back. It lasted here because Neyland was so good.

267

Wallace Wade was the Alabama coach back in 1928 when Tennessee beat them. Wade had taken two or three teams to the Rose Bowl, and they were on top.

After Wade went to Duke, he said of Neyland, "He could take his and beat yours, or he could take yours and beat his."

That is the supreme compliment. What he is saying is that you don't have much chance. Wade was a great football coach, too.

Neyland had three peaks. He was there about 26 years, minus however many seasons he was gone with his Army duties. It was either very good for a short time after Neyland, or people were raising hell that it was no good.

Neyland retired after the 1952 season, and Harvey Robinson took over in a difficult position because they lost a lot of great players. That was also the time Neyland got on the Football Rules Committee, and he hated free-substitution. At the first meeting after his retirement, Neyland got on the committee and got them to go back to the old rule of one appearance per quarter, so you had to play both offense and defense.

Neyland got that committee around the table. He reached over to Davey Nelson—it was his first year on the committee—and, as everybody raised their hands to vote for the measure for the new substitution rule, Neyland picked up Nelson's arm as if he were voting to approve. It was a 5–4 vote in favor, and Neyland said there will be no more chicken-shit two-platoon football.

Harvey Robinson lasted just two seasons. Robby had to teach guys to play both ways, but he didn't have the talent. He also used a defense Neyland didn't like, and of course, Neyland thought defense was all there was. That did not endear Robby to General Neyland, who was also the athletic director.

Robby was removed as coach, and then Bowden Wyatt came in and did well for several years. But in the last half of his tenure, they went downhill. He was probably the greatest leader I ever saw. Those guys would bust through the wall for him. He would get you so fired up. Neyland didn't try and do that; he was an engineer, and he wanted people thinking straight and doing their assignments.

When Doug Dickey came here in 1964, they were still playing both ways in college football. There was a little more liberal substitution, where someone could go in twice a quarter. Dickey finally brought in the T formation and the full-time quarterback and got rid of the single-wing, and college football went to a two-platoon system.

The program grew to where it is now gradually, not suddenly, from the late 1960s to 1990. Since 1990, it has been fairly obnoxious with its size.

Bob Woodruff, who had been an assistant under Bowden Wyatt, came up as athletic director after Neyland. There were some who wanted him to be coach and AD, but they hired Jim McDonald in 1963 when Wyatt was fired. He went 5–5, and they brought in Dickey from Florida. Of course, McDonald always hated Woodruff after that, but you have to give Dickey credit because he got it moving again.

They were down in ticket sales and support, and Woodruff went to businessmen in town and sold them as many tickets as they could take, people like Kerns Bakery and sporting good shops. The businesses, in turn, would give their customers tickets, and that really rescued the program financially. Woodruff caught a lot of hell for his tenure, but he was one of the smartest guys I knew.

It was okay back then that Woodruff was from Florida because there were no bitter feelings between the schools like there are now. That bitterness started in 1984 when Tennessee found out that the Florida coach, Charley Pell, had been cheating left and right, and Tennessee helped turn him in.

In the spring conference meeting in 1985, Woodruff and Ed Boling, the Tennessee president, got the SEC to take the 1984 championship away from Florida. They fined the school, and from that time on, Florida people hated Tennessee. The following year, when Tennessee went down to Gainesville for a game, they were threatening to kill Tennessee players. In 1985, the only game Tennessee lost was at Florida.

That 1985 team was when it really took off again here. People talk about how the program went to another level when Phillip Fulmer took over, but it was really going well with John Majors when Fulmer took over in 1993, and it hasn't stopped since.

Ben Byrd, a native of Knoxville, worked for *The Knoxville Journal* for more than 40 years as reporter, columnist, and sports editor. He won awards for his work and retired full-time as a newspaperman on December 31, 1991, when *The Journal* closed after 150 years.

HAYWOOD HARRIS
Sports Information
Director/Historian
1961–Present

The thing I have always been struck by is how lucky we were to get Bob Neyland as our football coach. He could have been sent to any campus in the country for the ROTC program and his work with the Army, but he was sent here. Neyland Stadium could be in Manhattan, Kansas, at Kansas State, for all we know, or maybe some place in Utah.

I think he is the greatest coach of all time, not just because he won football games, but also because of his influence on the game. It was a stroke of good fortune for Knoxville and the University of Tennessee.

Just look at what he has done—and I'm not just talking about winning games. He was the man who came up with the idea of putting a tarp on the field and communication between the press box and sideline. He was the one who got the idea going of scouting opponents.

The wide-tackle-6 defense was his defense, and he was the first to use that. You hear coaches down through the years say they use "the old Tennessee wide-tackle-6 defense." He was a pioneer in that regard, and I don't think he gets enough credit for that. People acknowledge that he was a genius, and he could have been anything he wanted to be.

Back then, Neyland made Tennessee one of the model programs around the country. He gave Tennessee quality football, and I think coaches, more

Haywood Harris, the longtime sports information director, keeps alive the culture of the Vols from the days of General Neyland.

than fans, were admirers of Neyland because they realized how technically sound he was. At one time, there were a tremendous number of coaches who came through the program and had the Neyland teaching in their back-ground.

The first game I went to was when I was 12 in 1942 against Fordham, a team that was supposed to be good enough that season to go on and play in the Rose Bowl. I saved my money all summer to come up with the $4 for a single ticket at the 50-yard line.

That was as big a thrill as I can remember to see Tennessee romp over Fordham 40–14. Some of the edge was lost later that week when the famous commentator Bill Stern came out with his "Onions and Orchids" segment and said, "Orchids to Tennessee for beating Fordham and knocking them out of a Rose Bowl berth so early in the season. And onions to the same Tennessee team for heating up the Fordham locker room at halftime."

That game confirmed me as a Tennessee fan for the way they played that day. I still can't get over the Texas game in 1951 when Tennessee won the Cotton Bowl and set the stage for being national champions the next year.

There were various rating services back then, and I remember in 1951 we were national champions and then lost in the Sugar Bowl to Maryland. We played terribly. The worst part was that it was Hank Lauricella's home town, and we went down there and played a poor game. I think we left it up there in Lexington when we beat Kentucky 28–0, in what I think is the most perfect game I have seen Tennessee play on offense and defense.

I remember the class that won the national championship. My ROTC instructor came in and told us we were going to have very good teams at Tennessee because he had just seen the freshmen practice. That was in 1948 when they were all freshmen. Two years later, he was right because they were very good in 1950, 1951, and 1952 with Lauricella, Jim Haslam, Bert Rechichar, and John Michels, among others.

There was as much fervor back then as there is now. It wasn't an all-day thing with this tailgating, which is what the women put in later, but there was a lot of excitement. I remember back in 1956, after we beat Georgia Tech in Atlanta, and the fans drove up and down Gay Street, bumper-to-bumper, honking their horns like it was V-J Day. The crowd took over Gay Street. There are more people now, but it was just as intense then. It was pretty good then and pretty good now.

There have been some valleys, but Tennessee fans never accepted anything less than winning seasons for any length of time. Neyland set the stage for that. He created the expectations and the groundwork.

Whenever things would drop off, there was always a coach to bring them back. It traces back to Neyland. He laid it out there for Bowden Wyatt, Doug

Dickey, Johnny Majors, and Phil Fulmer. You can see how it has grown over the years with the hard work of others, because the stadium gets bigger and bigger with their success.

Even when we had a down season, or might not be as strong as previous Tennessee teams, coaches with other schools would tell their players all about the Tennessee tradition, and warned them to get ready for a tough game. That is what it means to be Vol. When opponents have that kind of respect for your program when you are down, that shows something. The coaches would say, "They are Tennessee, forget what the record looks like."

A good example of that was in 1959 when we had a 5–4–1 team, and we beat LSU 14–13, when the Tigers were No. 1 in the country. We stopped them at the goal line on a two-point conversion. Billy Cannon, their great runner, was stopped short.

My favorite tradition is still the Last Tackle Drill. It is the last Thursday of the season over on the practice field. Coach Majors did it, and now Coach Fulmer does it. The whole squad lines up on both sides of a tunnel, and the coach gets up there and says something about the player in his final year and what he contributed to Tennessee. The player starts down this tunnel the players have formed, and at the other end is this tackling dummy dressed in either the Vanderbilt or Kentucky jersey, and he hits it.

It is a sentimental moment that can bring a tear to your eye. It is such a happy moment for some of these guys, not that they are finishing, but just recapitulating what they have done through their careers at Tennessee. The whole senior class, including the walk-ons, who paid the price without the benefit of the scholarship, participate in this ceremony. The walk-ons' participation is particularly moving because they played little or not much at all, but it means just as much to them. I remember one player, Mike Cunningham, who just broke down crying.

It is usually on Thanksgiving, but I don't mind leaving my house to come over here and see the Last Tackle Drill. The players get rung out emotionally on that thing.

The one thing I have noticed over the years as I have done books on Tennessee football is how little the players want to talk about themselves. They want to talk about coaches and teammates. They all love their Vol experience and they love to talk about it, especially the older guys. It becomes much more important to them as they look back.

I look back and realize how lucky I was that Gus Manning hired me as a part-time worker and recommended me for a job. I couldn't ask for a better job and a more wonderful life.

Since I retired from the full-time work, Gus Manning and I have had a chance to go back and research Tennessee football back through the years, not just the recent Vols or players from the '70s and '80s, but further back with Beattie Feathers, Bowden Wyatt, and Bobby Dodd, among others.

I looked at my job as an opportunity to help people enjoy the Vol experience as much as I did. That was the joy of the job as far as I was concerned. Any time I get to do some publicity on the local or on the national level for Tennessee, I'm thrilled.

Haywood Harris is considered the official historian of Tennessee football. After a newspaper career with *The Charlotte Observer* and *The Knoxville Journal*, Harris became sports information director at Tennessee in 1961. He has written three books about Tennessee football.

AL ROBERT NEYLAND · HACK, MAC, & DODD · JOHN MICHELS ·
ON · STEVE DeLONG · FRANK EMANUEL · RON WIDBY · BOB JO
LL · LESTER McCLAIN · BOBBY MAJORS · JAMIE ROTELLA · COND
COLQUITT · ROLAND JAMES · TIM IRWIN · WILLIE GAULT · REG
WILKERSON · HARRY GALBREATH · ERIC STILL · ANTONE DAVIS
ON GRANT · DARWIN WALKER · TRAVIS STEPHENS · JOHN HEN
OOD HARRIS · GENERAL ROBERT NEYLAND · HACK, MAC, & DC
MAJORS · BILL JOHNSON · STEVE DeLONG · FRANK EMANUEL
STEVE KINER · CHIP KELL · LESTER McCLAIN · BOBBY MAJORS
N · LARRY SEIVERS · CRAIG COLQUITT · ROLAND JAMES · TIM
IE JONES · TIM McGEE · BRUCE WILKERSON · HARRY GALBREA
NG · JEFF HALL · TEE MARTIN · DEON GRANT · DARWIN WALK
IT · ARRON SEARS · BEN BYRD · HAYWOOD HARRIS · GENERAL
DOUG ATKINS · JIM HASLAM · JOHNNY MAJORS · BILL JOHNSON
FLOWERS · CHARLIE ROSENFELDER · STEVE KINER · CHIP KE
WAY · MICKEY MARVIN · STANLEY MORGAN · LARRY SEIVERS ·
JIMMY COLQUITT · BILL MAYO · JOHNNIE JONES · TIM McGEI
SHULER · JOEY KENT · PEYTON MANNING · JEFF HALL · TEE MA
N · DUSTIN COLQUITT · JAMES WILHOIT · ARRON SEARS · BEN